WeightWatchers® momentum™

Slow Cook It

165 All-New Slow-Cooker Recipes

About Weight Watchers

Weight Watchers International, Inc., is the world's leading provider of weight-management services, operating globally through a network of company-owned and franchise operations. Weight Watchers holds over 50,000 weekly meetings worldwide, at which members receive group support and education about healthful eating patterns, behavior modification, and physical activity. Weight-loss and weight-management results vary by individual. We recommend that you attend Weight Watchers meetings to benefit from the supportive environment you'll find there and follow the comprehensive Weight Watchers program, which includes a food plan, an activity plan, and a behavioral component. In addition, Weight Watchers offers a wide range of products, publications, and programs for people interested in weight loss and weight control. For the Weight Watchers meeting nearest you, call **1-800-651-6000.** For information about bringing Weight Watchers to your workplace, call **1-877-ATWORK1.** Also visit us at our Web site, **WeightWatchers.ca,** and look for *Weight Watchers Magazine* at your newsstand or in your meeting room.

OSSO BUCO–STYLE
DRUMSTICKS, PAGE 95

WEIGHT WATCHERS PUBLISHING GROUP

EDITORIAL DIRECTOR	NANCY GAGLIARDI
CREATIVE DIRECTOR	ED MELNITSKY
PHOTO EDITOR	DEBORAH HARDT
MANAGING EDITOR	SARAH WHARTON
PRODUCTION MANAGER	ALAN BIEDERMAN
EDITORIAL ASSISTANT	KRISTINA LUCARELLI
FOOD EDITOR	EILEEN RUNYAN
EDITOR	CAROL PRAGER
NUTRITION CONSULTANT	U. BEATE KRINKE
RECIPE DEVELOPERS	MAUREEN LUCHEJKO
	SALLY-JO O'BRIEN
	JEAN PELLEGRINO
	PAUL PICCUITO
	SARAH REYNOLDS
	MIRIAM RUBIN
	MARLA SOCHET
PHOTOGRAPHER	ANN STRATTON
FOOD STYLIST	MICHAEL PEDERSON
PROP STYLIST	LYNDA WHITE
DESIGNER	SHELLEY CAMHI
ART DIRECTOR	DANIELA HRITCU

ON THE COVER: From top left, clockwise:
Escarole, Bean, and Chicken Soup, page 143; Kung Pao Chicken, page 86;
Spicy "Barbecued" Brisket, page 37; Stuffed Beef Rolls, page 40

About Our Recipes

We make every effort to ensure that you will have success with our recipes. For best results and for nutritional accuracy, please keep these guidelines in mind:

- Recipes in this book have been developed for members who are following the **Momentum™** plan. We include **POINTS**® values for every recipe. **POINTS** values are assigned based on calories, fat (grams), and fiber (grams) provided for a serving size of a recipe.

- All recipes feature approximate nutritional information; our recipes are analyzed for Calories (Cal), Total Fat (Fat), Saturated Fat (Sat Fat), Trans Fat (Trans Fat), Cholesterol (Chol), Sodium (Sod), Carbohydrates (Carb), Dietary Fiber (Fib), Protein (Prot), and Calcium (Calc).

- Nutritional information for recipes that include meat, poultry, and fish are based on cooked skinless boneless portions (unless otherwise stated), with the fat trimmed.

- We recommend that you buy lean meat and poultry, then trim it of all visible fat before cooking. When poultry is cooked with the skin on, we suggest removing the skin before eating.

- Before serving, divide foods—including any vegetables, accompaniments, or sauce—into portions of equal size according to the designated number of servings per recipe.

- Any substitutions made to the ingredients will alter the "Per serving" nutritional information and may affect the **POINTS** value.

- All fresh fruits, vegetables, and greens in recipes should be rinsed before using.

- All ♥™ Filling Extra suggestions have a **POINTS** value of **0** unless otherwise stated.

- All Filling Foods are highlighted in green.

- Recipes that work with the Simply Filling techinque are indicated.

CHICKEN AND HERB DUMPLING STEW, PAGE 93

Keep Warm

Off

Contents

CHAPTER 5
Beans and Grains

CHAPTER 6
Vegetarian Main Dishes and Sides

CHAPTER 7
Easy Sweets

STUFFED BREAST OF VEAL,
PAGE 127

Introduction

Slow cookers are back in a big way. In fact, surveys show that the number of households using slow cookers has almost doubled in the past 20 years. That statistic isn't surprising when you consider the remarkable array of healthful dishes that you can make with a slow cooker and the ease of using one: Simply prepare the ingredients, pop them into the insert, select the appropriate setting, and let the cooker work its magic for the next several hours. The convenience of up-front preparation, plus the inviting aroma that permeates your home—and perhaps greets you at the end of a long day—may persuade you to never again make a stew, soup, roast, or even dessert any other way!

The principle of slow cooking is simple: The cooker generates heat, a tight-fitting lid seals in the heat, and as the food simmers, it releases steam, which over the course of several hours slowly tenderizes the food, creating rich flavours. Even better, this method of slow, high-moisture cooking allows the healthful-minded cook to produce the fabulous, rich taste of many favorite dishes without using a lot of fat. Cooked in a slow cooker, lean meats that might be tough and skinless poultry that might be bland will develop the satisfying, mouthwatering taste you'll love.

TODAY'S SLOW COOKERS

Although slow cookers have come a long way since your mother's circa 1970s version, today's appliance has basically the same parts: a metal base (which houses low-watt electric coils), a stoneware insert, and a tight-fitting glass lid. The amount of energy used is so small that a slow cooker can be safely left on while you are away from home. A bonus: The stoneware insert can double as a serving dish.

Here's what's on today's slow-cooker market:

MANUAL SLOW COOKERS feature two or three settings (high, low, warm), a dishwasher-safe stoneware insert, and a glass lid.

PROGRAMMABLE SLOW COOKERS feature multiple time and temperature settings; a digital timer that counts down the cooking time; a control that automatically shifts the temperature to warm when the cooking time is up; a dishwasher-safe stoneware insert that's safe for microwaving, baking, and browning foods on the stovetop; and a glass lid.

ROUND AND OVAL SLOW COOKERS are available in a number of sizes: $1^1/_2$- to $3^1/_2$-quart for 1 to 3 servings, 4- to 5-quart for 4 to 6 servings, and 5- to 7-quart for 6 or more servings.

Still have mom's slow cooker? The new slow cookers heat up more quickly than some older models. If you have a classic appliance and you're following a recipe that calls for the food to cook at the low setting, for best results set the cooker on high for the first hour of cooking; then reduce the temperature to low and complete the recipe as directed.

AS EASY AS 1, 2, 3

In addition to reading the manufacturer's instructions that come with your slow cooker, follow these steps for best results:

1 **PREP SMART** Fat retains heat better than water. This means that foods with some fat, like meat, will cook in a slow cooker faster than foods with next to no fat, like vegetables. To make sure your ingredients are evenly cooked, we suggest that you cut any vegetables—particularly root vegetables, such as carrots, potatoes, and turnips—into pieces that are a bit smaller than the meat.

2 **FILL 'ER UP** Fill the slow cooker at least one half full but no more than three quarters full (just be sure to leave 2 inches between the food and the lid). Put the ingredients that take the longest to cook—like root vegetables—on the bottom and sides of the insert for maximum exposure to the heat. Place quicker-cooking ingredients, such as fish, shellfish, and thawed frozen vegetables, toward the centre.

3 **KEEP A LID ON IT** Unless the recipe instructs you to stir the food, resist the urge to lift the lid. Each time you uncover the slow cooker and stir the contents, the internal temperature drops by 9 to 12°C (10° to 15°F) (thus requiring the cooking time to increase by 20 to 30 minutes). If a recipe calls for stirring or you wish to check for doneness toward the end of the cooking time, replace the lid as quickly as possible.

THE GREAT BROWNING DEBATE

Is it worth the time and effort to brown meats and veggies before slow cooking, or will your food be just as tasty if you toss everything in the pot without browning it first? The good news is that you can create delicious dishes either way. But before you choose your method, keep these points in mind:

Pro Browning meats and vegetables on the stovetop begins the process of caramelization and increases a dish's depth of flavour and colour. Although some foods will brown somewhat during the slow-cooking process (particularly if they are not submerged in liquid), they will not develop the same colour and flavour of foods that have been browned first on the stovetop.

Con Stovetop browning involves more prep work (and cleanup); so if you're in a rush, opt for slow-cooker recipes that don't call for browning.

SLOW-COOKER FITNESS TEST

A properly working slow cooker cooks slowly enough to allow for unattended cooking yet fast enough to keep food out of the bacteria danger zone 4° to 60° C (40° to 140°F). Here's how to determine whether your slow cooker is working properly:

- Fill it one half to two thirds full with water.
- Cover and set on low for 8 hours.
- Uncover and quickly insert an instant read-thermometer into the water. The temperature should register 85° C (185°F).

If the temperature is lower, the slow cooker is not heating the food to a high enough temperature quickly enough to avoid potential food-safety problems and should be replaced.

SLOW-COOKER SAFETY Q&A

While using a slow-cooker is easy, you may have questions about slow cooking and food safety. Here are some answers:

Q: Is it safe to cook food for such long periods of time at a low temperature?
A: Yes! Slow cookers are designed to ensure that safe temperatures are reached before bacteria have time to grow. According to the USDA, bacteria in food are killed at 75° C (165°F). As long as the lid is kept on and the food is cooked for the amount of time called for, it will be safe. If you're not browning larger cuts of meat or poultry first, you might, as a precaution and to give the cooking process a head start, set the slow cooker on high for 1 to 2 hours before lowering the setting. Or prepare the recipe as directed, but bring the liquid ingredients to a simmer on the stovetop before adding them to the cooker, thereby jump-starting the heating process.

Q: Can I prep the ingredients for my slow-cooker recipe and refrigerate them in the insert overnight?
A: We don't recommend this. A chilled insert filled with uncooked ingredients will not reach the proper cooking temperature in the slow cooker in a reasonable amount of time, Instead, refrigerate the chopped ingredients in separate airtight containers overnight; then combine them in the insert when you're ready to begin cooking. You can brown vegetables ahead of time and refrigerate them overnight, but avoid browning meat and poultry ahead: Browning partially cooks food and, in the case of meat, raises the temperature to a level that might encourage bacteria to grow. Brown meat and poultry only right before you assemble the dish to be slow cooked

Q: Can I reheat leftovers in a slow cooker?
A: Although slow cookers can keep food warm up to 2 hours, they cannot reheat refrigerated leftovers safely because they take too long to come to the appropriate temperature. So use your stovetop or microwave for reheating. (Some inserts are microwavable and ovenproof up to 200° C (400°F); check the manufacturer's instructions.)

SLOW-COOKER SMARTS

Keep these slow-cooker secrets in mind and you'll be guaranteed successful results every time.

• A stoneware insert is sensitive to dramatic changes in temperature, so to avoid breakage or cracking, do not place the hot insert directly on a very cold surface.
• Power outage? If it lasts no more than 2 hours, finish cooking the food on the stovetop. If the power is out for more than 2 hours or you are unsure how long it has been out, discard the food.
• To simplify cleanup, spray the insert with nonstick spray before adding the ingredients, or use a disposable slow-cooker nylon liner (available to fit 3 L to 6 L) [3- to 6½-quart] slow cookers).
• Do not put frozen ingredients in a slow cooker (they can cool the cooker and slow the cooking process). Instead, completely defrost all frozen foods—including meat, poultry, seafood, and vegetables—in the refrigerator before adding them to the slow cooker.
• When cooking larger pieces of meat or poultry, use an instant-read meat thermometer to ensure that the meat is cooked to a safe temperature. For whole poultry, insert the thermometer into a thigh, without touching the bone, and make sure the temperature has reached 80° C (180°F).
• When cooking at a high altitude, allow an additional 30 minutes for each hour of cooking time specified in the recipe.

BIG, BIG BATCHES

Have an extra-large (4.5 L to 6 L [5- to 7-quart]) slow cooker and want to double a soup or stew recipe? It's easy. Just double the ingredients, with the following exceptions:

- Increase the liquid by half (or as needed). For example, if the recipe calls for 250 mL (1 cup) of liquid, add only 375 mL (1½ cups).
- With the exception of pungent spices, which should be increased only sparingly (see SEASON LATER, NOT SOONER below), up the seasonings and dried herbs by one quarter; then adjust to taste at the end of the cooking time.
- Up the amount of any thickening agent, such as flour, cornstarch, or cornmeal, by half, adding more at the end of the cooking time if the mixture is too thin.
- Big-batch cooking means more ingredients, which take more time to heat up, so consider getting a head start by heating the liquid ingredients on the stovetop before adding them to the slow cooker.

WANT TO MAKE A RECIPE SLOW-COOKER FRIENDLY?

If you enjoy slow cooking, the good news is that you're not limited to recipes specifically created for slow cookers. Follow these tips to adapt your favorite dishes:

PICK THE RIGHT RECIPE Slow cookers are ideal for braises, stews, and soups. Vegetarian dishes, especially those with root vegetables, also do very well in slow cookers.

SIZE TO FIT Note the number of servings your recipe makes—you may need to scale it up or down depending on the size of your slow cooker. (Oval-shaped cookers offer more cooking surface and are ideal for larger cuts of meat, whereas smaller round models are best for soups.)

REDUCE LIQUIDS Slow cooking retains more moisture than other cooking methods. That means you may want to reduce the amount of liquid in a recipe (start with half to three quarters of the amount called for). Any liquid left over after the dish has been slow cooked can be used to make a sauce. Just strain the liquid into a saucepan and simmer on the stovetop until reduced.

SEASON LATER, NOT SOONER Slow cooking mellows the seasoning of a dish, so plan to adjust the salt and pepper to taste before serving. At the beginning of the cooking time, add half the amount of dried herbs and spices called for; then taste and adjust the seasoning toward the end of the cooking time. On the other hand, flavourful spice blends, such as chili powder and curry powder, intensify with slow cooking, so use them conservatively. Fresh herbs are best added at the end of the cooking time.

ADJUST TIME AND TEMPERATURE Differences in slow-cooker models can make for variation in cooking times and temperatures. But as a general rule, cook food until tender. A recipe that calls for food to cook $1^1/_2$ to 2 hours on the stovetop will likely take about 4 hours on high in a slow cooker. Also keep in mind that 2 hours on low translates to about 1 hour on high. To ensure that meat and poultry are properly cooked, use an instant-read thermometer to check for doneness.

SLOW-COOKER BAKING TRICKS

Yes, you can make terrific "baked" goods in a slow cooker! In fact puddings, compotes, baked custards, and flans do particularly well. Just follow these helpful hints:

- Use a (3 to 5 L) 3- to 5-quart slow cooker and fill the insert one half to three quarters full.
- Avoid overbeating the batter. If using an electric mixer, follow all recommended mixing times.
- Many dessert recipes, such as custards and puddings, require cooking in a baking dish that is placed inside the stoneware insert. For more even cooking, some recipes call for enough hot or boiling water to be added to the insert until it reaches halfway up the outside of the baking dish. Add water to the insert only if it is called for in the recipe.
- Don't be tempted to double a dessert recipe: it's best to simply prepare the original recipe as many times as needed to serve more people.

FROM TOP:
BROCCOLI FRITTATA
BITES, PAGE 23,
PORK-PINEAPPLE
SKEWERS, PAGE 19,
AND MOO SHU ROLLS,
PAGE 18

Chapter 1

Snacks and Drinks

Your cooker may be slow,
but it's sure to get any gathering going
with a tasty selection of easy nibbles
and specialty drinks.

Moo Shu Rolls

prep 20 min • **slow-cook** 4 hrs • **serves** 10

◆ 250 g (8oz [½ pound]) ground lean beef (7% fat or less)

◆ 250 g (8oz [½ pound]) ground lean pork

◆ 1 large portobello mushroom cap, finely chopped

◆ 1 small onion, finely chopped

5 garlic cloves, finely chopped

◆ 60 mL (¼ cup) low-sodium chicken broth

30 mL (2 tablespoons) low-sodium soy sauce

30 mL (2 tablespoons) rice vinegar

2 mL (½ teaspoon) ground ginger

1 mL (¼ teaspoon) five-spice powder

◆ 20 Boston or Bibb lettuce leaves

◆ 3 carrots, shredded

◆ 10 thin scallions, sliced

◆ 5 radishes, thinly sliced

1 Combine beef, pork, mushroom, onion, and garlic in 5 or 6 L (5- or 6-quart) slow cooker. Mix broth, soy sauce, vinegar, ginger, and five-spice powder in small bowl; pour over beef mixture. Cover and cook until flavors are blended and sauce is slightly thickened, 4–5 hours on high or 8–10 hours on low.

2 Spoon 1 generous tablespoon beef mixture in centre of each lettuce leaf. Top each with about 15 mL (1 tablespoon) carrots, 15 mL (1 tablespoon) scallion, and 15 mL (1 tablespoon) radishes; roll up.

This recipe works with the Simply Filling technique.

PER SERVING (2 rolls): 94 Cal, 3 g Fat, 1 g Sat Fat, 0 g Trans Fat, 27 mg Chol, 144 mg Sod, 5 g Carb, 1 g Fib, 11 g Prot, 32 mg Calc. *POINTS value: 2.*

Pork-Pineapple Skewers

prep 20 min • **cook/slow-cook** 4 hrs 5 min • **serves** 8

- 500 g (16oz [1 pound]) boneless pork loin, trimmed and cut into ¾-inch cubes
- 30 mL (2 tablespoons) cornstarch
- 10 mL (2 teaspoons) Asian (dark) sesame oil
- 2 (250 mL [8-ounce]) cans pineapple chunks in juice
- 1 red onion, chopped
- 1 yellow bell pepper, diced
- 60 mL (¼ cup) ketchup
- 45 mL (3 tablespoons) rice vinegar
- 45 mL (3 tablespoons) honey
- 30 mL (2 tablespoons) low-sodium soy sauce
- 3 garlic cloves, minced
- 15 mL (1 tablespoon) minced peeled fresh ginger
- 30 mL (2 tablespoons) chopped fresh cilantro

1 Mix pork and 15 mL (1 tablespoon) cornstarch in large bowl. Heat oil in large nonstick skillet over medium-high heat. Add pork and cook, turning frequently, until browned, 3–4 minutes.

2 Drain pineapple, reserving juice from 1 can. (Refrigerate juice from remaining can for another use). Combine remaining 15 mL (1 tablespoon) cornstarch, pineapple and reserved juice, onion, bell pepper, ketchup, vinegar, honey, soy sauce, garlic, and ginger in 5- or 6-L (5- or 6-quart) slow cooker. Stir in pork. Cover and cook until pork is fork-tender, 4–5 hours on high or 8–10 hours on low.

3 At end of cooking time, stir cilantro into slow cooker. Thread pork and pineapple evenly on 8 (20 cm [8-inch]) wooden skewers. Serve with sauce.

PER SERVING (1 skewer with about 30 mL [2 tablespoons] sauce): 159 Cal, 3 g Fat, 1 g Sat Fat, 0 g Trans Fat, 32 mg Chol, 379 mg Sod, 21 g Carb, 1 g Fib, 12 g Prot, 12 mg Calc. *POINTS* value: 3.

Chicken, Apple, and Cheese Meatballs

prep 20 min • **slow-cook** 4 hrs • **serves** 12

- 500 g (16oz[1 pound]) ground skinless chicken breast
- 1 small onion, finely chopped
- 1 green apple, peeled and shredded
- 125 mL (½ cup) whole wheat bread crumbs (1 slice)
- 125 mL (½ cup) shredded low-fat Cheddar cheese
- 60 mL (¼ cup) finely chopped fresh parsley
- 30 mL (2 tablespoons) grated Parmesan cheese
- 1 large egg
- 3 mL (¾ teaspoon) salt
- 3 mL (¾ teaspoon) dried thyme

1 Combine all ingredients in large bowl. Form into 36 meatballs.

2 Transfer meatballs to 5- or 6-L (5- or 6-quart) slow cooker. Cover and cook until instant-read thermometer inserted in centre of meatball registers 75° C (165°F), 4–5 hours on high or 8–10 hours on low. Serve with toothpicks.

IN THE KITCHEN
Before rolling the meatballs, wet your hands with water so the chicken mixture will be less sticky.

PER SERVING (3 meatballs): 82 Cal, 2 g Fat, 1 g Sat Fat, 0 g Trans Fat, 43 mg Chol, 250 mg Sod, 4 g Carb, 1 g Fib, 11 g Prot, 61 mg Calc.
POINTS value: *2*.

Zesty Sausage and Tomato

prep 15 min • **cook/slow-cook** 2 hr 5 min • **serves** 12

500 g (1 pound) hot Italian turkey sausage links, casings removed

♦ 1   small red onion, finely chopped

♦ 1   carrot, finely chopped

♦ 1   red bell pepper, finely chopped

♦ 1   (830 g [28-ounce]) can crushed tomatoes with roasted garlic

1   (170 g [6-ounce]) can tomato paste with Italian seasonings

5   mL (1 teaspoon) dried oregano

5   mL (1 teaspoon) fennel seeds

5   mL (1 teaspoon) sugar

1   mL (¼ teaspoon) black pepper

24   baked whole wheat pita chips

1 Heat large nonstick skillet over medium-high heat. Add sausage, onion, carrot, and bell pepper; cook, breaking sausage apart with wooden spoon, until sausage is well browned, 7–8 minutes.

2 Transfer sausage mixture to 5- or 6- L (5- or 6-quart) slow cooker. Stir in crushed tomatoes, tomato paste, oregano, fennel seeds, sugar, and black pepper. Cover and cook until mixture simmers and thickens, 2–3 hours on high or 4–6 hours on low. Serve with pita chips.

♦ **FILLING EXTRA**

Prefer a mellower taste? At the end of the cooking time, stir 1 (250g [8-ounce]) package shredded fat-free mozzarella cheese into the slow cooker until the cheese melts. (The per-serving *POINTS* value will increase by *1*).

PER SERVING (⅓ cup with 2 pita chips): 149 Cal, 8 g Fat, 3 g Sat Fat, 0 g Trans Fat, 16 mg Chol, 593 mg Sod, 12 g Carb, 2 g Fib, 7 g Prot, 40 mg Calc. *POINTS* value: *3.*

Baja Shrimp Boil

prep 10 min • slow-cook 2 hrs • serves 4

- 500 g (1 pound) unpeeled large shrimp

  175 mL (¾ cup) dry white wine

  60 mL (4 tablespoons) chopped fresh flat-leaf parsley

  60 mL (4 tablespoons) snipped fresh dill

  Grated zest of 1 lemon

  7 mL (1½ teaspoons) butter

  2 mL (½ teaspoon) salt

  1 mL (¼ teaspoon) black pepper

1 Combine shrimp, wine, 30 mL (2 tablespoons) parsley, 30 mL (2 tablespoons) dill, lemon zest, butter, salt, and pepper in 5- or 6- L (5- or 6-quart) slow cooker. Cover and cook until shrimp are just opaque in centre and can be peeled easily, 2–3 hours on high or 4–6 hours on low.

2 At end of cooking time, stir remaining 30 mL (2 tablespoons) parsley and 30 mL (2 tablespoons) dill into slow cooker. Divide shrimp and cooking liquid evenly among 4 bowls.

◆ FILLING EXTRA

For a heartier snack, serve this saucy shrimp with 4 hot cooked small red potatoes (1 cooked potato per serving will increase the *POINTS* value by *1*).

PER SERVING (about 6 shrimp with 3 tablespoons cooking liquid): 80 Cal, 2 g Fat, 1 g Sat Fat, 0 g Trans Fat, 110 mg Chol, 432 mg Sod, 2 g Carb, 0 g Fib, 12 g Prot, 33 mg Calc. *POINTS* value: *2*.

Broccoli Frittata Bites

prep 15 min • cook/slow-cook 3 hrs 20 min • serves 10

10 mL (2 teaspoons) olive oil

♦ 1 large onion, chopped

♦ 1 (290 g [10-ounce]) box frozen chopped broccoli, thawed and drained

310 mL (1¼ cups) low-fat buttermilk

♦ 3 large eggs

125 mL (½ cup) all-purpose flour

5 mL (1 teaspoon) baking soda

2 mL (½ teaspoon) salt

1 mL (¼ teaspoon) freshly grated nutmeg

250 mL (1 cup) shredded low-fat Cheddar cheese

1 Spray 5- or 6- L (5- or 6-quart) slow cooker stoneware with nonstick spray.

2 Heat oil in large nonstick skillet over medium heat. Add onion and cook, stirring occasionally, until softened, about 3 minutes. Reduce heat and cook, stirring occasionally, until golden and very soft, about 15 minutes. Add broccoli and cook, stirring occasionally, until flavours are blended, 2–3 minutes.

3 Whisk buttermilk and eggs in medium bowl. Whisk in flour, baking soda, salt, and nutmeg just until blended. Stir in broccoli mixture and 175 mL (¾ cup) Cheddar until combined.

4 Transfer mixture to slow cooker; sprinkle remaining 60 mL (¼ cup) Cheddar over top. Cover and cook until toothpick inserted into centre comes out clean, 3–4 hours on high or 6–8 hours on low.

5 Transfer stoneware to rack and let frittata cool slightly, about 15 minutes. Cut frittata into 10 pieces. Serve warm or at room temperature.

♦ FILLING EXTRA
Prepare the recipe as directed but add 250 mL (1 cup) shredded carrots with the broccoli in step 2.

PER SERVING (1 piece): 100 Cal, 4 g Fat, 1 g Sat Fat, 0 g Trans Fat, 67 mg Chol, 406 mg Sod, 9 g Carb, 1 g Fib, 7 g Prot, 136 mg Calc.
POINTS value: *2.*

Mini Falafels

prep 20 min • **cook/slow-cook** 2 hrs 10 min • **serves** 10

◆ 1   (15-ounce) can chickpeas, rinsed and drained

◆ 1   small onion, coarsely chopped

125 mL (½ cup) whole wheat bread crumbs (1 slice)

60   mL (¼ cup) fresh cilantro or parsley leaves

◆ 1   large egg

Juice of 1 lemon

2   garlic cloves

7   mL (1½ teaspoons) garam masala

3   mL (¾ teaspoon) salt

1   mL (¼ teaspoon) black pepper

10   mL (2 teaspoons) olive oil

1 Put chickpeas, onion, bread crumbs, cilantro, egg, lemon juice, garlic, garam masala, salt, and pepper in food processor and pulse until coarsely chopped. With moistened hands, form into 20 patties.

2 Heat 5 mL (1 teaspoon) oil in large nonstick skillet over medium-high heat. Add 10 patties and cook until browned, about 3 minutes per side. Transfer patties to 5- or 6-L (5- or 6-quart) slow cooker. Repeat with remaining 5 mL (1 teaspoon) oil and 10 patties.

3 Cover and cook until falafels are firm and heated through, 2-3 hours on high or 4-6 hours on low.

◆ **FILLING EXTRA**

Top each falafel with 15 mL (1 tablespoon) plain fat-free yogourt and a sprinkling of finely chopped fresh cilantro.

PER SERVING (2 falafels): 76 Cal, 2 g Fat, 0 g Sat Fat, 0 g Trans Fat, 21 mg Chol, 239 mg Sod, 11 g Carb, 2 g Fib, 4 g Prot, 25 mg Calc.
POINTS value: *1.*

Caponata

prep 25 min • **cook/slow-cook** 3 hrs 5 min • **serves** 8

15 mL (1 tablespoon) olive oil

◆ 1 eggplant, diced

◆ 1 onion, chopped

2 mL (½ teaspoon) salt

◆ 1 (14½-ounce) can diced tomatoes

◆ 1 large red bell pepper, chopped

◆ 3 celery stalks, thinly sliced

30 mL (2 tablespoons) red-wine vinegar

◆ 30 mL (2 tablespoons) tomato paste

3 garlic cloves, finely chopped

2 mL (½ teaspoon) dried thyme

125 mL (½ cup) chopped fresh basil

◆ 60 mL (¼ cup) brine-cured Kalamata olives, pitted and chopped

1 Heat oil in large nonstick skillet over medium-high heat. Add eggplant, onion, and salt; cook, stirring occasionally, until vegetables are softened, about 6 minutes.

2 Transfer eggplant mixture to 5- or 6L (5- or 6-quart) slow cooker. Stir in tomatoes, bell pepper, celery, vinegar, tomato paste, garlic, and thyme. Cover and cook until vegetables are fork-tender, 3–4 hours on high or 6–8 hours on low.

3 Transfer caponata to large bowl and let cool to room temperature. Stir in basil and olives.

◆ **FILLING EXTRA**
Serve caponata atop 1 L (4 cups) cooked whole wheat couscous (125 mL [½ cup] cooked couscous per serving will up the *POINTS* value by *2*). This recipe works with the Simply Filling technique.

PER SERVING (175 mL [¾ cup]): 74 Cal, 3 g Fat, 0 g Sat Fat, 0 g Trans Fat, 0 mg Chol, 308 mg Sod, 12 g Carb, 4 g Fib, 2 g Prot, 44 mg Calc.
POINTS value: *1.*

Black Bean Salsa Dip

prep 10 min • slow-cook 1 hr • serves 6

- 2 (475 mL [15½-ounce]) cans low-sodium black beans, rinsed and drained
- 250 mL (1 cup) fat-free salsa
- 5 mL (1 teaspoon) ground cumin
- 1 garlic clove, finely chopped
- Grated zest and juice of 1 lime
- 60 mL (¼ cup) chopped fresh cilantro
- 60 mL (¼ cup) sliced scallions
- 24 celery sticks

1 Combine beans, salsa, cumin, and garlic in 5- or 6-L (5- or 6-quart) slow cooker. Cover and cook until beans are hot, 1–2 hours on high or 2–4 hours on low

2 At end of cooking time, stir lime juice and zest into slow cooker. With large spoon or potato masher, coarsely mash bean mixture. Stir in cilantro and scallions. Serve warm with celery sticks.

◆ FILLING EXTRA

For a cheesy-topped dip, prepare the recipe as directed, but after stirring in the cilantro and scallions, sprinkle the bean mixture with 125 mL (½ cup) shredded fat-free mozzarella cheese. Cover and cook on high until the cheese melts, about 10 minutes. This recipe works with the Simply Filling technique.

PER SERVING (125 mL (½ cup) salsa with 4 celery sticks): 159 Cal, 1 g Fat, 0 g Sat Fat, 0 g Trans Fat, 0 mg Chol, 275 mg Sod, 30 g Carb, 12 g Fib, 9 g Prot, 96 mg Calc. *POINTS* value: *2.*

Tomatillo-Pinto Bean Dip

prep 10 min • **slow-cook** 1 hr • **serves** 6

- ◆ 2 (450 mL [15-ounce]) cans pinto beans, rinsed and drained
- ◆ 1 (375 mL [12-ounce]) can tomatillos, drained and chopped
- ◆ 1 (4½-ounce) can chopped green chiles
- ◆ 1 small red onion, chopped
- ◆ 60 mL (¼ cup) vegetable broth or water
-    15 mL (1 tablespoon) cider vinegar
-    5 mL (1 teaspoon) chili powder
-    2 mL (½ teaspoon) ground cumin
-    2 mL (½ teaspoon) salt
-    .5 mL (⅛ teaspoon) cayenne
-    60 mL (¼ cup) chopped fresh cilantro
-    Juice of 1 lime
- ◆ 24 jicama sticks

1 Combine beans, tomatillos, chiles, onion, broth, vinegar, chili powder, cumin, salt, and cayenne in 5- or 6- L (5- or 6-quart) slow cooker. Cover and cook until slightly thickened, 1–2 hours on high or 2–4 hours on low.

2 At end of cooking time, stir cilantro and lime juice into slow cooker. Let mixture cool about 5 minutes. Puree in batches in food processor. Serve warm or at room temperature with jicama sticks.

IN THE KITCHEN
If you want to make this dip ahead, transfer to an airtight container and let cool completely. Cover and refrigerate up to 4 days. Let return to room temperature before serving. This recipe works with the Simply Filling technique.

PER SERVING (175 mL [⅓ cup] with 4 jicama sticks): 173 Cal, 1 g Fat, 0 g Sat Fat, 0 g Trans Fat, 0 mg Chol, 519 g Sod, 33 g Carb, 11 g Fib, 10 g Prot, 63 mg Calc. *POINTS* value: *3.*

Warm Cheese and Cannellini Dip

prep 10 min • slow-cook 1 hr • serves 12

- 3 (475 mL [15½-ounce]) cans cannellini (white kidney) beans, rinsed and drained

125 mL (½ cup) water

125 mL (½ cup) grated pecorino cheese

3 garlic cloves, thinly sliced

30 mL (2 tablespoons) olive oil

10 mL (2 teaspoons) Italian seasoning

1 mL (¼ teaspoon) salt

1 mL (¼ teaspoon) black pepper

Grated zest and juice of 1 small lemon

- 24 slices fennel

1 Combine beans, water, pecorino, garlic, oil, Italian seasoning, salt, and pepper in 5- or 6- L (5- or 6-quart) slow cooker. Cover and cook until pecorino melts and garlic is softened, 1–2 hours on high or 2–4 hours on low.

2 At end of cooking time, stir lemon zest and juice into slow cooker. With large spoon or potato masher, coarsely mash bean mixture. Serve warm or at room temperature with fennel slices.

IN THE KITCHEN

To make ahead, transfer this dip to a microwavable container and let cool. Cover and refrigerate up to 3 days. To serve, microwave, partially covered, on High until heated through, about 3 minutes, stirring once halfway through the cooking time.

PER SERVING (60 mL [¼ cup] with 2 fennel slices): 148 Cal, 4 g Fat, 1 g Sat Fat, 0 g Trans Fat, 5 mg Chol, 296 mg Sod, 21 g Carb, 6 g Fib, 9 g Prot, 101 mg Calc. *POINTS* value: 2.

Southern Artichoke Dip

prep 10 min • **slow-cook** 1 hr • **serves** 12

◆ 2 (420 g [14-ounce) cans artichoke hearts, drained and finely chopped

◆ 1 (290 g [10-ounce]) package frozen chopped collard greens, thawed and squeezed dry

250 mL (1 cup) grated Parmesan cheese

250 mL (1 cup) low-fat mayonnaise

125 mL (½ cup) light sour cream

2 shallots, chopped

1 mL (¼ teaspoon) hot pepper sauce

Grated zest of ½ lemon

◆ 2 red bell peppers, cut into strips

1 Combine artichoke hearts, collard greens, Parmesan, mayonnaise, sour cream, shallots, and pepper sauce in 5- or 6-L (5- or 6-quart) slow cooker. Cover and cook until Parmesan melts and dip is hot, 1–2 hours on high or 3–4 hours on low.

2 At end of cooking time, stir lemon zest into slow cooker. Serve with bell pepper strips.

IN THE KITCHEN
If you like, substitute a package of frozen chopped spinach or Swiss chard, thawed and squeezed dry, for the collard greens.

PER SERVING (75 mL [⅓ cup] with about 3 bell pepper strips): 128 Cal, 7 g Fat, 3 g Sat Fat, 0 g Trans Fat, 10 mg Chol, 464 mg Sod, 13 g Carb, 5 g Fib, 6 g Prot, 180 mg Calc. *POINTS* value: *2.*

Italian Snack Mix

prep 5 min • **slow-cook** 2 hrs 50 min • **serves** 20

60 mL (¼ cup) light stick butter

60 mL (¼ cup) grated Parmesan cheese

5 mL (1 teaspoon) garlic powder

5 mL (1 teaspoon) Italian seasoning

2 L (8 cups) multigrain oat cereal

500 mL (2 cups) tiny pretzel t wists

500 mL (2 cups) goldfish cheese crackers

1 Place butter in 5- or 6-L (5- or 6-quart) slow cooker. Cover and cook until melted, about 5 minutes on high. Add Parmesan, garlic powder, and Italian seasoning; mix well. Stir in cereal, pretzels, cheese crackers, and apricots.

2 Cook uncovered on high about 45 minutes, stirring every 15 minutes.

3 Reduce heat to low. Cook uncovered, stirring occasionally, until mixture is crisp and fragrant, 2–3 hours. Transfer mixture to large bowl and let cool completely.

PER SERVING (125 mL [½ cup]): 115 Cal, 3 g Fat, 1 g Sat Fat, 0 g Trans Fat, 5 mg Chol, 226 mg Sod, 20 g Carb, 2 g Fib, 3 g Prot, 70 mg Calc.
POINTS value: *2.*

Hot Chocolate Latte

prep 5 min • **slow-cook** 1 hr • **serves** 6

175 mL (¾ cup) confectioners' sugar

60 mL (¼ cup) unsweetened cocoa

2 mL (½ teaspoon) cinnamon

1 mL (¼ teaspoon) salt

500 mL (2 cups) low-fat (1%) milk

1.5 L (6 cups) brewed coffee

30 mL (2 tablespoons) semisweet chocolate chips

5 mL (1 teaspoon) vanilla extract

Whisk sugar, cocoa, cinnamon, and salt in 5- or 6-L (5- or 6-quart) slow cooker until smooth. Whisk in milk until blended. Stir in coffee, chocolate chips, and vanilla. Cover and cook until hot and flavours are blended, 1–2 hours on high or 2–4 hours on low. Ladle into mugs.

IN THE KITCHEN
Having a party? You can keep the latte hot in the slow cooker on low or warm up to 3 hours.

PER SERVING (generous 250 mL [1 cup]): 123 Cal, 2 g Fat, 1 g Sat Fat, 0 g Trans Fat, 4 mg Chol, 140 mg Sod, 25 g Carb, 3 g Fib, 4 g Prot, 109 mg Calc. *POINTS* value: *2.*

Mumbai Chai

prep 10 min • **slow-cook** 1 hr • **serves** 8

1.5 L (6 cups) low-fat (1%) milk

500 mL (2 cups) water

125 mL (½ cup) packed brown sugar

6 Darjeeling tea bags

8 whole cloves

8 cardamom pods

2 whole cinnamon sticks

1 (2-inch) piece peeled fresh ginger, sliced

10 mL (2 teaspoons) vanilla extract

1 Whisk milk, water, and brown sugar in 5- or 6-L (5- or 6-quart) slow cooker until smooth. Stir in tea bags, cloves, cardamom, cinnamon sticks, ginger, and vanilla. Cover and cook until hot and flavours are blended, 1–2 hours on high or 2–4 hours on low.

2 Pour chai through strainer into large heatproof bowl. Discard tea bags, cloves, cardamom, cinnamon sticks, and ginger. Ladle into mugs.

IN THE KITCHEN

To make serving easier, prepare the recipe as directed, but wrap the tea bags, cloves, cardamom, cinnamon sticks, and ginger in a cheesecloth bag tied with kitchen string. Then all you need to do is remove the bag with a slotted spoon in step 2 and serve the chai from the slow cooker.

PER SERVING (250 mL [1 cup]): 135 Cal, 2 g Fat, 1 g Sat Fat, 0 g Trans Fat, 9 mg Chol, 90 mg Sod, 23 g Carb, 0 g Fib, 6 g Prot, 231 mg Calc. *POINTS* value: *3.*

Glogg

1   L (4 cups) red wine

250 mL (1 cup) vodka

Zest of 1 orange, removed in strips with vegetable peeler

Zest of 2 lemons, removed in strips with vegetable peeler

4   (7.5 cm [3-inch]) cinnamon sticks

30 mL (2 tablespoons) sugar

12 cardamom pods

15 mL (1 tablespoon) whole cloves

60 mL (¼ cup) slivered almonds

30 mL (2 tablespoons) raisins

1 Combine wine, vodka, orange and lemon zests, cinnamon sticks, sugar, cardamom, and cloves in 4- or 5-L (4- or 5-quart) slow cooker. Cover and cook until hot and flavours are blended, 2–3 hours on high or 4–6 hours on low.

2 Remove orange and lemon zest strips, cinnamon stick, cardamom, and cloves with slotted spoon and discard. Divide almonds and raisins among 8 heat-resistant glasses or mugs then top evenly with glogg.

PER SERVING (about 125 mL [½ cup]): 194 Cal, 2 g Fat, 0 g Sat Fat, 0 g Trans Fat, 0 mg Chol, 6 mg Sod, 6 g Carb, 1 g Fib, 1 g Prot, 21 mg Calc.
POINTS value: *4.*

SOUTHWEST STEAK TACOS,
PAGE 39

Chapter 2

Beef, Pork and More

Love meat? Assemble your ingredients
and let the satisfying aromas from your
favourite dinners greet you at the door.

Harvest Pot Roast Dinner

prep 25 min • **cook/slow-cook** 5 hrs 15 min • **serves** 6

- ◆ 1   1 (625 g [1¼-pound]) bottom round steak, trimmed
- 2   mL (½ teaspoon) salt
- 2   mL (½ teaspoon) black pepper
- 10 mL (2 teaspoons) olive oil
- ◆ 2   large onions, sliced
- 3   garlic cloves, thinly sliced
- ◆ 500 mL (2 cups) low-sodium beef broth
- ◆ 45 mL (3 tablespoons tomato paste
- ◆ 3   large carrots, cut diagonally into ½-inch slices (1.25 cm)
- ◆ 2   stalks celery, cut diagonally into ½-inch slices (1.25 cm)
- 8   thyme sprigs, tied with kitchen string
- 1   bay leaf
- ◆ 500 g (16oz [1 pound]) baby red potatoes, scrubbed and halved

1 Sprinkle beef with salt and pepper. Heat oil in large nonstick skillet over medium-high heat. Add beef and cook until browned, 3–4 minutes per side. Transfer beef to 5- or 6-L (5- or 6-quart) slow cooker.

2 Spray skillet with nonstick spray and set over medium heat. Add onions and garlic; cover and cook, stirring occasionally, until onions are softened and lightly browned, about 8 minutes. Transfer onion mixture to slow cooker.

3 Combine 250 mL (1 cup) broth and tomato paste in skillet. Bring to boil, whisking constantly, about 1 minute. Pour broth mixture into slow cooker. Stir in remaining 250 mL (1 cup) broth, carrots, celery, thyme, and bay leaf. Press potatoes down into vegetable mixture. Cover and cook until beef and vegetables are fork-tender, 5–6 hours on high or 10–12 hours on low.

4 Transfer beef to cutting board and let stand 10 minutes. Transfer vegetables with slotted spoon to bowl. Discard thyme and bay leaf. Cut beef across grain into 12 slices. Serve with vegetables and gravy.

This recipe works with the Simply Filling technique.

PER SERVING (2 slices beef with generous 175 mL [¾ cup] vegetables and scant 45 mL [3 tablespoons] gravy): 279 Cal, 6 g Fat, 2 g Sat Fat, 0 g Trans Fat, 68 mg Chol, 362 mg Sod, 25 g Carb, 4 g Fib, 31 g Prot, 57 mg Calc.
POINTS value: *5.*

Spicy "Barbecued" Brisket

prep 20 min • **broil/cook/slow-cook** 7 hrs 10 min • **serves** 6

30 mL (2 tablespoons) chili powder

5 mL (1 teaspoon) kosher salt

3 mL (¾ teaspoon) black pepper

2 mL (½ teaspoon) garlic powder

750 g (24oz [1½ pounds]) beef brisket, trimmed

15 mL (3 teaspoons) canola oil

♦ 2 large onions, thinly sliced

250 mL (1 cup) ketchup

125 mL (½ cup) chili sauce

60 mL (¼ cup) molasses

30 mL (2 tablespoons) strong brewed coffee

2 mL (½ teaspoon) hot pepper sauce

1 Spray broiler rack with nonstick spray. Preheat broiler.

2 Mix chili powder, salt, pepper, and garlic powder in cup. Rub brisket with spice mixture. Transfer brisket to broiler rack. Drizzle top with 5 mL (1 teaspoon) oil. Broil brisket 12.5 cm (5 inches) from heat until browned, 4–6 minutes per side.

3 Meanwhile, heat remaining 10 mL (2 teaspoons) oil in large nonstick skillet over medium heat. Add onions and cook, stirring frequently, just until golden, about 8 minutes. Stir in ketchup, chili sauce, molasses, coffee, and pepper sauce.

4 Spread half of ketchup mixture over bottom of 5- or 6-L (5- or 6-quart) slow cooker. Top with brisket and remaining ketchup mixture. Cover and cook until brisket is fork-tender, 7–9 hours on low.

5 Transfer brisket to cutting board. Skim fat from sauce. Cut brisket across grain into 18 slices. Serve with sauce.

IN THE KITCHEN
This brisket makes excellent sandwiches. Divide the brisket, sauce, And 175 mL (¾ cup) prepared coleslaw among 4 split whole wheat hamburger rolls and up the per serving *POINTS* value by *3.*

PER SERVING (3 slices brisket with 75 mL [⅓ cup] sauce): 287 Cal, 9 g Fat, 3 g Sat Fat, 0 g Trans Fat, 38 mg Chol, 1,075 mg Sod, 31 g Carb, 3 g Fib, 22 g Prot, 65 mg Calc. *POINTS* value: *6.*

Steak with Merlot and Mushrooms

prep 20 min • broil/slow-cook/cook 4 hrs 10 min • serves 4

2 mL (½ teaspoon) salt

2 mL (½ teaspoon) dried thyme

2 mL (½ teaspoon) coarsely ground black pepper

1 mL (¼ teaspoon) garlic powder

♦ 1 (625 g [1¼-pound]) flank steak, trimmed

♦ 1 red onion, thinly sliced

♦ 150 mL (²/₃ cup) low-sodium beef broth

75 mL (¹/₃ cup) red wine (such as merlot)

♦ 60 mL (¼ cup) tomato paste

10 mL (2 teaspoons) olive oil

♦ 1 (250 g [8-ounce]) package cremini mushrooms, thickly sliced

♦ 1 (250 g [8-ounce]) package white mushrooms, thickly sliced

15 mL (1 tablespoon) all-purpose flour

1 Spray broiler rack with nonstick spray. Preheat broiler.

2 Mix salt, thyme, pepper, and garlic powder in cup. Rub thyme mixture all over steak. Transfer steak to broiler rack. Broil steak 12.5 cm (5 inches) from heat until lightly browned, about 5 minutes per side.

3 Scatter onion in bottom of 5- or 6-L (5- or 6-quart) slow cooker. Top with steak. Whisk broth, wine, and tomato paste in medium bowl until smooth. Pour broth mixture over steak. Cover and cook until steak and onion are fork-tender, 4–6 hours on high or 6–8 hours on low.

4 About 35 minutes before cooking time is up, heat oil in large nonstick skillet over medium-high heat. Add mushrooms and cook, stirring frequently, until lightly browned, about 8 minutes. Sprinkle with flour and cook, stirring constantly, about 1 minute. Stir mushroom mixture into slow cooker. Cover and cook on high until mixture simmers and thickens, about 25 minutes.

5 Transfer steak to cutting board. Cut steak across grain into 12 slices. Serve with sauce.

♦ FILLING EXTRA

Accompany this elegant steak dish with 750 mL (3 cups) cooked barley and 1L (4 cups) steamed broccoli rabe (175 mL [¾ cup] cooked barley and 250 mL [1 cup] cooked broccoli rabe per serving will up the *POINTS* value by *2*).

PER SERVING (3 slices steak with 150mL [²/₃ cup] sauce): 318 Cal, 9 g Fat, 2 g Sat Fat, 0 g Trans Fat, 102 mg Chol, 496 mg Sod, 13 g Carb, 2 g Fib, 46 g Prot, 36 mg Calc. *POINTS* value: *7*.

Southwest Steak Tacos

prep 15 min • cook/slow-cook 4 hrs • serves 8

- 500 g (1 pound) flank steak, trimmed
- 250 mL (1 cup) pale ale
- Juice from ½ orange
- Juice from 1 lime
- 2 mL (½ teaspoon) salt
- 1 mL (¼ teaspoon) black pepper
- 8 (15cm [6-inch]) corn tortillas
- 125 mL (½ cup) fat-free salsa
- 40 mL (8 teaspoons) fat-free plain yogourt
- ½ chopped red onion
- 16 cilantro sprigs

1 Combine steak, ale, orange juice, lime juice, salt, and pepper in 5- or 6-L (5- or 6-quart) slow cooker. Cover and cook until steak is fork-tender, 4–5 hours on high or 8–10 hours on low.

2 At end of cooking time, transfer steak to cutting board. Discard all but 30 mL (2 tablespoons) cooking liquid. With 2 forks, shred steak into small pieces; transfer to bowl and stir in reserved cooking liquid.

3 Heat tortillas according to package directions. Top each with 30 mL (2 tablespoons) steak, 15 mL (1 tablespoon) salsa, 5 mL (1 teaspoon) yogourt, 15 mL (1 tablespoon) red onion, and 2 cilantro sprigs.

◈ FILLING EXTRA
Add 1 chopped red onion and 1 diced poblano pepper with the steak in step 1.

PER SERVING (1 taco): 208 Cal, 8 g Fat, 3 g Sat Fat, 0 g Trans Fat, 40 mg Chol, 301 mg Sod, 15 g Carb, 1 g Fib, 18 g Prot, 58 mg Calc. *POINTS* value: 5.

Stuffed Beef Rolls

prep 20 min • cook/slow-cook 3 hrs 10 min • serves 6

125 mL (½ cup) raisins

250 mL (1 cup) garlic and herb seasoned dried bread crumbs

125 mL (½ cup) chopped fresh flat-leaf parsley

125 mL (½ cup) grated Asiago cheese

15 mL (1 tablespoon) olive oil

45 mL (3 tablespoons) water

♦ 6 (0.5 cm [¼-inch]-thick) slices top round steak, trimmed (125 g [4 ounces] each)

1 mL (¼ teaspoon) black pepper

375 mL (1½ cups) fat-free marinara sauce

1 To make filling, combine raisins, bread crumbs, parsley, Asiago, and oil in medium bowl. Add water, 15 mL (1 tablespoon) at a time, until mixture holds together when pressed with your fingertips.

2 Place 1 steak between 2 pieces of wax paper. Pound steak to 0.25 cm (⅛-inch) thickness. Repeat with remaining steaks. Remove and discard top sheets of wax paper. Press about 60 mL (¼ cup) filling onto each steak, leaving 1.25 cm (½ inch) border. From one short end, roll up each steak jelly-roll style. Tie each roll at 2.5 cm (1-inch) intervals with kitchen string. Sprinkle rolls with pepper.

3 Spray large nonstick skillet with nonstick spray and set over medium-high heat. Add rolls and cook, turning occasionally, until browned, about 8 minutes. Transfer rolls to 5- or 6-L (5- or 6-quart) slow cooker. Stir in marinara sauce. Cover and cook until rolls are fork-tender, 3–4 hours on high or 6–8 hours on low. Remove strings and serve with sauce.

IN THE KITCHEN
Serve these savory rolls with a side of medium-size pasta, such as penne or fusilli (½ cup cooked penne for each serving will up the *POINTS* value by *2*).

PER SERVING (1 roll with ¼ cup sauce): 310 Cal, 8 g Fat, 3 g Sat Fat, 1 g Trans Fat, 65 mg Chol, 772 mg Sod, 28 g Carb, 2 g Fib, 31 g Prot, 173 mg Calc. *POINTS* value: *6.*

Shredded Cuban-Style Beef and Black Beans

prep 20 min • **slow-cook** 10 hrs 5 min • **serves** 6

♦ 1 (425 mL [14½-ounce]) can diced tomatoes with jalapeños

♦ 75 mL (⅓ cup) tomato paste

60 mL (¼ cup) water

♦ 2 Cubanelle or yellow bell peppers, quartered lengthwise and sliced 0.5 cm (¼ inch) thick

♦ 1 (475 mL [15½-ounce])can low-sodium black beans, rinsed and drained

♦ 1 white onion, coarsely chopped

♦ 1 large carrot, sliced 1.25 cm (½ inch) thick

2 garlic cloves, minced

7 mL (1½ teaspoons) ground cumin

2 mL (½ teaspoon) dried oregano

1 mL (¼ teaspoon) salt

1 mL (¼ teaspoon) red pepper flakes

♦ 1 (625 g [1¼-pound]) bottom round steak, trimmed

1 Whisk tomatoes, tomato paste, and water in large bowl until blended. Stir in Cubanelle peppers, beans, onion, carrot, garlic, cumin, oregano, salt, and red pepper flakes. Transfer half of pepper mixture to 5- or 6-L (5- or 6-quart) slow cooker. Top with beef and remaining pepper mixture. Cover and cook until beef and vegetables are fork-tender, 10–12 hours on low.

2 At end of cooking time, transfer beef with slotted spoon to plate and let cool slightly, about 10 minutes. With 2 forks, shred beef into small pieces. Return beef to slow cooker. Cover and cook on high until heated through, about 5 minutes.

♦ **FILLING EXTRA**

Prepare the recipe as directed but add 1 (375 g [12-ounce]) bag frozen thawed corn kernels with the shredded beef in step 2 and increase the cooking time to 10–15 minutes. The per-serving *POINTS* value will increase by *1*. This recipe works with the Simply Filling technique.

PER SERVING (250 mL [1 cup]): 276 Cal, 5 g Fat, 1 g Sat Fat, 0 g Trans Fat, 68 mg Chol, 356 mg Sod, 26 g Carb, 8 g Fib, 36 g Prot, 87 mg Calc.
POINTS value: *5.*

Chuck Wagon Chili

prep 25 min • **cook/slow-cook** 4 hrs 10 min • **serves** 4

---

625 g (1¼ pounds) boneless chuck steak, trimmed and cut into 1.25 cm (½-inch) cubes

325 mL (1⅓ cups) beer

♦ **2** red onions, chopped

♦ **2** large carrots, diced

♦ **1** (250 g [8-ounce]) package cremini mushrooms, diced

3 garlic cloves, thinly sliced

♦ **60** mL (¼ cup) tomato paste

45 mL (3 tablespoons) honey

45 mL (3 tablespoons) chipotle chile powder

10 mL (2 teaspoons) ground cumin

5 mL (1 teaspoon) dried oregano

♦ **15** mL (1 tablespoon) cornmeal

60 mL (¼ cup) light sour cream

1 Spray large nonstick skillet with nonstick spray and set over medium-high heat. Add half of beef; cook, turning occasionally, until browned, about 4 minutes. Transfer beef to 5- or 6-L (5- or 6-quart) slow cooker. Repeat with remaining beef.

2 Add 75 mL (⅓ cup) beer to skillet. Bring to boil, scraping up browned bits from bottom of pan. Pour beer mixture into slow cooker; stir in onions, carrots, mushrooms, garlic, remaining 250 mL (1 cup) beer, tomato paste, honey, chile powder, cumin, and oregano. Cover and cook until beef and vegetables are fork-tender, 4–5 hours on high or 8–10 hours on low.

3 About 20 minutes before cooking time is up, gradually stir cornmeal into slow cooker until blended. Cover and cook on high until mixture simmers and thickens, about 15 minutes. Serve with sour cream.

♦ **FILLING EXTRA**
Serve this fiery chili with a 475 mL (15½-ounce) can of black or pinto beans, rinsed, drained, and heated according to package directions. This will up the per-serving *POINTS* value by *1*.

PER SERVING (325 mL (1⅓ cups) with 15 mL (1 tablespoon) sour cream): 337 Cal, 9 g Fat, 3 g Sat Fat, 1 g Trans Fat, 79 mg Chol, 208 mg Sod, 37 g Carb, 6 g Fib, 30 g Prot, 89 mg Calc. *POINTS* value: *7.*

Old-Fashioned Borscht

prep 30 min • **roast/slow-cook** 4 hrs 25 min • **serves** 6

- 750 g (24oz [1½ pounds]) bottom round steak, trimmed and cut into 1.25 cm (½-inch) cubes
- 4 small fresh beets, trimmed, peeled and chopped
- 2 onions, chopped
- 3 carrots, chopped
- 1 fennel bulb, chopped
- 250 mL (1 cup) chopped red cabbage
- 1 (425 mL [14½-ounce]) can diced tomatoes with roasted garlic
- 2 bay leaves
- 2 mL (½ teaspoon) salt
- 1 mL (¼ teaspoon) black pepper
- 1.5 L (6 cups) low-sodium beef broth
- 60 mL (¼ cup) chopped fresh dill

1 Adjust racks to divide oven into thirds. Preheat oven to 230°C (450°F).

2 Combine beef, beets, onions, carrots, fennel, and cabbage in large bowl; lightly spray with nonstick spray. Spread half of beef and vegetables in each of 2 large rimmed baking sheets. Roast 15 minutes. Stir vegetables, switch pans between racks, and roast until beef and vegetables are browned, about 10 minutes.

3 Transfer beef and vegetables to 5- or 6-L (5- or 6-quart) slow cooker. Stir in tomatoes, bay leaves, salt, and pepper. Pour broth over beef and vegetables. Cover and cook until beef and vegetables are fork-tender, 4–5 hours on high or 8–10 hours on low.

4 At end of cooking time, discard bay leaves and stir in dill.

◆ **FILLING EXTRA**
Add 2 peeled and chopped parsnips to the slow cooker with the other vegetables in step 2. This recipe works with the Simply Filling technique.

PER SERVING (400 mL [1⅔ cups]): 301 Cal, 7 g Fat, 2 g Sat Fat, 0 g Trans Fat, 84 mg Chol, 494 mg Sod, 21 g Carb, 5 g Fib, 41 g Prot, 88 mg Calc.
POINTS value: **6.**

Belgian Beef Stew

prep 25 min • **cook/slow-cook** 4 hrs 15 min • **serves** 6

- ◆ 500 g (16oz [1 pound]) bottom round steak, trimmed and cut into 2.5cm (1-inch) cubes
- 2 mL (½ teaspoon) salt
- 1 mL (¼ teaspoon) black pepper
- ◆ 3 medium red onions, sliced
- ◆ 125 mL (½ cup) low-sodium chicken broth
- ◆ 375 mL (12oz [¾ pound]) baby red potatoes, halved
- 2 shallots, finely chopped
- 30 mL (2 tablespoons) red-wine vinegar
- 15 mL (1 tablespoon) packed brown sugar
- 15 mL (1 tablespoon) horseradish mustard
- 15 mL (1 tablespoon) chopped fresh thyme or 5 mL (1 teaspoon) dried
- 2 bay leaves
- 1 (375 mL [12-ounce]) can dark beer
- ◆ 5 carrots, cut into 2.5 cm (1-inch) chunks
- 30 mL (2 tablespoons) all-purpose flour

1 Sprinkle both sides of the beef with salt and pepper. Spray large nonstick skillet with nonstick spray and set over medium-high heat. Add beef and cook, turning occasionally, until browned, about 6 minutes. Transfer beef with slotted spoon to 5- or 6-L (5- or 6-quart) slow cooker.

2 Add onions to skillet. Reduce heat and cook, stirring occasionally, until lightly browned, about 8 minutes. Stir in broth. Bring to boil, scraping up browned bits from bottom of pan. Pour onion mixture into slow cooker. Stir in potatoes, shallots, vinegar, brown sugar, mustard, thyme, and bay leaves. Pour 75 mL (⅓ cup) beer into small bowl and refrigerate. Pour remaining beer over beef and vegetables. Press potatoes down into vegetable mixture. Top with even layer of carrots. Cover and cook until beef and vegetables are fork-tender, 4–5 hours on high or 8–10 hours on low.

3 About 25 minutes before cooking time is up, whisk flour and reserved 75 mL (⅓ cup) beer until smooth; stir in about 60 mL (¼ cup) hot liquid from slow cooker until blended. Stir flour mixture into slow cooker. Cover and cook on high until mixture simmers and thickens, about 20 minutes. Discard bay leaves.

PER SERVING (250 mL [1 cup]): 231 Cal, 8 g Fat, 3 g Sat Fat, 0 g Trans Fat, 46 mg Chol, 341 mg Sod, 24 g Carb, 3 g Fib, 17 g Prot, 44 mg Calc. *POINTS* value: **5.**

Spiced Beef Stew

prep 30 min • cook/slow-cook 4 hrs 15 min • serves 4

15 mL (1 tablespoon) mustard seeds

7 mL (1½ teaspoons) curry powder

2 mL (½ teaspoon) salt

Pinch cayenne

10 mL (2 teaspoons) canola oil

◆ 625 g (20oz [1¼ pounds]) top round steak, trimmed and cut into 2.5cm (1-inch) cubes

◆ 1 large onion, thinly sliced

4 garlic cloves, thinly sliced

10 mL (2 teaspoons) grated peeled fresh ginger

◆ 250 mL (1 cup) low-sodium beef broth

◆ 1 (250 mL [8-ounce]) can tomato sauce

1 Place small heavy skillet over medium heat. Add mustard seeds and cook, stirring frequently, until lightly toasted and starting to pop, about 3 minutes. Stir in curry powder. Transfer curry mixture to cup; stir in salt and cayenne.

2 Heat oil in large nonstick skillet over medium-high heat. Add half of beef and cook, turning occasionally, until lightly browned, 3–4 minutes. Transfer beef with slotted spoon to 5- or 6-L (5- or 6-quart) slow cooker. Repeat with remaining beef.

3 Spray skillet with nonstick spray and set over medium heat. Add onion and garlic; cook, stirring frequently, until onion is softened, about 5 minutes. Add ginger and curry mixture; cook, stirring frequently, until fragrant, about 1 minute. Transfer onion mixture to slow cooker.

4 Add broth and tomato sauce to skillet. Bring to boil, scraping up browned bits from bottom of pan. Pour broth mixture into slow cooker; stir to mix well. Cover and cook until beef is fork-tender, 4–6 hours on high or 8–10 hours on low.

◆ **FILLING EXTRA**

If you like, top each serving of this zesty stew with 15 mL (1 tablespoon) plain fat-free yogourt and a sprinkling of chopped fresh cilantro. This recipe works with the Simply Filling technique.

PER SERVING (175 mL [¾ cup]): 245 Cal, 8 g Fat, 2 g Sat Fat, 0 g Trans Fat, 73 mg Chol, 650 mg Sod, 10 g Carb, 2 g Fib, 33 g Prot, 39 mg Calc.
POINTS value: *5.*

Hearty Beef and Vegetable Soup

- 1 (955 mL [32-ounce]) carton low-sodium beef broth

750 mL (3 cups) water

- 1 (175 mL [6-ounce]) can tomato paste

3 mL (¾ teaspoon) salt

- 500 g (16oz {1 pound}) top round steak, trimmed and cut into 2.5 cm (1-inch) cubes

- 3 large carrots, sliced 1.25 cm (½ inch) thick

- 2 celery stalks, sliced 1.25 cm (½ inch) thick

- 1 large leek, cleaned, halved lengthwise, and cut into 2.5 cm (1-inch) slices, white and light green parts only

- 1 (250 g [½-pound]) baking potato, peeled and diced

- 2 turnips, peeled and diced

- 175 mL (¾ cup) frozen peas, thawed

1 Whisk broth, water, tomato paste, and salt in 5- or 6-L (5- or 6-quart) slow cooker until smooth. Stir in beef, carrots, celery, leek, potato, and turnips. Cover and cook until beef and vegetables are fork-tender, 4–6 hours on high or 8–12 hours on low.

2 At end of cooking time, stir in peas. Cover and cook on high until peas are heated through, about 15 minutes.

IN THE KITCHEN

This soup freezes beautifully. Transfer to a freezer container and let cool. Cover and freeze up to 3 months. Let thaw in the refrigerator overnight. Transfer to a saucepan. Cover and cook over medium heat, stirring occasionally, until heated through, 10–15 minutes. This recipe works with the Simply Filling technique.

PER SERVING (500 mL [2 cups]): 213 Cal, 3 g Fat, 1 g Sat Fat, 0 g Trans Fat, 39 mg Chol, 667 mg Sod, 25 g Carb, 5 g Fib, 22 g Prot, 67 mg Calc.
POINTS value: *4.*

Beef Posole

22 mL (1½ tablespoons) chili powder

5 mL (1 teaspoon) cumin seeds

1 mL (¼ teaspoon) salt

♦ 625 g (1¼ pounds) top round steak, trimmed and cut into 1.25 cm (½-inch) cubes

10 mL (2 teaspoons) canola oil

♦ 375 mL (1½ cups) low-sodium chicken broth

♦ 1 (475 mL [15½-ounce]) can hominy, rinsed and drained

♦ 1 (425 mL [14½-ounce]) can diced tomatoes with green chiles

♦ 2 large carrots, sliced 1.25 cm (½ inch) thick

♦ 1 large red bell pepper, diced

♦ 1 white onion, coarsely chopped

60 mL (¼ cup) water

3 garlic cloves, minced

1 Combine chili powder, cumin seeds, and salt in medium bowl. Add beef and toss to coat. Heat oil in large nonstick skillet over medium-high heat. Add beef and cook, turning occasionally, until lightly browned, about 6 minutes. Transfer beef to 5- or 6-L (5- or 6-quart) slow cooker.

2 Add broth to skillet and bring to boil over medium heat, scraping up browned bits from bottom of pan. Pour broth mixture into slow cooker. Stir in hominy, tomatoes, carrots, bell pepper, onion, water, and garlic. Cover and cook until beef and vegetables are fork-tender, 4–6 hours on high or 8–12 hours on low.

♦ **FILLING EXTRA**
Serve this classic Mexican stew over 500 mL (2 cups) cooked brown rice (125 mL [½ cup] of cooked rice per serving will up the *POINTS* value by *2*). This recipe works with the Simply Filling technique.

PER SERVING (425 mL [1¾ cups]): 329 Cal, 9 g Fat, 2 g Sat Fat, 0 g Trans Fat, 73 mg Chol, 588 mg Sod, 28 g Carb, 7 g Fib, 35 g Prot, 83 mg Calc.
POINTS value: *7.*

Beef Burgoo

prep 15 min • **slow-cook** 4 hrs • **serves** 6

45 mL (3 tablespoons) all-purpose flour

2 mL (½ teaspoon) dried thyme, crumbled

1 mL (¼ teaspoon) salt

1 mL (¼ teaspoon) black pepper

0.5 mL ($\frac{1}{8}$ teaspoon) cayenne

◆ 500 g (16oz [1 pound]) bottom round steak, trimmed and cut into 2.5cm (1-inch) cubes

◆ 125 g (4oz [¼ pound]) boneless low-sodium ham steak, trimmed and diced

◆ 375 mL (1½ cups) low-sodium beef broth

◆ 1½ cups low-sodium beef broth

◆ 125 mL (½ cup) tomato puree

45 mL (3 tablespoons) bourbon

◆ 2 large onions, cut into thin wedges through root end

◆ 1 sweet potato, peeled and cut into 1.25 cm (½-inch) chunks

◆ 1 large carrot, sliced 1.25 cm (½ inch) thick

◆ 1 (290 g [10-ounce]) box frozen succotash, thawed succotash, thawed

1 Combine flour, thyme, salt, pepper, and cayenne in medium bowl. Add beef and toss to coat.

2 Transfer beef mixture and ham to 5- or 6 L (5- or 6-quart) slow cooker. Stir in broth, tomato puree, and bourbon. Add onions, potato, carrot, and succotash; stir to mix well. Cover and cook until beef and vegetables are fork-tender, 4–6 hours on high or 8–12 hours on low.

IN THE KITCHEN
No frozen succotash at your market? Substitute 250 mL (1 cup) each thawed frozen baby lima beans and frozen corn kernels.

PER SERVING: (generous 250 mL [1 cup]): 281 Cal, 5 g Fat, 2 g Sat Fat, 0 g Trans Fat, 63 mg Chol, 418 mg Sod, 25 g Carb, 5 g Fib, 31 g Prot, 48 mg Calc. *POINTS* value: *5.*

Saucy Cabbage Rolls

prep 35 min • **cook/slow-cook** 6 hrs 20 min • **serves** 6

- 1 (1 kg [2-pound]) head green cabbage, cored
- 75 mL (1/3 cup) bulgur
- 10 mL (2 teaspoons) olive oil
- 175 mL (¾ cup) shredded carrot
- 175 mL (¾ cup) chopped onion
- 2 garlic cloves, minced
- 500 g (16oz [1 pound]) ground lean beef (7% fat or less)
- 75 mL (1/3 cup) dried currants
- 1 large egg
- 1 mL (¼ teaspoon) ground allspice
- 3 mL (¾ teaspoon) salt
- 2 mL (½ teaspoon) black pepper
- 1 (796 mL [28-ounce]) can whole tomatoes in puree
- 125 mL (½ cup) tomato paste
- 60 mL (¼ cup) packed dark brown sugar
- 30 mL (2 tablespoons) cider vinegar

1 Bring large pot of water to boil. Add cabbage. Cover and cook until outer leaves peel off easily, 8–10 minutes. With slotted spoon and tongs, transfer cabbage to colander. Let stand until cool enough to handle, about 10 minutes.

2 Meanwhile, combine bulgur and enough boiling water to cover by 2.5 cm (1 inch) in heatproof bowl. Cover and let stand until bulgur is tender, about 20 minutes. Drain in colander, pressing down on bulgur to remove any excess liquid.

3 Remove 12 large leaves and pat dry with paper towels. Trim thick ribs from leaves. Cut enough of remaining cabbage into 2.5 cm (1-inch) chunks to equal 1L (4 cups) (reserve remaining cabbage for another use). Spread cut-up cabbage in bottom of 5- or 6-L (5- or 6-quart) slow cooker.

4 To make filling, heat oil in medium nonstick skillet over medium heat. Add carrot, onion, and garlic; cook, stirring frequently, until vegetables are softened, about 5 minutes. Transfer to medium bowl. Stir in bulgur, beef, currants, egg, allspice, salt, and pepper.

5 Place 60 mL (¼ cup) filling in centre of each cabbage leaf. Fold in sides and roll up. Put rolls, seam side down, in slow cooker.

6 Break up tomatoes with spoon in large bowl. Stir in tomato paste, brown sugar, and vinegar. Pour tomato mixture over rolls. Cover and cook until instant-read thermometer inserted into centre of roll registers 70 °C (160°F), 6–8 hours on low.

PER SERVING (2 rolls with 150 mL (2/3 cup) chopped cabbage and sauce): 298 Cal, 7 g Fat, 2 g Sat Fat, 0 g Trans Fat, 78 g Chol, 770 mg Sod, 40 g Carb, 7 g Fib, 21 g Prot, 135 mg Calc. *POINTS* value: **6.**

Mediterranean Beef, Orzo, and Feta Wraps

prep 30 min • **cook/slow-cook** 2 hrs 15 min • **serves** 4

30   mL (2 tablespoons) pine nuts

5   mL (1 teaspoon) dried oregano, crumbled

◆ 375 g (¾ pound) ground extra-lean beef (5% fat or less)

◆ 1   onion, coarsely chopped

◆ 1   red bell pepper, coarsely chopped

2   garlic cloves, minced

1   mL (¼ teaspoon) salt

1   mL (¼ teaspoon) black pepper

◆ 375 mL (1½ cups) canned crushed tomatoes

◆ 30   mL (2 tablespoons) tomato paste

◆ 125 mL (½ cup) whole wheat orzo

◆ 60   mL (¼ cup) crumbled fat-free feta cheese

4   (25 cm [10-inch]) fat-free flour tortillas, warmed

◆ 500 mL (2 cups) shredded romaine lettuce or spinach

1 Place small skillet over medium heat. Add pine nuts and cook, stirring frequently, until toasted, about 3 minutes. Add oregano and cook, stirring constantly, until fragrant, about 30 seconds. Transfer nut mixture to small bowl.

2 Spray large nonstick skillet with nonstick spray and set over medium-high heat. Add beef and brown, breaking it apart with wooden spoon, about 5 minutes. Drain off any fat; add onion, bell pepper, garlic, salt, and black pepper. Cook, stirring frequently, until vegetables are crisp-tender, 3–4 minutes. Transfer beef and vegetable mixture to 5- or 6-L (5- or 6-quart) slow cooker. Stir in tomatoes, tomato paste, and pine nut mixture. Cover and cook until vegetables are fork-tender, 2–3 hours on high or 4–6 hours on low.

3 About 20 minutes before cooking time is up, cook orzo according to package directions, omitting salt if desired.

4 At end of cooking time, stir orzo into slow cooker and sprinkle feta over top. Cover and cook on high until feta is heated through, about 5 minutes.

5 Spoon 250 mL (1 cup) beef mixture onto each tortilla. Top evenly with romaine. Fold in sides and roll up. Cut each roll in half.

PER SERVING (1 wrap): 385 Cal, 8 g Fat, 2 g Sat Fat, 0 g Trans Fat, 45 mg Chol, 1,085 mg Sod, 55 g Carb, 9 g Fib, 29 g Prot, 203 mg Calc.
POINTS value: *8.*

Latin-Style Meatball Soup

prep 25 min • **bake/slow-cook** 4 hrs 10 min • **serves** 6

- 1 large onion, coarsely chopped
- 500 g (1 pound) ground lean beef (7% fat or less)
- 75 mL (¹/₃ cup) plain dried bread crumbs
- 1 large egg
- 20 mL (4 teaspoons) chili powder
- 3 mL (¾ teaspoon) ground cumin
- 2 mL (½ teaspoon) salt
- 1 large red bell pepper, coarsely chopped
- 375 mL (1½ cups) frozen corn kernels, thawed
- 750 mL (3 cups) low-sodium chicken broth
- 1 (450 g [15-ounce]) can tomato sauce
- 1 (435 g [14½-ounce]) can diced tomatoes with green chiles
- 1 zucchini, cut lengthwise in half, then thinly sliced
- 1 lime, cut into 6 wedges

1 Preheat oven to 220°C (425°F). Lightly spray large rimmed baking sheet with nonstick spray.

2 Set aside 175 mL (¾ cup) chopped onion for sauce.

3 Combine beef, bread crumbs, remaining chopped onion, egg, 15 mL (3 teaspoons) chili powder, cumin, and salt in large bowl. Form into 30 meatballs. Place meatballs on baking sheet 2.5 cm (1 inch) apart. Bake until lightly browned, about 10 minutes.

4 Meanwhile, combine reserved 175 mL (¾ cup) chopped onion, bell pepper, corn, broth, tomato sauce, tomatoes, and remaining 5 mL (1 teaspoon) chili powder in 5- or 6-L (5- or 6-quart) slow cooker. Stir in meatballs and any juices. Cover and cook until instant-read thermometer inserted into centre of meatball registers 70°C (160°F), 4–6 hours on high or 8–10 hours on low.

5 At end of cooking time, stir zucchini into slow cooker. Cover and cook on high until tender, about 20 minutes. Serve with lime wedges.

IN THE KITCHEN
We use canned tomatoes with mild green chiles, but if you like your Latin fare with an extra kick, switch to diced tomatoes with jalapeño pepper.

PER SERVING (5 meatballs with 325 mL (1⅓ cups) broth and vegetables): 253 Cal, 7 g Fat, 3 g Sat Fat, 0 g Trans Fat, 78 mg Chol, 811 mg Sod, 27 g Carb, 5 g Fib, 23 g Prot, 80 mg Calc. *POINTS* value: *5.*

Beef, Pork and More 51

Best-Even Spaghetti and Meatballs

prep 25 min • **cook/slow-cook** 3 hrs 5 min • **serves** 4

- ◆ 1 large onion, coarsely chopped
- ◆ 1 medium red bell pepper, coarsely chopped
- 2 large garlic cloves, minced
- 60 mL (4 tablespoons) chopped fresh flat-leaf parsley
- 2 mL (½ teaspoon) salt
- 1 mL (¼ teaspoon) black pepper
- ◆ 1 (830 g [28-ounce]) can crushed tomatoes in puree
- ◆ 375 g (¾ pound) ground extra-lean beef (5% fat or less)
- ◆ 125 g (¼ pound) ground lean pork
- ◆ 60 mL (¼ cup) fat-free egg substitute
- 60 mL (4 tablespoons) shredded pecorino cheese
- 45 mL (3 tablespoons) seasoned dried bread crumbs
- 170 g (6 ounces) multigrain spaghetti

1 Set aside 30 mL (2 tablespoons) chopped onion for meatballs.

2 Spray medium nonstick skillet with nonstick spray and set over medium heat. Add remaining chopped onion, bell pepper, and garlic; cook, stirring frequently, until vegetables are crisp-tender, about 5 minutes. Stir in 30 mL (2 tablespoons) parsley, 1 mL (¼ teaspoon) salt, and 0.5 mL (⅛ teaspoon) black pepper. Transfer vegetable mixture to 5- or 6-L (5- or 6-quart) slow cooker. Stir in tomatoes.

3 Combine beef, pork, egg substitute, 45 mL (3 tablespoons) pecorino, bread crumbs, reserved 30 mL (2 tablespoons) chopped onion, and remaining 30 mL (2 tablespoons) parsley, 1 mL (¼ teaspoon) salt, and 0.5 mL (⅛ teaspoon) black pepper in large bowl. Form into 12 meatballs. Transfer meatballs to slow cooker; gently turn to coat with tomato mixture. Cover and cook until instant-read thermometer inserted into centre of meatball registers 70°C (160°F) , 3–4 hours on high or 6–8 hours on low.

4 About 20 minutes before cooking time is up, cook spaghetti according to package directions, omitting salt if desired.

5 Ladle meatballs and sauce over spaghetti. Serve, sprinkled with remaining 15 mL (1 tablespoon) pecorino.

IN THE KITCHEN
If you have a pot of rosemary on your windowsill or a plant in the garden, snip a large branch and chop about 15 mL (1 tablespoon) of the needles. Add the chopped rosemary to the sauce at the end of the cooking time. Let stand about 5 minutes to allow the flavours to blend before serving.

PER SERVING (3 meatballs with 175 mL (¾ cup) sauce and 175 mL (¾ cup) spaghetti): 447 Cal, 10 g Fat, 4 g Sat Fat, 0 g Trans Fat, 70 mg Chol, 1,016 mg Sod, 55 g Carb, 7 g Fib, 37 g Prot, 209 mg Calc. *POINTS* value: *9.*

Tex-Mex Chili Mac

prep 25 min • **cook/slow-cook** 5 hrs 15 min • **serves** 6

- 250 g (½ pound) ground lean beef (7% fat or less)
- 250 g (½ pound) ground lean pork
- 1 large red bell pepper, coarsely chopped
- 1 large green bell pepper, coarsely chopped
- 1 large onion, coarsely chopped
- **3 garlic cloves, minced**
- **30 mL (2 tablespoons) chili powder**
- **3 mL (¾ teaspoon) salt**
- **2 mL (½ teaspoon) black pepper**
- 1 (830 g [28-ounce]) can whole tomatoes in puree
- 125 mL (½ cup) tomato puree
- 125 g (4 ounces) whole wheat elbow macaroni
- **175 mL (¾ cup) shredded low-fat**
- 90 mL (6 tablespoons) chopped sweet white onion

1 Place large nonstick skillet over medium-high heat; add beef and pork. Brown meat, breaking it apart with wooden spoon, about 5 minutes. Drain off any fat; add bell peppers, onion, garlic, chili powder, salt, and black pepper. Cook, stirring frequently, until vegetables are crisp-tender, about 5 minutes. Transfer meat and vegetable mixture to 5- or 6-L (5- or 6-quart) slow cooker.

2 Add tomatoes to skillet and break up with spoon. Bring to boil, scraping up browned bits from bottom of pan. Stir in tomato puree. Pour tomato mixture into slow cooker; stir to mix well. Cover and cook until vegetables are fork-tender, 5–7 hours on low.

3 About 20 minutes before cooking time is up, cook macaroni according to package directions, omitting salt if desired.

4 At end of cooking time, stir macaroni into slow cooker. Cover and cook on low until macaroni is heated through, about 5 minutes. Serve, topped with Cheddar and sweet onion.

PER SERVING (310 mL (1¼ cups) chili with 30 mL (2 tablespoons) cheese and 15 mL (1 tablespoon) onion): 276 Cal, 7 g Fat, 3 g Sat Fat, 0 g Trans Fat, 48 mg Chol, 874 mg Sod, 30 g Carb, 6 g Fib, 25 g Prot, 179 mg Calc. *POINTS* value: *5.*

Ketchup and Mustard Meat Loaf

prep 20 min • **cook/slow-cook** 4 hrs 5 min • **serves** 4

- ½   onion, finely chopped
- 125 mL (½ cup) shredded carrot
- 30 mL (2 tablespoons) chopped fresh flat-leaf parsley
- 1   garlic clove, minced
- 5   mL (1 teaspoon) canola oil
- 2   mL (½ teaspoon) dried thyme
- 1   mL (¼ teaspoon) salt
- 1   mL (¼ teaspoon) black pepper
- 500 g (1 pound) lean meat loaf mix (beef, pork, and veal)
- 125 mL (½ cup) seasoned dried bread crumbs
- 125 mL (½ cup) ketchup
- 60 mL (¼ cup) fat-free egg substitute
- 30 mL (2 tablespoons) whole-grain mustard

1 Spray 5- or 6-L (5- or 6-quart) slow cooker stoneware with nonstick spray. Make foil handles (see **IN THE KITCHEN** below).

2 Spray medium nonstick skillet with nonstick spray and set over medium heat. Add onion, carrot, parsley, garlic, oil, thyme, salt, and pepper; cook, stirring frequently, until vegetables are softened, 4–5 minutes. Transfer to large bowl and let cool slightly, about 5 minutes. Stir in meat loaf mix, bread crumbs, 60 mL (¼ cup) ketchup, egg substitute, and 15 mL (1 tablespoon) mustard just until blended. Form into 10 cm x 17 cm (4 x 7-inch) loaf.

3 Transfer loaf to slow cooker so that centre is on top of crossed foil strips. Mix remaining 60mL (¼ cup) ketchup and 15 mL (1 tablespoon) mustard in small bowl. Spread mixture over top and sides of meat loaf. Cover and cook until instant-read thermometer inserted into centre of meat loaf registers 70°C (160°F), 4–6 hours on high or 8–10 hours on low.

4 Using foil handles, transfer meat loaf to cutting board and let stand 5 minutes. Cut into 12 slices.

IN THE KITCHEN

To make removing the meat loaf from the slow cooker easy, make foil handles: Fold 1 (60 cm [24-inch]) sheet of foil lengthwise in half twice. Repeat with another sheet of foil to make 2 strips. Press the foil strips into the stoneware, so that they form a cross on the bottom and the ends hang over the top edge of the slow cooker.

PER SERVING (3 slices): 282 Cal, 10 g Fat, 3 g Sat Fat, 0 g Trans Fat, 74 mg Chol, 763 mg Sod, 22 g Carb, 2 g Fib, 27 g Prot, 101 mg Calc.
POINTS value: *6.*

Pork Roast with Dried Plums

prep 20 min • broil/slow-cook 4 hrs 10 min • serves 6

15 mL (1 tablespoon) packed dark brown sugar

3 mL (¾ teaspoon) dried oregano

2 mL (½ teaspoon) salt

2 mL (½ teaspoon) coarsely ground black pepper

♦ 1 (750 g [1½-pound]) bone-in pork loin roast, trimmed

5 mL (1 teaspoon) olive oil

1 orange

45 mL (3 tablespoons) all-purpose flour

♦ 175 mL (¾ cup) low-sodium chicken broth

75 mL (⅓ cup) red wine or unsweetened grape juice

175 mL (¾ cup) pitted dried plums, halved

1 7.5cm (3-inch) cinnamon stick

1 Spray broiler rack with nonstick spray. Preheat broiler.

2 Mix brown sugar, oregano, salt, and pepper in cup. Rub pork with oil, then with brown sugar mixture. Transfer pork to broiler rack. Broil pork 12.5 cm (5 inches) from heat until lightly browned, 6–8 minutes per side. Transfer pork to 5- or 6- L (5- or 6- quart) slow cooker.

3 Meanwhile, with swivel-blade vegetable peeler, cut 2 (7.5cm [3-inch]) strips peel from orange. Squeeze juice from half of orange (reserve remaining orange for another use). Put flour in medium bowl. Gradually whisk in broth, orange juice, and wine until smooth. Pour broth mixture into slow cooker. Stir in dried plums, orange peel, and cinnamon stick. Cover and cook until pork is fork-tender, 4–6 hours on high or 8–10 hours on low, turning pork and basting it with sauce once halfway through cooking time.

4 Transfer pork to cutting board and let stand 5 minutes. Remove and discard bone from pork; cut pork into 12 slices. Serve with sauce.

PER SERVING (2 slices pork with about 75 mL [5 tablespoons] sauce): 235 Cal, 7 g Fat, 2 g Sat Fat, 0 g Trans Fat, 52 mg Chol, 237 mg Sod, 23 g Carb, 2 g Fib, 20 g Prot, 29 mg Calc. *POINTS* value: *5.*

Pork Charcuterie

prep 20 min • broil/slow-cook/cook 4 hrs 25 min • serves 4

3 mL (¾ teaspoon) dried thyme

3 mL (¾ teaspoon) coarsely ground black pepper

2 mL (½ teaspoon) dill seeds

1 mL (¼ teaspoon) salt

♦ 1 (750 g [1½-pound]) bone-in pork loin roast, trimmed

2 large onions, thinly sliced

2 garlic cloves, thinly sliced

60 mL (¼ cup) all-purpose flour

150 mL (²⁄₃ cup) water

60 mL (¼ cup) dry white wine

60 mL (¼ cup) finely chopped dill pickles

7 mL (1½ teaspoons) whole-grain mustard

1 Spray broiler rack with nonstick spray. Preheat broiler.

2 Mix thyme, pepper, dill seeds, and salt in cup. Spray pork with nonstick spray, then rub with herb mixture. Transfer pork to broiler rack. Broil pork 5 inches from heat until lightly browned, 6–8 minutes per side.

3 Combine onions and garlic in 5- or 6-L (5- or 6-quart) slow cooker. Top with pork. Put flour in medium bowl. Gradually whisk in water and wine until smooth. Pour wine mixture into slow cooker. Cover and cook until pork is fork-tender, 4–6 hours on high or 8–12 hours on low.

4 Transfer pork to cutting board. Cover with foil and keep warm. Transfer cooking liquid and onions to small saucepan and bring to boil. Reduce heat and simmer until mixture is slightly thickened and reduced to about 625 mL (2½ cups), about 10 minutes. Whisk in pickles and mustard. Remove and discard bone from pork; cut pork into 8 slices. Serve with sauce.

♦ FILLING EXTRA

Serve this hearty roast with 500 mL (2 cups) steamed baby carrots and 500 mL (2 cups) cooked quinoa and up the per-serving *POINTS* value by *2.*

PER SERVING (2 slices pork with about 150 mL [²⁄₃ cup] sauce): 247 Cal, 11 g Fat, 4 g Sat Fat, 0 g Trans Fat, 56 mg Chol, 287 mg Sod, 15 g Carb, 2 g Fib, 21 g Prot, 42 mg Calc. *POINTS* value: *5.*

Pork with Two Beans

prep 25 min • broil/slow-cook 3 hrs 10 min • serves 4

◆ 1 (625 g [1¼-pound]) pork tenderloin, trimmed and cut crosswise in half

2 small garlic cloves, cut into 12 slices

5 mL (1 teaspoon) olive oil

5 mL (1 teaspoon) fennel seeds

2 mL (½ teaspoon) dried rosemary, crumbled

2 mL (½ teaspoon) salt

2 mL (½ teaspoon) coarsely ground black pepper

1 mL (¼ teaspoon) red pepper flakes

◆ 125 mL (½ cup) tomato puree

◆ 125 mL (½ cup) low-sodium chicken broth

30 mL (2 tablespoons) white-wine vinegar

◆ 500 mL (2 cups) frozen Italian-cut green beans, thawed

◆ 250 mL (1 cup) canned cannellini (white kidney) beans, rinsed and drained

1 Spray broiler rack with nonstick spray. Preheat broiler.

2 Cut about 6 (1.25 cm [½-inch]) slits in each piece of pork and insert 1 garlic slice in each. Mix fennel seeds, rosemary, salt, black pepper, and red pepper flakes in cup. Rub spice mixture all over pork. Transfer pork to broiler rack. Broil pork 12.5 cm (5 inches) from heat until lightly browned, 5–7 minutes per side.

3 Combine tomato puree, broth, and vinegar in 5- or 6-L (5- or 6-quart) slow cooker. Top with pork. Cover and cook until pork is fork-tender, 3–4 hours on high or 6–8 hours on low.

4 About 35 minutes before cooking time is up, stir green and cannellini beans into slow cooker. Cover and cook on high until beans are heated through, about 30 minutes.

5 Transfer pork to cutting board. Cut each piece into 8 slices. Serve with beans and sauce.

IN THE KITCHEN
Frozen Italian-cut green beans (sometimes called pole beans) are widely available in 500 g (16-ounce) bags. This recipe works with the Simply Filling technique.

PER SERVING (4 slices pork with about 225 mL (⅔ cup)beans and sauce): 260 Cal, 7 g Fat, 2 g Sat Fat, 0 g Trans Fat, 56 mg Chol, 626 mg Sod, 19 g Carb, 5 g Fib, 32 g Prot, 83 mg Calc. *POINTS* value: *5.*

BBQ Pork Chops

prep 20 min • broil/cook/slow-cook 3 hrs 10 min • serves 4

15 mL (1 tablespoon) paprika

2 mL (½ teaspoon) garlic powder

2 mL (½ teaspoon) salt

2 mL (½ teaspoon) coarsely ground black pepper

♦ 4 (170 g [6-ounce]) bone-in centre-cut pork loin chops, trimmed

5 mL (1 teaspoon) olive oil

♦ 1 large onion, thinly sliced

♦ 250 mL (1 cup) tomato puree

60 mL (¼ cup) ketchup

30 mL (2 tablespoons) honey

2 mL (½ teaspoon) chipotle chile powder

1 Preheat broiler. Spray large rimmed baking sheet with nonstick spray.

2 Mix paprika, garlic powder, salt, and pepper in cup. Rub pork with oil, then with spice mixture. Transfer pork to baking sheet. Broil pork 12.5 cm (5 inches) from heat until lightly browned, about 4 minutes per side.

3 Meanwhile, spray large nonstick skillet with nonstick spray and set over medium heat. Add onion and cook, stirring frequently, until softened, about 5 minutes. Stir in tomato puree, ketchup, honey, and chile powder. Spread half of sauce in bottom of 5- or 6-L (5- or 6-quart) slow cooker. Top with pork and any juices and remaining sauce. Cover and cook until pork is fork-tender, 3–4 hours on low.

♦ FILLING EXTRA

Serve these smoky chops with baked sweet potatoes (1 medium baked potato topped with 15 mL (1 tablespoon) fat-free sour cream per serving will up the *POINTS* value by *2*).

PER SERVING (1 pork chop and about 125 mL [½ cup] sauce): 300 Cal, 11 g Fat, 3 g Sat Fat, 0 g Trans Fat, 76 mg Chol, 759 mg Sod, 23 g Carb, 3 g Fib, 29 g Prot, 34 mg Calc. *POINTS* value: *6.*

Double Mushroom—Smothered Pork Chops

prep 25 min • **cook/slow-cook** 3 hrs 5 min • **serves** 4

♦ 4   (125 g [¼-pound]) boneless centre-cut pork loin chops, trimmed

2   mL (½ teaspoon) salt

1   mL (¼ teaspoon) black pepper

1   (300 g [10¾-ounce]) can low-sodium, low-fat condensed cream of mushroom soup

60   mL (¼ cup) water

♦ 4   carrots, chopped

♦ 1   (290 g [10-ounce]) package sliced cremini mushrooms

5   mL (1 teaspoon) steak sauce

5   mL (1 teaspoon) dried thyme

2   mL (½ teaspoon) dried oregano

1 Sprinkle pork with salt and pepper. Spray large nonstick skillet with nonstick spray and set over medium-high heat. Add pork and cook until browned, about 2 minutes per side.

2 Combine soup, water, carrots, mushrooms, steak sauce, thyme, and oregano in 5- or 6-L (5- or 6-quart) slow cooker. Top with pork. Cover and cook until pork and vegetables are fork-tender, 3–4 hours on high or 6–8 hours on low.

♦ FILLING EXTRA

For a satisfying side dish, toss 8 (90 g [3-ounce]) hot cooked baby potatoes with a light spray of olive oil nonstick spray and salt and black pepper to taste. This will increase the per-serving *POINTS* value by *2.*

PER SERVING (1 pork chop with 125 mL [½ cup] vegetables): 230 Cal, 8 g Fat, 3 g Sat Fat, 0 g Trans Fat, 64 mg Chol, 637 mg Sod, 14 g Carb, 3 g Fib, 25 g Prot, 41 mg Calc. *POINTS* value: *5.*

Hoisin Pork Rolls

prep 25 min • **slow-cook** 2 hrs • **serves** 4

- 60 mL (¼ cup) water
- 35 mL (1 tablespoon + 4 teaspoons) hoisin sauce
- 30 mL (2 tablespoons) dry sherry
- 30 mL (2 tablespoons) low-sodium soy sauce
- 2 garlic cloves, crushed through a press
- 25 mL (1 tablespoon + 2 teaspoons) cornstarch
- 5 mL (1 teaspoon grated peeled fresh ginger
- 5 mL (1 teaspoon) sugar
- ◆ 625 g (1¼ pounds) pork tenderloin, trimmed and cut into matchstick strips
- ◆ 1 (250 g [8-ounce]) package sliced mushrooms
- ◆ 500 mL (2 cups) matchstick carrots
- ◆ 125 mL (½ cup) drained canned bamboo shoots
- ◆ 500 mL (2 cups) loosely packed shredded romaine lettuce
- 125 mL (½ cup) coarsely chopped fresh cilantro
- ◆ 125 mL (½ cup) thinly sliced scallions
- 4 (22 cm [9-inch]) fat-free flour tortillas

1 Whisk water, 1 tablespoon hoisin sauce, sherry, soy sauce, garlic, cornstarch, ginger, and sugar in 5- or 6-L (5- or 6-quart) slow cooker until smooth. Add pork and mix well. Stir in mushrooms, carrots, and bamboo shoots.

2 Cover and cook until pork and vegetables are fork-tender, 2–3 hours on high or 4–6 hours on low, stirring once halfway through cooking time.

3 Combine romaine, cilantro, and scallions in medium bowl. Spread each tortilla with 5 mL (1 teaspoon) remaining hoisin sauce. Top each with generous 175 mL (¾ cup) pork mixture and 175 mL (¾ cup) romaine mixture. Fold in sides and roll up.

IN THE KITCHEN
If the sauce gets too thick, add 15 mL (1 tablespoon) hot water to the slow cooker when stirring the pork mixture halfway through the cooking time in step 2.

PER SERVING (1 roll): 388 Cal, 6 g Fat, 2 g Sat Fat, 0 g Trans Fat, 57 mg Chol, 1,066 mg Sod, 53 g Carb, 8 g Fib, 35 g Prot, 169 mg Calc. *POINTS* value: *7.*

Pork and Pepper Stew

prep 25 min • **broil/slow-cook** 3 hrs 10 min • **serves** 6

45   mL (3 tablespoons) all-purpose flour

3   garlic cloves, minced

2   mL (½ teaspoon) dried marjoram

2   mL (½ teaspoon) dried sage

2   mL (½ teaspoon) salt

2   mL (½ teaspoon) black pepper

♦ 625 g (1¼ pounds) boneless pork loin, trimmed and cut into 2.5 cm (1-inch) cubes

10   mL (2 teaspoons) olive oil

♦ 3 assorted-colour bell peppers, cut into thin strips

♦ 375 mL (1½ cups) canned crushed tomatoes

60   mL (¼ cup) dry sherry or low-sodium chicken broth

1 Preheat broiler. Spray large rimmed baking sheet with nonstick spray.

2 Combine flour, garlic, marjoram, sage, salt, and black pepper in medium bowl. Add pork and toss to coat. Transfer pork to baking sheet and spread in single layer, shaking excess flour into bowl. Reserve flour. Drizzle pork with oil. Broil pork 12.5 cm (5 inches) from heat, turning frequently, until lightly browned, 8–10 minutes.

3 Transfer pork and any juices to 5- or 6-L (5- or 6-quart) slow cooker. Stir in bell peppers, tomatoes, sherry, and reserved flour mixture until blended. Cover and cook until pork and bell peppers are fork-tender, 3–4 hours on high or 6–8 hours on low.

♦ **FILLING EXTRA**

For a hearty side dish, spray a broiler rack with nonstick spray and preheat the broiler. Cut 1 (500 g [16-ounce]) tube refrigerated fat-free polenta into 8 rounds. Transfer the polenta to the broiler rack and broil 12.5 cm (5 inches) from the heat until lightly browned and heated through, 3–4 minutes. The per-serving *POINTS* value will increase by *2*.

PER SERVING (generous 175 mL [¾ cup]): 218 Cal, 9 g Fat, 3 g Sat Fat, 0 g Trans Fat, 60 mg Chol, 125 mg Sod, 10 g Carb, 2 g Fib, 23 g Prot, 35 mg Calc. *POINTS* value: *5*.

Pork Cacciatore

prep 15 min • slow-cook 4 hrs • serves 4

- 500 mL (2 cups) canned crushed tomatoes
- 1 (375 g [12-ounce]) package mushrooms, quartered
- 60 mL (¼ cup) dry white wine
- 2 garlic cloves, minced
- 30 mL (2 tablespoons) all-purpose flour
- 2 mL (½ teaspoon) dried oregano
- 2 mL (½ teaspoon) salt
- 1 mL (¼ teaspoon) red pepper flakes
- 500 g (1 pound) boneless pork loin, trimmed and cut into 2.5cm (1-inch) cubes

1 Combine tomatoes, mushrooms, wine, and garlic in in 5- or 6-L (5- or 6-quart) slow cooker.

2 Mix flour, oregano, salt, and red pepper flakes in medium bowl. Add pork and toss to coat. Stir pork and flour mixture into slow cooker. Cover and cook until pork and mushrooms are fork-tender, 4–6 hours on high or 8–12 hours on low.

◆ FILLING EXTRA

Serve this Italian favorite over 750 mL (3 cups) cooked whole wheat fusilli and increase the per-serving *POINTS* value by *2.*

PER SERVING (about 250 mL [1 cup]): 247 Cal, 9 g Fat, 3 g Sat Fat, 0 g Trans Fat, 72 mg Chol, 516 mg Sod, 12 g Carb, 2 g Fib, 29 g Prot, 52 mg Calc. *POINTS* value: *5.*

Pork Goulash

45	mL (3 tablespoons) all-purpose flour
15	mL (1 tablespoon) paprika
3	mL (¾ teaspoon) dried marjoram
2	mL (½ teaspoon) salt
2	mL (½ teaspoon) black pepper
◆ 625	g (1¼ pounds) boneless pork loin, trimmed and cut into 2.5 cm (1-inch) cubes
10	mL (2 teaspoons) olive oil
◆ 500	mL (2 cups) coarsely chopped green cabbage
◆ 1	large onion, coarsely chopped
◆ 2	large carrots, sliced
◆ 250	mL (1 cup) low-sodium chicken broth
◆ 125	mL (½ cup) tomato puree
60	mL (¼ cup) dry white wine
625	mL (2½ cups) water
◆ 75	mL (⅓ cup) barley
◆ 90	mL (6 tablespoons) fat-free sour cream

1 Preheat broiler. Spray large rimmed baking sheet with nonstick spray.

2 Combine flour, paprika, marjoram, salt, and pepper in medium bowl. Add pork and toss to coat. Transfer pork to baking sheet and spread in single layer, shaking excess flour into bowl. Reserve flour. Drizzle pork with oil. Broil pork 12.5 cm (5 inches) from heat, turning frequently, until lightly browned, about 8 minutes.

3 Transfer pork and any juices to 5- or 6-L (5- or 6-quart) slow cooker. Stir in cabbage, onion, carrots, broth, tomato puree, wine, and reserved flour mixture. Cover and cook until pork and vegetables are fork-tender, 4–6 hours on high or 8–12 hours on low.

4 About 40 minutes before cooking time is up, bring water to boil in medium saucepan. Stir in barley. Cover, reduce heat, and simmer until barley is tender, about 35 minutes. Drain.

5 At end of cooking time, stir barley into slow cooker. Serve, topped with sour cream.

◆ **FILLING EXTRA**
In addition to the sour cream, top each serving of goulash with 30 mL (2 tablespoons) sliced scallions.

PER SERVING (generous 175 mL (¾ cup) stew with 15 mL (1 tablespoon) sour cream): 281 Cal, 10 g Fat, 3 g Sat Fat, 0 g Trans Fat, 62 mg Chol, 373 mg Sod, 24 g Carb, 5 g Fib, 25 g Prot, 63 mg Calc. *POINTS* value: *6.*

Pork Stew with Olive Gremolata

prep 25 min • **broil/slow-cook** 4 hrs 10 min • **serves** 4

3   garlic cloves

10   mL (2 teaspoons) olive oil

5   mL (1 teaspoon) dried rosemary

2   mL (½ teaspoon) salt

1   mL (¼ teaspoon) black pepper

♦ 625 g (1¼ pounds) pork tenderloin, trimmed and cut into 2.5 cm (1-inch) cubes

♦ 1   orange

♦ 375 g (¾ pound) red baby potatoes, halved

♦ 2   large carrots, sliced 1.25 cm (½ inch) thick

♦ 250 mL (1 cup) low-sodium chicken broth

♦ 10   brine-cured Kalamata olives, pitted and chopped

1 Preheat broiler. Spray rimmed baking sheet with nonstick spray.

2 Mince 2 garlic cloves. Transfer minced garlic to large bowl; stir in oil, rosemary, salt and pepper. Add pork and toss to coat. Transfer pork to baking sheet and spread in single layer. Broil pork 12.5 cm (5 inches) from heat, turning frequently, until lightly browned, 8–10 minutes.

3 Meanwhile, with swivel-blade peeler, remove 2 (10 cm [4-inch]) strips orange peel. Grate enough of remaining peel to equal 10 mL (2 teaspoons). Chop segments from half of orange (reserve remaining orange for another use). Wrap grated peel in plastic wrap and refrigerate.

4 Combine potatoes and carrots in 5- or 6-L (5- or 6-quart) slow cooker. Top with pork and any juices, broth, orange strips, and chopped orange. Cover and cook until pork and vegetables are fork-tender, 4–5 hours on high or 8–10 hours on low.

5 To make gremolata, about 10 minutes before cooking time is up, mince remaining 1 garlic clove. Transfer garlic to small bowl; stir in olives and grated orange peel. Stir gremolata into slow cooker. Cover and cook on high until flavours are blended, about 5 minutes.

This recipe works with the Simply Filling technique.

PER SERVING (325 mL [1⅓ cups]): 291 Cal, 9 g Fat, 2 g Sat Fat, 0 g Trans Fat, 56 mg Chol, 491 mg Sod, 25 g Carb, 4 g Fib, 30 g Prot, 69 mg Calc.
POINTS value: *6.*

Kentucky Pork Chili

prep 20 min • **slow-cook** 4 hrs • **serves** 6

- 500 g (1 pound) pork tenderloin, trimmed and cut into 1.25 cm (½-inch) cubes
- 2 medium onions, chopped
- 2 zucchini, diced
- 1 (430 g [14½-ounce]) can fire-roasted diced tomatoes with green chiles
- 1 (450 g [15-ounce]) can red kidney beans, rinsed and drained
- 250 mL (1 cup) shredded carrots
- 60 mL (¼ cup) orange marmalade
- 2 strips turkey bacon, chopped
- 30 mL (2 tablespoons) bourbon or low-sodium chicken broth
- 2 garlic cloves, finely chopped
- 45 mL (3 tablespoons) chili powder
- 5 mL (1 teaspoon) dried oregano
- 1 mL (¼ teaspoon) black pepper
- 30 mL (2 tablespoons) cornmeal

1 Put pork in food processor and pulse until medium to finely chopped. Transfer pork to 5- or 6-L (5- or 6-quart) slow cooker. Stir in onions, zucchini, tomatoes, beans, carrots, marmalade, bacon, bourbon, garlic, chili powder, oregano, and pepper. Cover and cook until pork and vegetables are fork-tender, 4–5 hours on high or 8–10 hours on low.

2 About 20 minutes before cooking time is up, gradually stir cornmeal into slow cooker until blended. Cover and cook on high until mixture simmers and thickens, about 15 minutes.

♦ **FILLING EXTRA**
Garnish each serving of the chili with a sprinkling of chopped red onion and 15 mL (a tablespoon) fat-free sour cream.

PER SERVING (250 mL [1 cup]): 260 Cal, 6 g Fat, 2 g Sat Fat, 0 g Trans Fat, 45 mg Chol, 625 mg Sod, 31 g Carb, 7 g Fib, 21 g Prot, 99 g Calc.
POINTS value: *5.*

Ham and Vegetable Chowder

prep 25 min • cook/slow-cook 4 hrs 5 min • serves 6

15 mL (1 tablespoon) olive oil

♦ 1 large onion, chopped

2 garlic cloves, minced

5 mL (1 teaspoon) caraway seeds

5 mL (1 teaspoon) caraway seeds

2 mL (½ teaspoon) dried thyme

1 bay leaf

1 mL (¼ teaspoon) salt

♦ 1 kg (2 pounds) baking potatoes, peeled and cut into 2.5 cm (1-inch) chunks

♦ 750 mL (3 cups) coarsely chopped green cabbage

♦ 750 mL (3 cups) low-sodium chicken broth

375 mL (1½ cups) water

♦ 250 g (½ pound) boneless low-sodium ham steak, trimmed and diced

♦ 375 mL (1½ cups) frozen corn kernels, thawed

1 Heat oil in medium nonstick skillet over medium heat. Add onion and garlic; cook, stirring frequently, until softened, 6–8 minutes. Add caraway seeds, thyme, bay leaf, and salt; cook, stirring frequently, until fragrant, about 1 minute.

2 Transfer onion mixture to 5- or 6-L (5- or 6-quart) slow cooker. Stir in potatoes, cabbage, broth, water, and ham. Cover and cook until vegetables are fork-tender, 4–6 hours on high or 8–12 hours on low.

3 About 35 minutes before cooking time is up, stir corn into slow cooker. Cover and cook on high until corn is just tender, about 30 minutes. Discard bay leaf.

IN THE KITCHEN
If you prefer a thicker soup, with a potato masher, coarsely mash about half of the potatoes right in the slow cooker. This recipe works with the Simply Filling technique.

PER SERVING (400 mL [1⅔ cups]): 261 Cal, 5 g Fat, 1 g Sat Fat, 0 g Trans Fat, 18 mg Chol, 479 mg Sod, 42 g Carb, 5 g Fib, 14 g Prot, 51 mg Calc.
POINTS value: *5.*

New Orleans Red Beans and Rice

prep 20 min • **cook/slow-cook** 3 hrs 10 min • **serves** 6

15   mL (1 tablespoon) olive oil

♦ 1   large onion, chopped

♦ 1   large green bell pepper,
       coarsely chopped

♦ 2   celery stalks, coarsely chopped

3   garlic cloves, minced

♦ 250 g (½ pound) boneless low-
       sodium ham steak, trimmed
       and diced

10   mL (2 teaspoons) Creole
     seasoning

♦ 2   (450g [15-ounce]) cans red
       kidney beans, rinsed and
       drained

♦ 1   (830g [28-ounce]) can whole
       tomatoes in puree, coarsely
       chopped

♦ 750 mL (3 cups) hot cooked
       brown rice

1 Heat oil in large nonstick skillet over medium-high heat. Add onion, bell pepper, celery, and garlic; cook, stirring frequently, until vegetables are crisp-tender, about 8 minutes. Add ham and Creole seasoning; cook, stirring frequently, until ham is heated through, 1–2 minutes.

2 Transfer ham mixture to 5- or 6-L (5- or 6-quart) slow cooker. Stir in beans and tomatoes. Cover and cook until vegetables are fork-tender, 3–4 hours on high or 6–8 hours on low.

3 Divide rice among 6 shallow bowls. Top evenly with bean mixture. Serve, sprinkled with scallions.

IN THE KITCHEN

For best results, select a ham steak that's about 1.25 cm (½ inch) thick. Avoid buying thinly sliced ham—it will fall apart in the slow cooker.

PER SERVING (325 mL [1⅓ cups] bean mixture with 125 mL [½ cup] rice and about 30 mL [2 tablespoons] scallions): 350 Cal, 6 g Fat, 1 g Sat Fat, 0 g Trans Fat, 18 mg Chol, 991 mg Sod, 57 g Carb, 12 g Fib, 20 g Prot, 112 mg Calc. *POINTS* value: *7.*

Three-Herb Leg of Lamb

prep 15 min • **cook/slow-cook** 3 hrs 10 min • **serves** 6

1   shallot, minced

30 mL (2 tablespoons) chopped fresh rosemary or 10 mL (2 teaspoons) dried

15 mL (1 tablespoon) chopped fresh thyme or 5 mL (1 teaspoon) dried

15 mL (1 tablespoon) chopped fresh oregano or 5 mL (1 teaspoon) dried

10 mL (2 teaspoons) extra-virgin olive oil

2   mL (½ teaspoon) salt

1   mL (¼ teaspoon) black pepper

◆ 1   kg (2 pounds) butterflied boneless leg of lamb, trimmed

30 mL (2 tablespoons) tarragon mustard

◆ 125 mL (½ cup) low-sodium chicken broth

1 Mix shallot, rosemary, thyme, oregano, 5 mL (1 teaspoon) oil, salt, and pepper in bowl. Rub lamb with mustard, then press on herb mixture.

2 Heat remaining 5 mL (1 teaspoon) oil in large nonstick skillet over medium-high heat. Add lamb and cook until browned on all sides, about 8 minutes. Transfer lamb to 5- or 6-L (5- or 6-quart) slow cooker.

3 Add broth to skillet and bring to boil, scraping up browned bits from bottom of pan. Pour broth mixture over lamb. Cover and cook until lamb is fork-tender, 3–4 hours on high or 6–8 hours on low.

4 Transfer lamb to cutting board and cut into 12 slices.

◆ **FILLING EXTRA**
Serve this savory lamb with 1 L (4 cups) cooked whole wheat couscous (150 mL [⅔ cup] cooked couscous per serving will up the *POINTS* value by *2*). This recipe works with the Simply Filling technique.

PER SERVING (2 slices): 212 Cal, 9 g Fat, 3 g Sat Fat, 0 g Trans Fat, 87 mg Chol, 434 mg Sod, 1 g Carb, 0 g Fib, 28 g Prot, 27 mg Calc.
POINTS value: *5.*

Herbed Lamb with White Beans

prep 20 min • **broil/slow-cook** 3 hrs 10 min • **serves** 4

- 500 g (1 pound) boneless leg of lamb, trimmed and cut into 3.75 cm (1½-inch) cubes
- 5 mL (1 teaspoon) olive oil
- 2 garlic cloves, minced
- 3 mL (¾ teaspoon) dried thyme, crumbled
- 2 mL (½ teaspoon) salt
- 1 mL (¼ teaspoon) black pepper
- 375 mL (1½ cups) canned crushed tomatoes
- 1 red onion, coarsely chopped
- 125 mL (½ cup) water
- 15 mL (1 tablespoon) balsamic vinegar
- 1 (475g [15½-ounce]) can cannellini (white kidney) beans, rinsed and drained

1 Preheat broiler. Spray large rimmed baking sheet with nonstick spray.

2 Combine lamb and oil in large bowl. Add garlic, thyme, salt, and pepper; toss to coat. Transfer lamb to baking sheet and spread in single layer. Broil lamb 12.5 cm (5 inches) from heat, turning frequently, until lightly browned, 8–10 minutes.

3 Transfer lamb and any juices to 5- or 6-L (5- or 6-quart) slow cooker. Stir in tomatoes, onion, water, and vinegar. Cover and cook until lamb and onion are fork-tender, 3–4 hours on high or 6–8 hours on low.

4 About 20 minutes before cooking time is up, stir beans into slow cooker. Cover and cook on high until beans are heated through, about 15 minutes. With whisk, coarsely mash about 125 mL (½ cup) beans to thicken sauce.

IN THE KITCHEN
If you have fresh thyme growing in the garden or on a windowsill, use it in this dish. Add 10 mL (2 heaping teaspoons) fresh thyme leaves in step 2, then stir in 5 mL (1 teaspoon) just before serving. This recipe works with the Simply Filling technique.

PER SERVING (about 310 mL [1¼ cups]): 320 Cal, 9 g Fat, 3 g Sat Fat, 0 g Trans Fat, 78 mg Chol, 718 mg Sod, 26 g Carb, 6 g Fib, 33 g Prot, 117 mg Calc. *POINTS* value: *6.*

Lamb and Spinach Stew

prep 20 min • broil/slow-cook 3 hrs 10 min • serves 4

- 30 mL (2 tablespoons) coarsely chopped fresh rosemary
- 2 garlic cloves, minced
- 2 mL (½ teaspoon) dried oregano
- 2 mL (½ teaspoon) salt
- 1 mL (¼ teaspoon) black pepper
- ◆ 500 g (1 pound) boneless leg of lamb, trimmed and cut into 2.5 cm (1-inch) cubes
- 5 mL (1 teaspoon) olive oil
- ◆ 750 mL (3 cups) frozen cut spinach (from 500 g [16-ounce] bag), thawed and squeezed dry
- ◆ 250 mL (1 cup) low-sodium chicken broth
- ◆ 1 bunch scallions, thinly sliced
- ◆ 2 stalks celery, sliced

1 Preheat broiler. Spray large rimmed baking sheet with nonstick spray.

2 Mix rosemary and garlic on cutting board. Sprinkle with oregano, salt, and pepper; finely chop until mixture is well blended. Combine lamb, oil, and herb mixture in large bowl. Transfer to baking sheet and spread in single layer. Broil lamb 12.5 cm (5 inches) from heat, turning frequently, until lightly browned, 8–10 minutes.

3 Transfer lamb and any juices to 5- or 6-L (5- or 6-quart) slow cooker. Stir in spinach, broth, scallions, and celery. Cover and cook until lamb and celery are fork-tender, 3–4 hours on high or 6–8 hours on low.

◆ **FILLING EXTRA**

Top this savory stew with 15 mL (1 tablespoon) plain fat-free Greek yogourt **per serving.** This recipe works with the Simply Filling technique.

PER SERVING (about 250 mL [1 cup]): 238 Cal, 10 g Fat, 3 g Sat Fat, 0 g Trans Fat, 78 mg Chol, 470 mg Sod, 9 g Carb, 4 g Fib, 29 g Prot, 170 mg Calc. *POINTS* value: *5.*

Lamb Stew with Peppers and Vinegar

prep 20 min • broil/cook/slow-cook 4 hrs 10 min • serves 4

- 625 g (1¼ pounds) boneless leg of lamb, trimmed and cut into 2.5 cm (1-inch) cubes
- 2 mL (½ teaspoon) salt
- 1 mL (¼ teaspoon) black pepper
- 1 red onion, thinly sliced
- 3 garlic cloves, minced
- 30 mL (2 tablespoons) coarsely chopped fresh rosemary
- 2 anchovy fillets, patted dry and cut up
- 3 assorted-colour bell peppers, cut into 2.5cm (1-inch) chunks
- 30 mL (2 tablespoons) + 75 mL (⅓ cup) water
- 60 mL (¼ cup) red-wine vinegar
- 4 canned whole tomatoes in puree, drained and chopped
- 45 mL (3 tablespoons) tomato paste
- 1 mL (¼ teaspoon) red pepper flakes

1 Preheat broiler. Spray large rimmed baking sheet with nonstick spray.

2 Combine lamb, salt, and black pepper in large bowl. Transfer to baking sheet and spread in single layer. Broil lamb 12.5 cm (5 inches) from heat, turning frequently, until lightly browned, 8–10 minutes. Transfer lamb and any juices to 5- or 6-L (5- or 6-quart) slow cooker.

3 Meanwhile, spray large nonstick skillet with nonstick spray and set over medium heat. Add onion, garlic, and rosemary; cook, stirring frequently, until onion is softened, about 4 minutes. Stir in anchovies. Add bell peppers and 30 mL (2 tablespoons) water; cook, stirring frequently, until bell peppers are crisp-tender, about 5 minutes.

4 Transfer bell pepper mixture to slow cooker. Add vinegar to skillet and bring to boil, scraping up browned bits from bottom of pan. Stir vinegar mixture, tomatoes, tomato paste, red pepper flakes, and remaining 75 mL (⅓ cup) water into slow cooker. Cover and cook until lamb and vegetables are fork-tender, 4–6 hours on high or 8–10 hours on low.

IN THE KITCHEN
Sweet bell peppers work best in this recipe—try red, yellow, or orange peppers.

PER SERVING (250 mL [1 cup]): 292 Cal, 10 g Fat, 4 g Sat Fat, 0 g Trans Fat, 99 mg Chol, 669 mg Sod, 16 g Carb, 4 g Fib, 33 g Prot, 74 g Calc.
POINTS value: **6.**

Greek Meatballs

prep 25 min • **slow-cook** 4 hrs • **serves** 4

♦ 250 g (½ pound) ground lean lamb

♦ 250 g (½ pound) ground extra-lean beef (5% fat or less)

♦ 60 mL (¼ cup) fat-free egg substitute

♦ 125 mL (½ cup) chopped scallions

75 mL (⅓ cup) plain dried bread crumbs

60 mL (4 tablespoons) finely chopped walnuts

60 mL (4 tablespoons) chopped fresh flat-leaf parsley

2 mL (½ teaspoon) dried mint

2 mL (½ teaspoon) dried oregano

2 mL (½ teaspoon) cinnamon

2 mL (½ teaspoon) salt

♦ 1 (425 mL [14½-ounce]) can diced tomatoes

♦ 250 mL (1 cup) tomato puree

♦ 60 mL (¼ cup) tomato paste

1 Combine lamb, beef, egg substitute, scallions, bread crumbs, 30 mL (2 tablespoons) walnuts, 30 mL (2 tablespoons) parsley, mint, oregano, 1 mL (¼ teaspoon) cinnamon, and salt in medium bowl. Form into 16 meatballs.

2 Combine diced tomatoes, tomato puree, tomato paste, and remaining 1 mL (¼ teaspoon) cinnamon in 5- or 6-L (5- or 6-quart) slow cooker. Transfer meatballs to slow cooker; turn gently to coat with tomato mixture. Cover and cook until instant-read thermometer inserted into centre of meatball registers 70°C (160°F), 4–6 hours on low.

3 Divide meatballs and sauce evenly among 4 bowls. Serve, sprinkled evenly with remaining 30 mL (2 tablespoons) walnuts and 30 mL (2 tablespoons) parsley.

♦ FILLING EXTRA

Whole-grain spelt, an old-world variety of wheat, has become more popular due to its high protein content and mild flavour. Cook 250 g (½ pound) spelt or whole wheat spaghetti according to package directions to serve with these saucy meatballs. The per-serving *POINTS* value will increase by *4.*

PER SERVING (4 meatballs with 125 mL [½ cup] sauce, 7 mL [½ tablespoon] walnuts and 7 mL [½ tablespoon] parsley): 309 Cal, 12 g Fat, 3 g Sat Fat, 0 g Trans Fat, 69 mg Chol, 969 mg Sod, 22 g Carb, 5 g Fib, 30 g Prot, 126 mg Calc. *POINTS* value: *6.*

Veal Stew Primavera

prep 25 min • **broil/cook/slow-cook** 4 hrs 10 min • **serves** 4

60 mL (¼ cup) all-purpose flour

5 mL (1 teaspoon) dried marjoram

2 mL (½ teaspoon) salt

1 mL (¼ teaspoon) black pepper

♦ 625 g (1¼ pounds) boneless leg of veal, trimmed and cut into 2.5 cm (1-inch) cubes

20 mL (4 teaspoons) whole-grain mustard

♦ 250 mL (1 cup) low-sodium chicken broth

150 mL (²/₃ cup) water

60 mL (¼ cup) dry white wine

♦ 250 mL (1 cup) frozen pearl onions, thawed

♦ 250 mL (1 cup) baby carrots

10 mL (2 teaspoons) olive oil

♦ 1 (375 g [12-ounce]) package mushrooms, quartered

♦ 250 g (½ pound) fresh asparagus, trimmed and cut into 5 cm (2-inch) pieces

1 Preheat broiler. Spray large rimmed baking sheet with nonstick spray.

2 Combine flour, marjoram, salt, and pepper in medium bowl. Add veal and toss to coat. Transfer veal to baking sheet and spread in single layer, shaking excess flour into bowl. Reserve flour. Broil veal 12.5 cm (5 inches) from heat, turning frequently, until golden, about 10 minutes. Transfer veal and any juices to 5- or 6-L (5- or 6-quart) slow cooker.

3 Meanwhile, combine mustard and reserved flour in medium bowl. Gradually whisk in broth, water, and wine until smooth. Transfer broth mixture to slow cooker. Stir in onions and carrots. Cover and cook until mixture simmers and thickens and veal is fork-tender, 4–6 hours on high or 8–12 hours on low.

4 About 30 minutes before cooking time is up, heat oil in large nonstick skillet over medium-high heat. Add mushrooms and cook, stirring frequently, until golden, about 8 minutes. Stir mushrooms and asparagus into slow cooker. Cover and cook on high until asparagus is tender, about 20 minutes, stirring once halfway through cooking time.

PER SERVING (325 mL [1⅓ cups]): 297 Cal, 10 g Fat, 3 g Sat Fat, 0 g Trans Fat, 122 mg Chol, 501 mg Sod, 17 g Carb, 3 g Fib, 35 g Prot, 68 mg Calc. *POINTS* value: **6.**

**OSSO BUCCO–STYLE
DRUMSTICKS, PAGE 95**

Chapter 3

Poultry from the Pot

Fill 'er up, plug 'er in and sit back while your family's favourite birds (chicken, turkey, duck, and cornish hens) are deliciously transformed into dinner.

Rotisserie-Style Chicken

prep • 25 min slow-cook 4 hrs • serves 8

- ◆ 3 carrots, sliced
- ◆ 1 onion, quartered and thinly sliced
- ◆ ½ turnip, peeled and cubed
- 10 mL (2 teaspoons) paprika
- 5 mL (1 teaspoon) chili powder
- 2 mL (½ teaspoon) dried thyme, crumbled
- 2 mL (½ teaspoon) dried oregano, crumbled
- 2 mL (½ teaspoon) onion powder
- 5 mL (1 teaspoon) kosher salt
- 2 mL (½ teaspoon) black pepper
- 1 mL (¼ teaspoon) cayenne
- ◆ 1 (2kg [4-pound]) chicken, skinned

1 Combine carrots, onion, and turnip in 5- or 6-L (5- or 6-quart) slow cooker. Mix paprika, chili powder, thyme, oregano, onion powder, salt, pepper, and cayenne in cup. Rub spice mixture all over chicken, sprinkling any remaining mixture inside body.

2 Place chicken on top of vegetables in slow cooker. Cover and cook until instant-read thermometer inserted into thigh registers 80°C (180°F) and vegetables are fork-tender, 4–6 hours on high.

3 Transfer chicken to cutting board and cut into 8 pieces. Serve with vegetables and any accumulated broth.

IN THE KITCHEN
To remove the skin from a whole chicken, place it, breast side down, on a cutting board. With kitchen shears or a sharp knife, cut the skin along the backbone. Holding the skin with a paper towel, gently pull it away from the meat. This recipe works with the Simply Filling technique.

PER SERVING (1 piece chicken with scant 125 mL [½ cup] vegetables and about 3 tablespoons broth): 193 Cal, 7 g Fat, 2 g Sat Fat, 0 g Trans Fat, 81 mg Chol, 300 mg Sod, 5 g Carb, 1 g Fib, 27 g Prot, 32 mg Calc. *POINTS* value: *4.*

Country Captain Chicken

◆ 1 (425 g [14½-ounce]) can fire-roasted diced tomatoes with garlic

◆ 1 onion, quartered and thinly sliced

◆ 1 yellow or red bell pepper, coarsely chopped

◆ 30 mL (2 tablespoons) tomato paste

15 mL (1 tablespoon) grated peeled fresh ginger

10 mL (2 teaspoons) curry powder

2 mL (½ teaspoon) cinnamon

2 mL (½ teaspoon) salt

◆ 1 (1.8kg [3½-pound]) chicken, cut into 8 pieces and skinned

30 mL (2 tablespoons) cold water

15 mL (1 tablespoon) cornstarch

◆ 1 Granny Smith apple, peeled and thinly sliced

◆ 250 mL (1 cup) frozen edamame or peas, thawed

20 mL (4 teaspoons) toasted coconut

20 mL (4 teaspoons) dried currants

1 Combine tomatoes, onion, bell pepper, tomato paste, ginger, curry powder, cinnamon, and salt in 5- or 6-L (5- or 6-quart) slow cooker. Top with chicken. Cover and cook until chicken is fork-tender, 3–4 hours on high or 6–8 hours on low.

2 About 25 minutes before cooking time is up, mix water and cornstarch in small bowl until smooth. Stir cornstarch mixture, apple, and edamame into slow cooker. Cover and cook on high until mixture simmers and thickens and apples are just tender, about 20 minutes. Serve, sprinkled with coconut and currants.

◆ **FILLING EXTRA**
Country Captain is traditionally served with white rice, but our healthful version is equally tasty accompanied by 1 L (4 cups) cooked brown rice (125 mL [½ cup] cooked rice for each serving will increase the *POINTS* value by *2*).

PER SERVING (1 piece chicken with about 150 mL [⅔ cup] vegetables and sauce and 2 mL [½ teaspoon] each coconut and currants): 224 Cal, 8 g Fat, 2 g Sat Fat, 0 g Trans Fat, 71 mg Chol, 325 mg Sod, 13 g Carb, 3 g Fib, 26 g Prot, 54 mg Calc. *POINTS* value: *5.*

Chicken with Fennel and Orange

prep 25 min • **slow-cook** 3 hrs • **serves** 4

- 250 mL (1 cup) low-sodium chicken broth

8 small shallots, peeled

- **3** carrots, sliced

3 mL (¾ teaspoon) crushed dried rosemary

3 mL (¾ teaspoon) salt

1 mL (¼ teaspoon) black pepper

- **1** (1.5 to 1.8 kg [3- to 3½-pound]) chicken, wings discarded, cut into 6 pieces, and skinned

- **1** (500 g [1-pound]) fennel bulb, halved and cut into 16 wedges through the root end

- **1** navel orange

1 Combine broth, shallots, carrots, rosemary, salt, and pepper in 6-L (5- or 6-quart) slow cooker. Top with chicken and fennel. Cover and cook until chicken and vegetables are fork-tender, 3–4 hours on high or 6–8 hours on low.

2 Meanwhile, grate zest from half of orange; transfer to small bowl. Remove peel and pith from orange. Cut orange in half; thickly slice and combine with zest.

3 Transfer chicken to cutting board; cut each breast in half the short way. Transfer chicken to platter. Stir orange mixture into slow cooker; pour over chicken.

◈ FILLING EXTRA
Perk up the flavour of this Mediterranean-inspired dish by adding 8 brine-cured Kalamata olives, **pitted and chopped with the orange mixture in step 3.** This recipe works with the Simply Filling technique.

PER SERVING (2 pieces chicken with 250 mL [1 cup] vegetables and sauce): 357 Cal, 11 g Fat, 3 g Sat Fat, 0 g Trans Fat, 121 mg Chol, 656 mg Sod, 22 g Carb, 5 g Fib, 43 g Prot, 109 mg Calc. *POINTS* value: *7.*

Apple Cider Chicken

prep 25 min • **slow-cook** 3 hrs • **serves** 4

- ◆ 3 parsnips, peeled, halved lengthwise, and sliced
- ◆ 2 sweet potatoes, peeled and cut into 2.5 cm (1-inch) chunks
- ◆ 1 onion, quartered and thinly sliced
- 175 mL (¾ cup) apple cider
- 30 mL (2 tablespoons) whole-grain mustard
- 2 garlic cloves, thinly sliced
- 5 mL (1 teaspoon) dried thyme
- 3 mL (¾ teaspoon) salt
- ◆ 2 (375g [¾-pound]) bone-in chicken breasts, skinned
- 30 mL (2 tablespoons) cold water
- 15 mL (1 tablespoon) cornstarch
- ◆ 1 Gala or Fuji apple, peeled and thinly sliced
- ◆ 60 mL (¼ cup) fat-free sour cream

1 Combine parsnips, potatoes, onion, cider, mustard, garlic, thyme, and salt in 5- or 6-L (5- or 6-quart) slow cooker. Top with chicken. Cover and cook until chicken and vegetables are fork-tender, 3–4 hours on high or 6–8 hours on low.

2 About 25 minutes before cooking time is up, mix water and cornstarch in small bowl until smooth. Stir cornstarch mixture and apple into slow cooker. Cover and cook on high until mixture simmers and thickens and apple is just tender, about 20 minutes.

3 Transfer chicken to cutting board; cut each breast in half the short way. Transfer chicken to platter; pour over vegetables and sauce. Serve, topped with sour cream.

◆ FILLING EXTRA
Add 1 peeled and thinly sliced Bosc pear along with the apple in step 2.

PER SERVING (1 piece chicken with 250 mL [1 cup] vegetables and sauce and 15 mL [1 tablespoon] sour cream): 345 Cal, 5 g Fat, 1 g Sat Fat, 0 g Trans Fat, 77 mg Chol, 651 mg Sod, 45 g Carb, 7 g Fib, 31 g Prot, 102 mg Calc. *POINTS* value: *7.*

Braised Chicken and Artichokes

◆ 500 g (1 pound) baby red potatoes, scrubbed and halved

175 mL (¾ cup) dry white wine

3   garlic cloves, thinly sliced

7   mL (1½ teaspoons) dried tarragon

5   mL (1 teaspoon) salt

1   mL (¼ teaspoon) black pepper

0.5 mL (⅛ teaspoon) ground allspice (optional)

◆ 2   (375 g [¾-pound]) bone-in chicken breasts, skinned

◆ 1   (275 g [9-ounce]) box frozen artichoke hearts, thawed

◆ 500 mL (2 cups) frozen pearl onions, thawed

1   lemon, cut into wedges

1 Combine potatoes, wine, garlic, 5 mL (1 teaspoon) tarragon, salt, pepper, and allspice (if using) in 5- or 6-L (5- or 6-quart) slow cooker. Top with chicken. Cover and cook until chicken and potatoes are fork-tender, 3–4 hours on high or 6–8 hours on low.

2 About 30 minutes before cooking time is up, stir artichokes and onions into slow cooker. Cover and cook on high until vegetables are tender, about 25 minutes.

3 Stir in remaining 2 mL (½ teaspoon) tarragon. Transfer chicken to cutting board; cut each breast in half the short way. Transfer chicken to platter; pour over vegetables and sauce. Serve with lemon wedges.

◆ **FILLING EXTRA**
Add 500 mL (2 cups) frozen thawed peas along with the artichokes and onions in step 2 and up the per-serving *POINTS* value by *1*.

PER SERVING (1 piece chicken with 425 mL (1¾ cups) vegetables and sauce): 376 Cal, 6 g Fat, 2 g Sat Fat, 0 g Trans Fat, 106 mg Chol, 734 mg Sod, 36 g Carb, 10 g Fib, 43 g Prot, 88 mg Calc. *POINTS* value: *7*.

Classic Chicken Noodle Soup

prep 20 min • **slow-cook/cook** 4 hrs 25 min • **serves** 6

♦ 2 (250 g [½-pound]) bone-in chicken breasts, skinned

♦ 1 onion, chopped

♦ 3 celery stalks, sliced

♦ 2 carrots, sliced

6 fresh parsley sprigs

2 garlic cloves, peeled

1 bay leaf

15 mL (1 tablespoon) chopped fresh thyme or 5 mL (1 teaspoon) dried

2 mL (½ teaspoon) salt

1 mL (¼ teaspoon) black pepper

♦ 2 (1 L [32-ounce]) cartons low-sodium chicken broth

375 mL (1½ cups) no-yolk egg noodles

60 mL (¼ cup) chopped fresh dill

1 Combine chicken, onion, celery, carrots, parsley, garlic, bay leaf, thyme, salt, and pepper in 5- or 6-L (5- or 6-quart) slow cooker. Pour broth over chicken and vegetables. Cover and cook until chicken and vegetables are fork-tender, 4–5 hours on high or 8–10 hours on low.

2 At end of cooking time, remove parsley, garlic, and bay leaf with slotted spoon and discard. Transfer chicken to plate and let stand until cool enough to handle, about 10 minutes. Remove and discard bones from chicken; cut chicken into bite-size pieces.

3 Meanwhile, cook noodles according to package directions, omitting salt if desired.

4 Stir chicken and noodles into slow cooker. Cover and cook on high until chicken is hot, about 5 minutes. Serve, sprinkled with dill.

♦ **FILLING EXTRA**
Add 375 mL (1½ cups) thawed frozen shelled edamame to the slow cooker with the chicken and noodles in step 4 and increase the cooking time to 15 minutes. (The per-serving *POINTS* value will increase by *1*).

PER SERVING (500 mL [2 cups]): 210 Cal, 4 g Fat, 2 g Sat Fat, 0 g Trans Fat, 47 mg Chol, 428 mg Sod, 21 g Carb, 2 g Fib, 23 g Prot, 72 mg Calc.
POINTS value: *4.*

Vietnamese Soupy Noodles and Chicken

prep 25 min • **slow-cook/cook** 4 hrs 30 min • **serves** 4

◆ 2 (250 g [½-pound]) bone-in chicken breasts, skinned

6 fresh cilantro sprigs

◆ 3 scallions, cut and separated into white and green parts

1 lemongrass stalk, trimmed and finely chopped

2 garlic cloves, bruised

5 mL (1 teaspoon) coriander seeds

1 (7.5 cm [3-inch]) cinnamon stick

2 mL (½ teaspoon) salt

0.5 mL (⅛ teaspoon) black pepper

◆ 2 (1 kg [32-ounce]) cartons low-sodium chicken broth

125 g (¼ pound) rice noodles

Fresh cilantro, basil, and mint sprigs, for garnish

4 lime wedges, for garnish

1 Combine chicken, 6 cilantro sprigs, white parts of scallions, lemongrass, garlic, coriander seeds, cinnamon stick, salt, and pepper in 5- or 6-L (5- or 6-quart) slow cooker. Pour broth over chicken and vegetables. Cover and cook until chicken is fork-tender, 4–5 hours on high or 8–10 hours on low.

2 At end of cooking time, transfer chicken with slotted spoon to plate and let stand until cool enough to handle, about 10 minutes. Remove and discard bones from chicken; cut chicken into bite-size pieces.

3 Meanwhile, cook noodles according to package directions. Drain and rinse under cold running water. Strain broth through large sieve into large bowl. Discard vegetables and spices.

4 Stir chicken and noodles into slow cooker. Cover and cook on high until chicken and noodles are hot, about 10 minutes.

5 Finely slice green parts of scallions. Ladle soup into bowls; sprinkle evenly with scallion greens. Garnish with cilantro, basil, and mint sprigs and lime wedges.

IN THE KITCHEN
If you don't have a fine sieve to strain the broth in step 3, use a colander lined with cheesecloth.

PER SERVING (625 mL [2½ cups]): 293 Cal, 6 g Fat, 2 g Sat Fat, 0 g Trans Fat, 70 mg Chol, 562 mg Sod, 27 g Carb, 1 g Fib, 31 g Prot, 63 mg Calc.
POINTS value: *6.*

Chicken with Figs

♦ 1 (625 g [1¼-pound]) butternut squash, peeled and cut into 2 cm (¾-inch) chunks

♦ 3 parsnips, peeled and sliced

125 mL (½ cup) dried Calimyrna figs

60 mL (¼ cup) + 30 mL (2 tablespoons) cold water

45 mL (3 tablespoons) packed dark brown sugar

30 mL (2 tablespoons) red-wine vinegar

2 garlic cloves, cut into thin strips

3 mL (¾ teaspoon) salt

1 mL (¼ teaspoon) black pepper

♦ 4 (125 g [¼-pound]) skinless, boneless chicken breasts

15 mL (1 tablespoon) cornstarch

30 mL (2 tablespoons) port or unsweetened apple juice

1 Combine squash, parsnips, figs, 60 mL (¼ cup) water, brown sugar, vinegar, garlic, salt, and pepper in 5- or 6-L (5- or 6-quart) slow cooker. Top with chicken. Cover and cook until chicken and vegetables are fork-tender, 3–4 hours on high or 6–8 hours on low.

2 About 25 minutes before cooking time is up, mix remaining 30 mL (2 tablespoons) water and cornstarch in small bowl until smooth. Stir cornstarch mixture and port into slow cooker. Cover and cook on high until mixture simmers and thickens, about 20 minutes.

♦ **FILLING EXTRA**
Serve this subtle fruity chicken with 500 mL (2 cups) cooked quinoa 125 mL [½ cup] for each serving will up the *POINTS* value by *2*).

PER SERVING (1 chicken breast with 250 mL [1 cup] vegetables and sauce): 339 Cal, 6 g Fat, 2 g Sat Fat, 0 g Trans Fat, 58 mg Chol, 508 mg Sod, 49 g Carb, 7 g Fib, 24 g Prot, 122 mg Calc. *POINTS* value: *6.*

Spanish Chicken with Chorizo

prep 20 min • **slow-cook** 3 hrs • **serves** 4

- ◆ 1 (435 g [14½-ounce]) can diced tomatoes with basil, garlic, and oregano
- 45 mL (3 tablespoons) balsamic vinegar
- ◆ 30 mL (2 tablespoons) tomato paste
- 15 mL (1 tablespoon) paprika
- 1 mL (¼ teaspoon) salt
- ◆ 1 large onion, chopped
- ◆ 2 stalks celery, sliced
- 60 mL (¼ cup) chopped chorizo sausage
- ◆ 4 (125 g [¼-pound]) skinless, boneless chicken breasts
- ◆ 1 large yellow or red bell pepper, coarsely chopped
- ◆ 15 mL (1 tablespoon) cornmeal
- ◆ 250 mL (1 cup) frozen peas, thawed

1 Combine tomatoes, vinegar, tomato paste, paprika, and salt in 6-L (5- or 6-quart) slow cooker. Stir in onion, celery, and chorizo. Top with chicken and bell pepper. Cover and cook until chicken and vegetables are fork-tender, 3–4 hours on high or 6–8 hours on low.

2 About 20 minutes before cooking time is up, gradually stir cornmeal into slow cooker until blended. Stir in peas. Cover and cook on high until mixture simmers and thickens and peas are just tender, about 15 minutes.

◆ **FILLING EXTRA**
Instead of the usual side of rice, serve this dish with 500 mL (2 cups) cooked instant polenta (125 mL [½ cup] cooked polenta per serving will increase the *POINTS* value by *2*).

PER SERVING (1 chicken breast with 175 mL [¾ cup]vegetables and sauce): 272 Cal, 6 g Fat, 2 g Sat Fat, 0 g Trans Fat, 75 mg Chol, 533 mg Sod, 22 g Carb, 5 g Fib, 31 g Prot, 83 mg Calc. *POINTS* value: *5.*

Mushroom and Cheese–Stuffed Chicken Breasts

prep 20 min • **cook/slow-cook** 2 hrs 10 min • **serves** 4

10 mL (2 teaspoons) olive oil

◆ 125 g (¼ pound) cremini mushrooms, finely chopped

2 mL (½ teaspoon) salt

1 mL (¼ teaspoon) black pepper

2 garlic cloves, finely chopped

30 mL (2 tablespoons) dry vermouth

75 mL (⅓ cup) crumbled goat cheese with herbs

◆ 4 (125 g [¼-pound]) skinless, boneless chicken breasts

◆ 125 mL (½ cup) low-sodium chicken broth

1 To make stuffing, heat 5 mL (1 teaspoon) oil in medium nonstick skillet over medium-high heat. Add mushrooms, 1 mL (¼ teaspoon) salt, and 0.5 mL (1/8 teaspoon) pepper; cook, stirring occasionally, until mushrooms are browned, 3–4 minutes. Add garlic and cook, stirring constantly, until fragrant, about 1 minute. Add vermouth and cook until evaporated, 1–2 minutes. Remove skillet from heat. Let mushroom mixture cool slightly, about 10 minutes. Stir in goat cheese.

2 With tip of sharp knife, cut horizontal slit through thickest portion of each chicken breast to form pocket. Fill each pocket with 30 mL (2 tablespoons) stuffing. Close pockets and secure with toothpicks.

3 Sprinkle chicken with remaining 1 mL (¼ teaspoon) salt and 0.5 mL (⅛ teaspoon) pepper. Heat remaining 1 teaspoon oil in skillet over medium-high heat. Add chicken and cook until browned, about 2 minutes per side. Transfer chicken to 5- or 6-L (5- or 6-quart) slow cooker.

4 Add broth to skillet. Bring to boil, scraping up browned bits from bottom of pan. Pour broth mixture into slow cooker. Cover and cook until chicken is fork-tender, 2–3 hours on high or 4–6 hours on low.

PER SERVING (1 chicken breast with about 37 mL [2½ tablespoons broth]): 196 Cal, 8 g Fat, 3 g Sat Fat, 0 g Trans Fat, 71 mg Chol, 580 mg Sod, 3 g Carb, 0 g Fib, 27 g Prot, 75 mg Calc. *POINTS* value: *5.*

Kung Pao Chicken

prep 20 min • **slow-cook** 3 hrs • **serves** 4

- 45 mL (3 tablespoons) hoisin sauce
- 45 mL (3 tablespoons) dry sherry or low-sodium chicken broth
- 45 mL (3 tablespoons) ketchup
- 30 mL (2 tablespoons) low-sodium soy sauce
- 30 mL (2 tablespoons) thin strips peeled fresh ginger
- 1 mL (¼ teaspoon) red pepper flakes
- ♦ 500 g (1 pound) skinless, boneless chicken breasts, cut into 2 cm (¾-inch) cubes
- ♦ 1 (250 g [8-ounce]) can sliced water chestnuts, drained
- 30 mL (2 tablespoons) cold water
- 15 mL (1 tablespoon) cornstarch
- ♦ 750 mL (3 cups) frozen sliced bell peppers and onions, thawed

1 Combine hoisin sauce, sherry, ketchup, soy sauce, ginger, and red pepper flakes in 5- or 6-L (5- or 6-quart) slow cooker. Stir in chicken and water chestnuts. Cover and cook until chicken is fork-tender, 3–4 hours on high or 6–8 hours on low.

2 About 20 minutes before cooking time is up, mix water and cornstarch in small bowl until smooth. Stir cornstarch mixture and bell peppers and onions into slow cooker. Cover and cook on high until mixture simmers and thickens and bell peppers and onions are crisp-tender, about 15 minutes.

IN THE KITCHEN
Like your Chinese food extra-spicy? Increase the red pepper flakes to 2 mL (½ teaspoon).

PER SERVING (310 mL [1¼ cups]): 249 Cal, 4 g Fat, 1 g Sat Fat, 0 g Trans Fat, 71 mg Chol, 660 mg Sod, 24 g Carb, 3 g Fib, 28 g Prot, 39 mg Calc.
POINTS value: *5.*

Jerk Chicken with Plantains

prep 20 min • **slow-cook** 3 hrs • **serves** 4

- 1 (435 g [14½-ounce]) can diced tomatoes with peppers, celery, and onion
- 15 mL (1 tablespoon) tomato paste
- 2 garlic cloves, minced
- 10 mL (2 teaspoons) dry Jamaican jerk seasoning
- 10 mL (2 teaspoons) smoked paprika
- 2 mL (½ teaspoon) ground allspice
- 2 mL (½ teaspoon) salt
- 2 small black plantains, peeled, halved lengthwise, and sliced
- 4 (125 g [½-pound]) whole chicken legs, skinned
- 500 mL (2 cups) frozen cut green beans, thawed

1 Combine tomatoes, tomato paste, garlic, jerk seasoning, paprika, allspice, and salt in 5- or 6-L (5- or 6-quart) slow cooker. Top with plantains and chicken. Cover and cook until chicken and plantains are fork-tender, 3–4 hours on high or 6–8 hours on low.

2 About 25 minutes before cooking time is up, stir green beans into slow cooker. Cover and cook on high until green beans are crisp-tender, about 20 minutes.

PER SERVING (1 chicken leg with scant 250 mL [1 cup] vegetables and sauce): 349 Cal, 8 g Fat, 3 g Sat Fat, 0 g Trans Fat, 83 mg Chol, 562 mg Sod, 43 g Carb, 6 g Fib, 31 g Prot, 105 mg Calc. *POINTS* value: *7*.

African Peanut Chicken

prep 25 min • **slow-cook** 3 hrs • **serves** 8

◆ 1 (14½-ounce) can diced tomatoes with garlic and onions

◆ 4 carrots, halved lengthwise and sliced

◆ 2 parsnips, peeled, halved lengthwise, and sliced

45 mL (3 tablespoons) low-fat peanut butter

45 mL (3 tablespoons) cayenne pepper sauce

7 mL (1½ teaspoons) ground cumin

2 mL (½ teaspoon) cinnamon

◆ 4 (125 g [¼-pound]) skinless chicken thighs

◆ 4 (125 g [¼-pound]) skinless chicken drumsticks

30 mL (2 tablespoons) cold water

15 mL (1 tablespoon) cornstarch

60 mL (¼ cup) chopped fresh cilantro (optional)

1 Combine tomatoes, carrots, parsnips, peanut butter, pepper sauce, cumin, and cinnamon in 5- or 6-L (5- or 6-quart) slow cooker. Top with chicken. Cover and cook until chicken and vegetables are fork-tender, 3–4 hours on high or 6–8 hours on low.

2 About 20 minutes before cooking time is up, mix water and cornstarch in small bowl until smooth. Stir cornstarch mixture into slow cooker. Cover and cook on high until mixture simmers and thickens, about 15 minutes. Stir in cilantro (if using).

◆ FILLING EXTRA

Serve 1L (4 cups) cooked whole wheat couscous to soak up all the delicious nutty sauce (125 mL [½ cup] cooked couscous per serving will increase the *POINTS* value by *1*).

PER SERVING (1 piece chicken with 125 mL [½ cup]vegetables and sauce): 172 Cal, 6 g Fat, 2 g Sat Fat, 0 g Trans Fat, 42 mg Chol, 313 mg Sod, 13 g Carb, 3 g Fib, 17 g Prot, 58 mg Calc. *POINTS* value: *3.*

Thai-Style Chicken Thighs

prep 20 min • **slow-cook** 3 hrs • **serves** 4

- 1 large onion, quartered and thinly sliced
- 250 mL (1 cup) mango or pineapple salsa
- 1 garlic clove, finely chopped
- 15 mL (3 teaspoons) Asian fish sauce
- 4 (150 g [5-ounce]) skinless chicken thighs
- 2 red bell peppers, coarsely chopped
- 1 green bell pepper, coarsely chopped
- 1¼ cup chopped fresh mint, basil, or cilantro
- Juice of 1 lime

1 Combine onion, salsa, garlic, and 2 teaspoons fish sauce in 6-L (5- or 6-quart) slow cooker. Top with chicken and bell peppers. Cover and cook until chicken and bell peppers are fork-tender, 3–4 hours on high or 6–8 hours on low.

2 Transfer chicken to platter. Stir mint, lime juice, and remaining 5 mL (1 teaspoon) fish sauce into slow cooker. Pour vegetables and sauce over chicken.

◆ FILLING EXTRA
Serve this Thai specialty with 500 mL (2 cups) cooked brown basmati rice and up the per-serving *POINTS* value by *2.*

PER SERVING (1 chicken thigh with 60 mL [¾ cup] vegetables and sauce): 200 Cal, 8 g Fat, 2 g Sat Fat, 0 g Trans Fat, 57 mg Chol, 604 mg Sod, 11 g Carb, 3 g Fib, 21 g Prot, 50 mg Calc. *POINTS* value: *4.*

Tangy Cherry Chicken

prep 20 min • **slow-cook** 3 hrs • **serves** 4

- 250 mL (1 cup) low-sodium chicken broth
- 45 mL (3 tablespoons) honey
- 45 mL (3 tablespoons) balsamic vinegar
- 7 mL (1½ teaspoons) five-spice powder or apple or pumpkin pie spice
- 3 mL (¾ teaspoon) salt
- 5 carrots, sliced
- 1 large red onion, quartered and thinly sliced
- 30 mL (2 tablespoons) thin strips peeled fresh ginger
- 125 mL (½ cup) dried cherries
- 4 (150 g [5-ounce]) skinless chicken thighs
- 30 mL (2 tablespoons) cold water
- 15 mL (1 tablespoon) cornstarch

1 Whisk broth, honey, 37 mL (2½ tablespoons) vinegar, five-spice powder, and salt in 5- or 6-L (5- or 6-quart) slow cooker. Stir in carrots, onion, and ginger. Sprinkle with cherries and top with chicken. Cover and cook until chicken and vegetables are fork-tender, 3–4 hours on high or 6–8 hours on low.

2 About 25 minutes before cooking time is up, mix water and cornstarch in small bowl until smooth. Stir cornstarch mixture into slow cooker. Cover and cook on high until mixture simmers and thickens, about 20 minutes. At end of cooking time, stir in remaining 7 mL (½ tablespoon) vinegar.

FILLING EXTRA
Round out the meal with 4 cooked small red potatoes and 1 L (4 cups) steamed green beans. A cooked small potato and 250 mL (1 cup) cooked beans will up the *POINTS* value by *1.*

PER SERVING (1 chicken thigh with 175 mL (¾ cup) vegetables and sauce): 342 Cal, 8 g Fat, 2 g Sat Fat, 0 g Trans Fat, 57 mg Chol, 570 mg Sod, 46 g Carb, 4 g Fib, 22 g Prot, 83 mg Calc. *POINTS* value: *7.*

Mojo Chicken

1	lime
75	mL (1/3 cup) frozen orange juice concentrate, thawed
45	mL (3 tablespoons) honey
6	mL (1¼ teaspoons) ground cumin
5	mL (1 teaspoon) dried oregano, crumbled
1	mL to 2mL (¼ to ½ teaspoon) chipotle chile powder
3	mL (¾ teaspoon) salt
♦ 1	sweet onion, quartered and thinly sliced
♦ 4	(125 g [¼-pound]) skinless chicken thighs
♦ 2	yellow squash, cut into 2 cm (¾-inch) chunks
♦ 2	small zucchini, cut into 2 cm (¾-inch) chunks
60	mL (¼ cup) chopped fresh cilantro

1 Grate zest from lime; cut lime into 4 wedges.

2 Whisk lime zest, orange juice concentrate, honey, cumin, oregano, chile powder, and salt in 5- or 6-L (5- or 6-quart) slow cooker. Stir in onion. Top with chicken, yellow squash, and zucchini. Cover and cook until chicken and vegetables are fork-tender, 3–4 hours on high or 6–8 hours on low.

3 Transfer chicken to platter. Stir cilantro into slow cooker. Pour vegetables and sauce over chicken. Serve with lime wedges.

IN THE KITCHEN
Don't have chipotle chile powder on hand? Use 2 mL (½ teaspoon) each chili powder, smoked paprika, and your favorite brand of hot pepper sauce instead.

PER SERVING (1 chicken thigh with 175 mL [¾ cup] vegetables and sauce and 1 lime wedge): 312 Cal, 10 g Fat, 3 g Sat Fat, 0 g Trans Fat, 70 mg Chol, 518 mg Sod, 32 g Carb, 3 g Fib, 27 g Prot, 81 mg Calc. *POINTS* value: *6.*

Chicken, Sausage, and White Bean Stew

prep 30 min • cook/slow-cook 3 hrs 10 min • serves 6

- ◆ 4 carrots, quartered lengthwise and sliced
- ◆ 1 leek, cleaned and chopped, white and light green parts only
- 2 garlic cloves, finely chopped
- 7 mL (1½ teaspoons) herbes de Provence or Italian seasoning
- ◆ 3 (150 g [5-ounce]) skinless chicken thighs
- 3 slices turkey bacon, cut into 0.5 cm (¼-inch) slices
- 125 mL (½ cup) dry white wine
- ◆ 125 mL (½ cup) low-sodium chicken broth
- 1 mL (¼ teaspoon) salt
- 1 mL (¼ teaspoon) black pepper
- 90 g (3 ounces) turkey kielbasa, halved lengthwise and sliced (175 mL [¾ cup])
- ◆ 1 (540 mL [19-ounce]) can cannellini (white kidney) beans, rinsed and drained

1 Combine carrots, leek, garlic, and herbes de Provence in 5- or 6-L (5- or 6-quart)slow cooker.

2 Spray large nonstick skillet with nonstick spray and set over medium-high heat. Add chicken and cook until browned, about 4 minutes. Turn chicken and sprinkle bacon around it; cook, stirring bacon occasionally, until chicken and bacon are browned, about 4 minutes.

3 Transfer chicken and bacon to slow cooker. Add wine, broth, salt, and pepper to skillet; bring to boil, scraping up browned bits from bottom of pan. Pour broth mixture over chicken. Top with kielbasa and beans. Cover and cook until chicken and vegetables are fork-tender, 3–4 hours on high or 6–8 hours on low.

4 At end of cooking time, transfer chicken with slotted spoon to plate and let stand until cool enough to handle, about 15 minutes. Remove and discard bones from chicken; cut chicken into bite-size pieces. Stir chicken into slow cooker. Cover and cook on high until chicken is hot, about 2 minutes.

IN THE KITCHEN
If leeks aren't readily available, switch to 1 small finely chopped red onion.

PER SERVING (about 375 mL [1½ cups]): 242 Cal, 7 g Fat, 2 g Sat Fat, 0 g Trans Fat, 42 mg Chol, 651 mg Sod, 23 g Carb, 5 g Fib, 21 g Prot, 98 mg Calc. *POINTS* value: *5.*

Chicken and Herb Dumpling Stew

prep 25 min • **slow-cook** 3 hrs • **serves** 4

- ◆ 375 g (¾ pound) skinless, boneless chicken thighs, cut into 2 cm (¾-inch) chunks
- ◆ 3   large carrots, sliced
- ◆ 250 g (½ pound) red potatoes, scrubbed and diced
- 1   mL (¼ teaspoon) salt
- 1   mL (¼ teaspoon) black pepper
- ◆ 1   (425 mL [14½-ounce]) can seasoned chicken broth with vegetables and herbs
- 22 mL (1½ tablespoons) water
- 15 mL (1 tablespoon) cornstarch
- ◆ 375 mL (1½ cups) frozen pearl onions, thawed
- ◆ 250 mL (1 cup) frozen peas, thawed
- 250 mL (1 cup) low-fat buttermilk baking mix
- 15 mL (1 tablespoon) chopped fresh dill
- ◆ 75 mL (5 tablespoons) fat-free milk

1 Combine chicken, carrots, potatoes, salt, and pepper in 5- or 6-L (5- or 6-quart) slow cooker. Pour in broth. Press chicken mixture down into broth. Cover and cook until chicken and vegetables are fork-tender, 3–4 hours on high or 6–8 hours on low.

2 About 50 minutes before cooking time is up, whisk water and cornstarch in small bowl until smooth. Stir cornstarch mixture, onions, and peas into slow cooker. Cover and cook on high until mixture simmers and thickens, about 15 minutes.

3 Meanwhile, combine baking mix and dill in medium bowl. Stir in milk just until soft dough forms.

4 Drop dough by rounded 30 mL (2 tablespoonfuls) onto simmering stew, making 4 dumplings. Cover and cook until toothpick inserted into centre of dumpling comes out clean, about 30 minutes.

PER SERVING (about 375 mL [1½ cups] stew with 1 dumpling): 373 Cal, 9 g Fat, 2 g Sat Fat, 0 g Trans Fat, 53 mg Chol, 1,001 mg Sod, 49 g Carb, 6 g Fib, 24 g Prot, 206 mg Calc. *POINTS* value: *7.*

Chipotle Chicken Chili

prep 25 min • cook/slow-cook 4 hrs 10 min • serves 6

- 500 g (1 pound) skinless, boneless chicken thighs, cut into 1.25 cm (½-inch) cubes
- **30 mL (2 tablespoons) + 5 mL (1 teaspoon) chipotle chile powder**
- 1 large red onion, chopped
- 2 large red bell peppers, diced
- 1 (425 mL [14½-ounce]) can diced tomatoes in sauce
- Juice of 1 orange
- **15 mL (1 tablespoon) packed brown sugar**
- **10 mL (2 teaspoons) ground cumin**
- **1 bay leaf**
- **7 mL (1½ teaspoons) unsweetened cocoa**
- **2 mL (½ teaspoon) instant espresso powder**
- 1 (275 g [9-ounce]) box frozen corn kernels, thawed
- 30 mL (2 tablespoons) cornmeal
- **75 mL (⅓ cup) chopped pistachios**

1 Spray large nonstick skillet with nonstick spray and set over medium-high heat. Add half of chicken and 2 mL (½ teaspoon) chile powder; cook, stirring occasionally, until browned, about 5 minutes. Transfer chicken mixture to 5- or 6-L (5- or 6-quart) slow cooker. Repeat with remaining chicken and 2 mL (½ teaspoon) chile powder.

2 Add remaining 30 mL (2 tablespoons) chile powder, onion, bell peppers, tomatoes, orange juice, brown sugar, cumin, bay leaf, cocoa, and espresso powder to slow cooker; mix well. Press chicken and vegetables down so they form even layer. Top with corn, leaving 1.25 cm (½-inch) border from side of slow cooker. Cover and cook until chicken and vegetables are fork-tender, 4–5 hours on high or 8–10 hours on low.

3 About 20 minutes before cooking time is up, gradually stir cornmeal into slow cooker until blended. Cover and cook on high until mixture simmers and thickens, 15 minutes. Serve, sprinkled with pistachios.

◆ **FILLING EXTRA**
Try this recipe with 1 (375 g [12-ounce]) bag thawed frozen corn kernels instead of the 275 g (9-ounce box).

PER SERVING (about 175 mL [¾ cup]): 287 Cal, 11 g Fat, 3 g Sat Fat, 0 g Trans Fat, 51 mg Chol, 223 mg Sod, 33 g Carb, 7 g Fib, 19 g Prot, 65 mg Calc. *POINTS* value: *6.*

Osso Buco–Style Drumsticks

prep 25 min • slow-cook 3 hrs • serves 4

- 425 mL (14½-ounce) can diced tomatoes with roasted garlic and onions
- 4   carrots, chopped
- 2   stalks celery, chopped
- 60 mL (¼ cup) red wine
- 30 mL (2 tablespoons) chopped sun-dried tomatoes (not oil-packed)
- 5   mL (1 teaspoon) Italian seasoning
- 1   mL (¼ teaspoon) red pepper flakes
- 1   mL (¼ teaspoon) salt
- 8   (125 g [¼-pound]) skinless chicken drumsticks
- 60 mL (¼ cup) plain dried bread crumbs

TOPPING

- 45 mL (3 tablespoons) chopped fresh parsley
- Grated zest of ½ lemon

1 Combine canned tomatoes, carrots, celery, wine, sun-dried tomatoes, Italian seasoning, red pepper flakes, and salt in 5- or 6-L (5- or 6-quart) slow cooker. Add chicken. Press chicken down into tomato mixture. Cover and cook until chicken and vegetables are fork-tender, 3–4 hours on high or 6–8 hours on low.

2 About 20 minutes before cooking time is up, gradually stir bread crumbs into slow cooker until blended. Cover and cook on high until mixture simmers and thickens, about 15 minutes.

3 Meanwhile, to make topping, combine parsley and lemon zest in bowl. Divide stew evenly among 4 plates. Serve, sprinkled with topping.

◆ FILLING EXTRA

For an additional *1 POINTS* value per serving, prepare the recipe as directed, but after adding the bread crumbs in step 2, stir in 500 mL (2 cups) thawed frozen baby lima beans.

PER SERVING (2 chicken drumsticks with 250 mL [1 cup] vegetables and sauce and about 10 mL [2 teaspoons] topping): 223 Cal, 5 g Fat, 1 g Sat Fat, 0 g Trans Fat, 97 mg Chol, 509 mg Sod, 17 g Carb, 4 g Fib, 28 g Prot, 107 mg Calc. *POINTS* value: *4.*

Meatball Heroes

prep 25 min • **slow-cook** 3 hrs • **serves** 4

375 mL (1½ cups) fat-free
marinara sauce

60 mL (4 tablespoons) plain
dried bread crumbs

◆ 500 g (1 pound) ground skinless
chicken or turkey breast

1 shallot, minced

60 mL (¼ cup) chopped fresh
parsley

3 mL (¾ teaspoon) Italian
seasoning

1 mL (¼ teaspoon) black
pepper

45 mL (3 tablespoons) low-fat
(1%) milk or water

45 mL (3 tablespoons) grated
pecorino cheese

1 (250 g [½-pound])
multigrain baguette, split

1 Mix marinara sauce and 1 tablespoon bread crumbs in 5- or 6-L (5- or 6-quart) slow cooker.

2 Combine chicken, shallot, parsley, Italian seasoning, pepper, milk, pecorino, and remaining 45 mL (3 tablespoons) bread crumbs in large bowl. With moistened hands, form into 12 meatballs.

3 Add meatballs, a few at a time, to slow cooker. Cover and cook until instant-read thermometer inserted into centre of meatball registers 77°C (170°F), 3–4 hours on high or 6–8 hours on low.

4 At end of cooking time, cut baguette crosswise into 8 equal pieces. Spoon 3 meatballs and 30 mL (2 tablespoons) sauce onto bottom half of each piece. Cover with top halves of baguette. Serve with remaining sauce.

◆ **FILLING EXTRA**
Cut 1 fennel bulb into thin wedges to serve alongside the heroes.

PER SERVING (1 hero with 60 mL [¼ cup] sauce): 385 Cal, 7 g Fat, 2 g Sat Fat, 0 g Trans Fat, 75 mg Chol, 914 mg Sod, 43 g Carb, 4 g Fib, 37 g Prot, 164 mg Calc. *POINTS* value: *7.*

Turkey with Chili-Orange Sauce

prep 20 min • **slow-cook** 3 hrs 20 min • **serves** 4

125 mL (½ cup) dry white wine or low-sodium chicken broth

60 mL (¼ cup) frozen orange juice concentrate

4 shallots, sliced

45 mL (3 tablespoons) low-sodium soy sauce

5 mL (1 teaspoon) Asian chili garlic sauce

5 mL (1 teaspoon) ancho chile powder

♦ 1 skinless, boneless turkey-breast half (about 750 g [1½ pounds])

30 mL (2 tablespoons) cold water

15 mL (1 tablespoon) cornstarch

30 mL (2 tablespoons) low-sugar orange marmalade

5 mL (1 teaspoon) white-wine vinegar

1 Combine wine, orange juice concentrate, shallots, soy sauce, chili garlic sauce, and chile powder in 5- or 6-L (5- or 6-quart) slow cooker. Top with turkey. Cover and cook until turkey is fork-tender, 3–4 hours on high or 6–8 hours on low.

2 At end of cooking time, transfer turkey to cutting board; cover with foil and keep warm. Whisk water and cornstarch in small bowl until smooth. Stir cornstarch mixture into slow cooker. Cover and cook on high until mixture simmers and thickens, about 20 minutes. Stir in marmalade and vinegar.

3 Cut turkey into 12 slices and serve with sauce.

PER SERVING (3 slices turkey with about 75 mL [⅓ cup] sauce): 275 Cal, 2 g Fat, 1 g Sat Fat, 0 g Trans Fat, 114 mg Chol, 504 mg Sod, 20 g Carb, 1 g Fib, 42 g Prot, 42 mg Calc. *POINTS* value: *5.*

Mexicali Turkey Breast

prep 30 min • slow-cook 3 hrs 20 min • serves 4

15 mL (1 tablespoon) smoked paprika

5 mL (1 teaspoon) chili powder

5 mL (1 teaspoon) dried thyme, crumbled

1 mL (¼ teaspoon) salt

♦ 1 small red onion, finely chopped

♦ 250 mL (1 cup) mild chunky fat-free salsa

♦ 1 skinless, boneless turkey-breast half (about 750g [1½ pounds])

5 mL (1 teaspoon) olive oil

♦ 3 poblano peppers, coarsely chopped

♦ 22 mL (1½ tablespoons) cornmeal

♦ 250 mL (1 cup) frozen corn kernels, thawed

5 mL (1 teaspoon) balsamic vinegar

1 Mix paprika, chili powder, thyme, and salt in cup. Combine onion, salsa, and 15 mL (1 tablespoon) paprika mixture in 5- or 6-L (5- or 6-quart) paprika mixture in 5- or 6-quart slow cooker. Rub all sides of turkey with oil, then remaining paprika mixture.

2 Transfer turkey to slow cooker. Place poblanos around both sides of turkey. Cover and cook until turkey and vegetables are fork-tender, 3–4 hours on high or 6–8 hours on low.

3 At end of cooking time, transfer turkey to cutting board; cover with foil and keep warm. Gradually stir cornmeal into slow cooker until blended. Stir in corn. Cover and cook on high until mixture simmers and thickens and corn is just tender, about 20 minutes. Stir in vinegar.

4 Cut turkey into 12 slices. Serve with vegetables and sauce.

This recipe works with the Simply Filling technique.

PER SERVING (3 slices turkey with 175 mL [¾ cup] vegetables and sauce): 285 Cal, 4 g Fat, 1 g Sat Fat, 0 g Trans Fat, 114 mg Chol, 621 mg Sod, 20 g Carb, 4 g Fib, 43 g Prot, 59 mg Calc. *POINTS* value: *5.*

Sicilian Turkey Roll

prep 40 min • **cook/slow-cook** 3 hrs 10 min • **serves** 4

◆ 1   large onion, chopped

125 mL (½ cup) dry white wine or low-sodium chicken broth

2   mL (½ teaspoon) salt

5   mL (1 teaspoon) olive oil

◆ 500 ml (2 cups) chopped fresh Swiss chard leaves

2   garlic cloves, finely chopped

45   mL (3 tablespoons) raisins, chopped

2   mL (½ teaspoon) dried marjoram

◆ 1   skinless, boneless turkey breast half (about 750 g [1½ pounds])

1   mL (¼ teaspoon) black pepper

4   (15 g [½-ounce]) slices prosciutto or baked ham

45   mL (3 tablespoons) grated pecorino cheese

1 Set aside 175 mL (¾ cup) chopped onion for filling. Mix remaining chopped onion, wine, and 1 mL (¼ teaspoon) salt in 5- or 6-L (5- or 6-quart) slow cooker.

2 Heat oil in large nonstick skillet over medium heat. Add reserved 175 mL (¾ cup) chopped onion and cook until softened, about 5 minutes. Add Swiss chard and garlic; cook, stirring occasionally, until vegetables are tender and liquid has evaporated, about 3 minutes. Stir in raisins and marjoram. Remove skillet from heat and let filling cool slightly, about 10 minutes.

3 Place turkey, skinned side up, on cutting board. Holding sharp knife parallel to board and starting at one long side, cut three quarters of way through and open up half breast like a book. Cover with sheet of plastic wrap. With meat mallet or rolling pin, gently pound to 1.25 cm (½-inch) thickness. Sprinkle with remaining 1 mL (¼ teaspoon) salt and pepper. Lay prosciutto onto turkey leaving 1.25 cm (½-inch) border. Spread filling evenly over prosciutto, then sprinkle with pecorino. Starting at one narrow end, roll up jelly-roll fashion. Tie with kitchen string at 2.5 cm (1-inch) intervals.

4 Transfer roll to slow cooker. Cover and cook until turkey is fork-tender, 3–4 hours on high or 6–8 hours on low. Transfer roll to cutting board. Remove string and cut into 12 slices. Serve with sauce.

PER SERVING (3 slices turkey with 75 mL [5 tablespoons] sauce): 290 Cal, 6 g Fat, 2 g Sat Fat, 0 g Trans Fat, 127 mg Chol, 585 mg Sod, 11 g Carb, 2 g Fib, 46 g Prot, 108 mg Calc. *POINTS* value: *6.*

Hot-and-Spicy Turkey Curry

prep 15 min • **slow-cook** 4 hrs • **serves** 4

- ◆ 1 red onion, sliced
- ◆ 375 g (¾ pound) Yukon Gold potatoes, scrubbed and cut into 2 cm (1-inch) chunks
- ◆ 500 g (1 pound) turkey cutlets, cut into 2 cm (1-inch) chunks
- 2 mL (½ teaspoon) salt
- ◆ 375 mL (1½ cups) low-sodium chicken broth
- 10 mL (2 teaspoons) Thai green curry paste
- 10 mL (2 teaspoons) curry powder
- ◆ 1 (500 g [16-ounce]) bag frozen broccoli, thawed
- 125 mL (½ cup) light coconut milk
- 30 mL (2 tablespoons) chopped fresh cilantro

1 In single layers, place onion, potatoes, and turkey in 5- or 6-L (5- or 6-quart)slow cooker. Sprinkle with salt. Mix broth, curry paste, and curry powder in bowl; pour over chicken and vegetables. Cover and cook until chicken and vegetables are fork-tender, 4–5 hours on high or 8–10 hours on low.

2 About 25 minutes before cooking time is up, stir broccoli and coconut milk into slow cooker. Cover and cook on high until broccoli is crisp-tender, about 20 minutes. Serve, sprinkled with cilantro.

◆ **FILLING EXTRA**
Serve this saucy curry with 500 mL (2 cups) cooked bulgur (125 mL [½ cup] cooked bulgur for each serving will increase the *POINTS* value by *1*).

PER SERVING (425mL [1¾ cups]): 260 Cal, 5 g Fat, 2 g Sat Fat, 0 g Trans Fat, 64 mg Chol, 489 mg Sod, 26 g Carb, 5 g Fib, 5 g Prot, 56 mg Calc.
POINTS value: *5.*

Spicy Asian Turkey

prep 20 min • **slow-cook** 3 hrs 20 min • **serves** 6

- 1 (500 g [1-pound]) bag baby carrots
- 60 mL (¼ cup) Thai sweet red chili sauce
- 30 mL (2 tablespoons) thin strips peeled fresh ginger
- 30 mL (2 tablespoons) rice-wine vinegar
- 15 mL (1 tablespoon) low-sodium soy sauce
- 2 (500 g [1-pound]) turkey thighs, skinned
- 30 mL (2 tablespoons) cold water
- 15 mL (1 tablespoon) cornstarch
- 1 (450 mL [15-ounce]) can baby corn, drained
- 500 mL (2 cups) frozen sugar-snap peas, thawed
- 60 mL (¼ cup) chopped fresh cilantro

1 Combine carrots, chili sauce, ginger, vinegar, and soy sauce in 5- or 6-L (5- or 6-quart) slow cooker. Top with turkey. Cover and cook until turkey and carrots are fork-tender, 3–4 hours on high or 6–8 hours on low.

2 At end of cooking time, transfer turkey with slotted spoon to plate and let stand until cool enough to handle, about 20 minutes.

3 Meanwhile, whisk water and cornstarch in small bowl until smooth; stir in about 60 mL (¼ cup) hot liquid from slow cooker until blended. Stir cornstarch mixture into slow cooker. Stir in corn and snap peas. Cover and cook on high until mixture simmers and thickens and snap peas are crisp-tender, about 20 minutes.

4 Remove and discard bones from turkey; cut turkey into bite-size pieces. Stir turkey into slow cooker. Cover and cook on high until turkey is hot, about 2 minutes. Serve, sprinkled with cilantro.

PER SERVING (about 375mL [1½ cups]): 251 Cal, 5 g Fat, 1 g Sat Fat, 0 g Trans Fat, 94 mg Chol, 545 mg Sod, 25 g Carb, 5 g Fib, 28 g Prot, 78 mg Calc. *POINTS* value: 5.

Turkey Picadillo

prep 15 min • **slow-cook** 3 hrs 20 min • **serves** 4

- ◆ 1 (425 mL [14½-ounce]) can diced tomatoes with garlic, drained
- ◆ 1 green bell pepper, chopped
- ◆ 45 mL (3 tablespoons) tomato paste
- 30 mL (2 tablespoons) honey
- 30 mL (2 tablespoons) chili powder
- 10 mL (2 teaspoons) unsweetened cocoa
- 7 mL (1½ teaspoons) ground cumin
- 3 mL (¾ teaspoon) salt
- ◆ 2 (500 g [1-pound]) turkey thighs, skinned
- ◆ 30 mL (2 tablespoons) cornmeal
- ◆ 375 mL (1½ cups) frozen corn kernels, thawed
- 45 mL (3 tablespoons) dried currants
- 15 mL (1 tablespoon) cayenne pepper sauce

1 Combine tomatoes, bell pepper, tomato paste, honey, chili powder, cocoa, cumin, and salt in 5- or 6-L (5- or 6-quart) slow cooker. Top with turkey. Cover and cook until turkey and bell pepper are fork-tender, 3–4 hours on high or 6–8 hours on low.

2 At end of cooking time, transfer turkey with slotted spoon to plate and let stand until cool enough to handle, about 20 minutes.

3 Meanwhile, gradually stir cornmeal into slow cooker until blended. Stir in corn, currants, and pepper sauce. Cover and cook on high until mixture simmers and thickens and corn is just tender, about 20 minutes.

4 Remove and discard bones from turkey; cut turkey into bite-size pieces. Ladle vegetables and sauce evenly among 4 bowls. Top evenly with turkey.

IN THE KITCHEN
For another *1 POINTS* value per serving, sprinkle this classic Latin-American dish with 60 mL (¼ cup) sliced almonds.

PER SERVING (175 mL [¾ cup] turkey with 175 mL [¾ cup] vegetables and sauce): 371 Cal, 7 g Fat, 2 g Sat Fat, 0 g Trans Fat, 140 mg Chol, 920 mg Sod, 40 g Carb, 6 g Fib, 41 g Prot, 99 mg Calc. *POINTS* value: *7.*

Cranberry-Orange Turkey

prep 25 min • **slow-cook** 3 hrs 15 min • **serves** 4

- ◆ 250 mL (1 cup) fresh or thawed frozen cranberries
- ◆ 3 carrots, chopped
- 125 mL (½ cup) low-sugar orange marmalade
- 7 mL (1½ teaspoons) ground ginger
- 2 mL (½ teaspoon) five-spice powder or apple or pumpkin pie spice
- 3 mL (¾ teaspoon) salt
- ◆ 2 (375 g [¾-pound]) turkey drumsticks, skinned
- 30 mL (2 tablespoons) cold water
- 15 mL (1 tablespoon) cornstarch
- ◆ 500 mL (2 cups) frozen sugar-snap peas, thawed
- ◆ 2 large scallions, chopped

1 Combine cranberries, carrots, marmalade, ginger, five-spice powder, and salt in 5- or 6-L (5- or 6-quart) slow cooker. Top with turkey. Cover and cook until turkey and carrots are fork-tender, 3–4 hours on high or 6–8 hours on low.

2 At end of cooking time, transfer turkey with slotted spoon to plate and let stand until cool enough to handle, about 20 minutes.

3 Meanwhile, whisk water and cornstarch in small bowl until smooth; stir in about 60 mL (¼ cup) hot liquid from slow cooker until blended. Stir cornstarch mixture into slow cooker. Stir in snap peas. Cover and cook on high until mixture simmers and thickens and snap peas are crisp-tender, about 15 minutes. Stir in scallions.

4 Remove and discard bones from turkey; with 2 forks, shred turkey into small pieces. Ladle vegetables and sauce evenly among 4 bowls. Top evenly with turkey.

◆ **FILLING EXTRA**
Serve 500 mL (2 cups) cooked wild rice with this Thanksgiving-inspired stew (125 mL [½ cup] cooked rice per serving will increase the *POINTS* value by *1*).

PER SERVING (175 mL [¾ cup] turkey with 175 mL [¾ cup] vegetables and sauce): 281 Cal, 4 g Fat, 1 g Sat Fat, 0 g Trans Fat, 91 mg Chol, 545 mg Sod, 35 g Carb, 5 g Fib, 27 g Prot, 91 mg Calc. *POINTS* value: *5.*

Creamy Turkey Meatballs

prep 20 min • bake/slow-cook 1 hr 15 min • serves 4

3 slices firm white bread, torn into small pieces

500 g (1 pound) ground skinless turkey breast

2 shallots, finely chopped

1 large egg

30 mL (2 tablespoons) whole-grain mustard

2 mL (½ teaspoon) salt

1 mL (¼ teaspoon) black pepper

1 mL (¼ teaspoon) ground allspice

125 mL (½ cup) low-sodium chicken broth

5 mL (1 teaspoon) steak sauce

125 mL (½ cup) fat-free sour cream

1 Preheat oven to 230°C (450°F). Lightly spray large rimmed baking sheet with nonstick spray.

2 Pulse bread in food processor or blender to fine crumbs. Combine bread crumbs, turkey, shallots, egg, 15 mL (1 tablespoon) mustard, salt, pepper, and allspice in large bowl. Form into 36 meatballs. Place meatballs on baking sheet 2.5 cm (1 inch) apart. Bake until lightly browned, about 15 minutes.

3 Transfer meatballs to 5- or 6-L (5- or 6-quart) slow cooker. Mix broth, remaining 15 mL (1 tablespoon) mustard, and steak sauce in small bowl; pour over meatballs. Cover and cook until instant-read thermometer inserted in centre of meatball registers 78°C (170°F) and sauce thickens slightly, 1–2 hours on high or 2–4 hours on low.

4 At end of cooking time, stir sour cream into slow cooker.

PER SERVING (9 meatballs with 45 mL [3 tablespoons] sauce): 225 Cal, 3 g Fat, 0 g Sat Fat, 0 g Trans Fat, 129 mg Chol, 750 mg Sod, 15 g Carb, 0 g Fib, 33 g Prot, 87 mg Calc. *POINTS* value: 5.

Turkey Strata

250 g (½ pound) sweet Italian turkey sausage links, casings removed

♦ 1   onion, chopped

♦ 1   (290 g [10-ounce] box frozen chopped broccoli, thawed and squeezed dry

7   mL (1½ teaspoons) dried tarragon

5   slices day-old whole wheat bread, cubed (about 1.3 L [5 cups])

250 mL (1 cup) shredded low-fat Italian cheese blend

625 mL (2½ cups) low-fat (1%) milk

♦ 375 mL (1½ cups) fat-free egg substitute

15   mL (1 tablespoon) Dijon mustard

3   mL (¾ teaspoon) salt

1   mL (¼ teaspoon) black pepper

1 Spray large nonstick skillet with nonstick spray and set over medium heat. Add sausage and onion; cook, breaking sausage apart with wooden spoon, until sausage is no longer pink, about 6 minutes. Add broccoli and tarragon; increase heat and cook, stirring occasionally, until broccoli is crisp-tender, about 3 minutes.

2 Spray 5- or 6-quart slow cooker stoneware with nonstick spray. In single layers, place 625 mL (2½ cups) bread, half sausage mixture, and 125 mL (½ cup) cheese blend in slow cooker. Repeat with remaining 625 mL (2½ cups) bread, sausage mixture, and 125 mL (½ cup) cheese blend.

3 Whisk milk, egg substitute, mustard, salt, and pepper in large bowl; pour over bread-sausage mixture. Cover and cook until knife inserted into centre of strata comes out clean, 3–4 hours on low.

4 Transfer stoneware to rack and let strata cool slightly, 30 minutes. Cut strata into 6 wedges.

IN THE KITCHEN

Want to make this dish but don't have day-old bread handy? Not a problem. Just lightly toast the slices, let cool, and cut into cubes.

PER SERVING (1 wedge): 270 Cal, 8 g Fat, 3 g Sat Fat, 0 g Trans Fat, 47 mg Chol, 1,019 mg Sod, 21 g Carb, 4 g Fib, 29 g Prot, 414 mg Calc. *POINTS* value: *5.*

Vietnamese Cornish Hens

- ½ large butternut squash, peeled and cut into 2 cm (¾-inch) slices
- 1 onion, quartered and thinly sliced
- 2 (750 g [1½-pound]) Cornish hens, halved and skinned
- 1 lime
- 45 mL (3 tablespoons) packed brown sugar
- 10 mL (2 teaspoons) Asian fish sauce
- 5 mL (1 teaspoon) Sriracha (hot chili sauce) or cayenne pepper sauce
- 3 mL (¾ teaspoon) ground ginger

1 Combine squash and onion in 5- or 6-L (5- or 6-quart) slow cooker. Top with hens so backbones face toward edge of slow cooker.

2 Grate zest from lime; cut lime into 4 wedges. Combine lime zest, brown sugar, fish sauce, chili sauce, and ginger in small bowl; spoon evenly over hens. Cover and cook until hens and vegetables are fork-tender, 3–4 hours on high or 6–8 hours on low.

3 Transfer hens and vegetables with slotted spoon to serving platter; cover with foil and keep warm. Transfer cooking liquid to medium skillet and bring to boil. Boil until mixture is syrupy glaze and reduced to about 75 mL (⅓ cup), about 7 minutes. Serve with hens and lime wedges.

PER SERVING (½ hen with 175 mL [¾ cup] vegetables and 20 mL [4 teaspoons] glaze): 325 Cal, 7 g Fat, 2 g Sat Fat, 0 g Trans Fat, 179 mg Chol, 366 mg Sod, 26 g Carb, 3 g Fib, 41 g Prot, 85 mg Calc. *POINTS* value: 6.

Cornish Hens with Fines Herbes

prep 20 min • slow-cook/cook 3 hrs 5 min • serves 4

15 mL (1 tablespoon) each chopped fresh parsley, tarragon, chervil, and chives

25 mL (5 teaspoons) unsalted butter, softened

3 mL (¾ teaspoon) salt

1 mL (¼ teaspoon) black pepper

◆ 2 (750 g [1½-pound]) Cornish hens

◆ 175 mL (¾ cup) low-sodium chicken broth

30 mL (2 tablespoons) quick-cooking tapioca

0.5 mL (⅛ teaspoon) ground mace or nutmeg

60 mL (¼ cup) fat-free half-and-half

1 Combine parsley, tarragon, chervil, and chives in cup. Transfer 15 mL (1 tablespoon) herb mixture to another cup; cover and refrigerate. Mash remaining 45 mL (3 tablespoons) herb mixture, butter, 2 mL (½ teaspoon) salt, and 0.5 mL (⅛ teaspoon) pepper with wooden spoon in small bowl until blended. With fingertips, gently separate skin from meat on breasts, thighs, and legs of hens. Pat meat dry with paper towels. Spread butter mixture evenly on meat under skin. Transfer hens to 5- or 6-L (5- or 6-quart) slow cooker.

2 Mix broth, tapioca, mace, and remaining 1 mL (¼ teaspoon) salt and 0.5 mL (⅛ teaspoon) pepper in bowl. Pour broth mixture over hens. Cover and cook until hens are fork-tender, 3–4 hours on high or 6–8 hours on low.

3 Transfer hens to cutting board; cover with foil and keep warm. Strain sauce through sieve into small saucepan, pressing solids through sieve with rubber spatula. Bring sauce to boil; stir in reserved 15 mL (1 tablespoon) herb mixture and half-and-half. Remove saucepan from heat.

IN THE KITCHEN
Fines herbes is a delicious combination of parsley, tarragon, chervil, and chives often used in French cooking. But you can simplify this dish by substituting 60 mL (¼ cup) chopped fresh tarragon.

PER SERVING (½ hen with 75 mL [⅓ cup] sauce): 263 Cal, 10 g Fat, 4 g Sat Fat, 0 g Trans Fat, 159 mg Chol, 653 mg Sod, 7 g Carb, 0 g Fib, 33 g Prot, 51 mg Calc. *POINTS* value: *6.*

Smoky Duck Chili

prep 25 min • **cook/slow-cook** 4 hrs 10 min • **serves** 6

♦ 500 g (1 pound) skinless, boneless duck breasts, cut into 1.25 cm (½-inch) cubes

Grated zest and juice of 1 orange

♦ 6 carrots, sliced

♦ 1 red onion, sliced

♦ 1 (425 mL [14½-ounce]) can diced tomatoes with roasted garlic

♦ 1 (250 mL [8-ounce]) can tomato sauce (no salt added)

♦ 1 (450 mL [15-ounce]) can black beans, rinsed and drained

30 mL (2 tablespoons) chipotle chile powder

15 mL (1 tablespoon) chopped fresh rosemary or 5 mL (1 teaspoon) dried

5 mL (1 teaspoon) ground coriander

60 mL (¼ cup) chopped fresh cilantro

1 Spray large nonstick skillet with nonstick spray and set over medium-high heat. Add half of duck and cook, turning occasionally, until browned, about 4 minutes. Transfer duck to 5- or 6-L (5- or 6-quart) slow cooker. Repeat with remaining duck.

2 Add orange juice to skillet. Bring to boil, scraping up browned bits from bottom of pan. Pour orange juice mixture into slow cooker. Stir in carrots, onion, diced tomatoes, tomato sauce, beans, orange zest, chile powder, rosemary, and coriander. Cover and cook until duck and vegetables are fork-tender, 4–5 hours on high or 8–10 hours on low. Serve, sprinkled with cilantro.

IN THE KITCHEN

Chipotle chile powder is readily available in the spice aisle at the supermarket. It's made from smoked dried jalapeño peppers, giving this dish a rich complex flavour.

PER SERVING (about 250 mL [1 cup]): 318 Cal, 5 g Fat, 1 g Sat Fat, 0 g Trans Fat, 81 mg Chol, 589 mg Sod, 50 g Carb, 11 g Fib, 23 g Prot, 151 mg Calc. *POINTS* value: *6.*

Fruited Duck Stew

prep 25 min • **cook/slow-cook** 4 hrs 35 min • **serves** 6

- 1.3 kg (2½ pounds) skinless, boneless duck breasts
- 1.3 kg (2½ pounds) whole duck legs, skinned
- 2 mL (½ teaspoon) salt
- 2 mL (½ teaspoon) black pepper
- 1 onion, sliced
- 1 (500 g [16-ounce]) bag shredded red cabbage
- 250 mL (1 cup) red wine
- 15 mL (1 tablespoon) chopped fresh thyme or 5 mL (1 teaspoon) dried
- 250 mL (1 cup) low-sodium chicken broth
- 125 mL (½ cup) dried cranberries
- 75 mL (⅓ cup) dried peaches or apricots, thinly sliced
- 45 mL (3 tablespoons) balsamic vinegar
- 15 mL (1 tablespoon) honey
- 10 mL (2 teaspoons) cornstarch

1 Sprinkle duck with salt and pepper. Heat large nonstick skillet over medium-high heat. Add half of duck and cook until browned, about 5 minutes per side. Transfer duck to 5- or 6-L (5- or 6-quart) slow cooker. Repeat with remaining duck.

2 Add onion to skillet. Reduce heat and cook, stirring occasionally, until browned, about 5 minutes. Remove skillet from heat; stir in cabbage, wine, and thyme. Transfer cabbage mixture to slow cooker; stir in broth, cranberries, and peaches. Cover and cook until duck and vegetables are fork-tender, 4–5 hours on high or 8–10 hours on low.

3 At end of cooking time, transfer duck with slotted spoon to cutting board and let stand until cool enough to handle, about 15 minutes. Whisk vinegar, honey, and cornstarch in small bowl until smooth; stir in about 60 mL (¼ cup) hot liquid from slow cooker until blended. Stir cornstarch mixture into slow cooker. Cover and cook on high until mixture simmers and thickens, about 10 minutes.

4 Remove and discard bones from duck legs; cut leg and breast meat into 3.5 cm (1½-inch) pieces. Stir duck into slow cooker. Cover and let stand until duck is heated through, about 5 minutes.

PER SERVING (about 250 mL [1 cup]): 360 Cal, 4 g Fat, 1 g Sat Fat, 0 g Trans Fat, 153 mg Chol, 337 mg Sod, 32 g Carb, 4 g Fib, 51 g Prot, 82 mg Calc. *POINTS* value: *7.*

PORK AND TOMATILLO
STEW, PAGE 119

Chapter 4

Big Batch Winners

When a crowd is coming, a slow cooker can save you. Try these meals to serve 8 or more. Plus, we give directions for freezing and reheating.

Corned Beef with Beet Relish

prep 20 min • **slow-cook/cook** 4 hrs • **serves** 6 plus leftovers

- 500 g (1 pound) leeks, cleaned and cut into 5cm (2-inch) pieces, white and light green parts only
- 3 garlic cloves, chopped
- 1 (1.5 kg [3-pound]) lean corned beef brisket, trimmed
- 750 g (1½ pounds) red potatoes, scrubbed and cut into 5 cm (2-inch) chunks
- 250 mL (1 cup) baby carrots
- ½ head Savoy cabbage, cut into 8 wedges
- 375 mL (1½ cups) low-sodium chicken broth
- 500 g (1 pound) beets, trimmed
- 60 mL (¼ cup) prepared horseradish
- 15 mL (1 tablespoon) cider vinegar
- 15 mL (1 tablespoon) chopped fresh dill
- 1 mL (¼ teaspoon) salt

1 Combine leeks and garlic in 5- or 6-L (5- or 6-quart) slow cooker. Top with beef. Place potatoes and carrots around beef. Top vegetables with cabbage. Pour broth over vegetables. Cover and cook until beef and vegetables are fork-tender, 4–5 hours on high or 8–10 hours on low.

2 Meanwhile, to make relish, bring beets and enough cold water to cover to a boil in large saucepan. Reduce heat; partially cover and simmer until fork-tender, 45–50 minutes. Drain and let cool. Peel and coarsely chop. Put beets, horseradish, vinegar, dill, and salt in food processor and pulse until finely chopped.

3 Transfer beef to cutting board and cut crosswise into 2 pieces. Transfer half of beef to freezer container. Top with half of vegetables (about 750 mL [3 cups]) and 250 mL (1 cup) cooking liquid and let cool. Cover and freeze up to 2 months. Transfer half of relish (175 mL [¾ cup]) to another airtight container. Cover and refrigerate up to 1 week (serve with grilled beef, pork, or chicken). Discard remaining cooking liquid. Cut remaining piece of beef across grain into 12 slices. Serve with remaining 750 mL (3 cups) vegetables and 175 mL (¾ cup) relish.

TO REHEAT
Thaw the beef, vegetables, and cooking liquid in the refrigerator overnight. Transfer to a Dutch oven. Cover and cook over medium heat, stirring occasionally, until heated through, 25–30 minutes. Discard the cooking liquid before serving.

PER SERVING (2 slices beef with 125 mL [½ cup] vegetables and 30 mL [2 tablespoons] relish): 187 Cal, 8 g Fat, 3 g Sat Fat, 0 g Trans Fat, 39 mg Chol, 574 mg Sod, 19 g Carb, 4 g Fib, 10 g Prot, 51 mg Calc. *POINTS* value: *4.*

Roast Beef with Tomatoes and Mushrooms

prep 20 min • cook/slow-cook 4 hrs 30 min • serves 4 plus leftovers

- 1 (1.3 kg [2½-pound]) eye-round roast, trimmed
- 5 mL (1 teaspoon) salt
- 2 mL (½ teaspoon) black pepper
- 5 mL (1 teaspoon) olive oil
- 2 red onions, sliced
- 1 (290g [10-ounce]) package sliced cremini mushrooms
- 2 shallots, finely chopped
- 15 mL (1 tablespoon) chopped fresh oregano or 5 mL (1 teaspoon) dried
- 1 (825 g [28-ounce]) can fire-roasted tomatoes, chopped
- 125 mL (½ cup) low-sodium beef broth

1 Sprinkle beef with 2 mL (½ teaspoon) salt and 1 mL (¼ teaspoon) pepper. Heat oil in large nonstick skillet over medium-high heat. Add beef and cook, turning frequently, until browned, about 6 minutes. Transfer beef with tongs to 5- or 6-L (5- or 6-quart) slow cooker.

2 Add onions, mushrooms, shallots, and oregano to skillet. Reduce heat and cook, stirring occasionally, until vegetables are softened, 6–7 minutes. Add tomatoes, broth, remaining 2 mL (½ teaspoon) salt and 1 mL (¼ teaspoon) pepper; cook, stirring occasionally, until mixture slightly thickens, 5–6 minutes. Pour tomato mixture over beef. Cover and cook until beef is fork-tender, 4–5 hours on high or 8–10 hours on low.

3 Transfer beef to cutting board; cover with foil and keep warm. Pour sauce into large saucepan; bring to boil over medium-high heat. Boil, stirring occasionally, until slightly thickened and reduced by about one third, 15–18 minutes.

4 Cut beef crosswise into 2 pieces. Transfer half of beef to freezer container. Top with half of sauce and vegetables (about 500 mL [2 cups]) and let cool. Cover and freeze up to 2 months. Cut remaining piece of beef into 8 slices. Serve with remaining 500 mL (2 cups) sauce and vegetables.

TO REHEAT

Thaw the beef, and the sauce and vegetable mixture in the refrigerator overnight. Transfer to a small baking dish; cover with foil. Bake in a 180°C (350°F) oven until heated through, about 25 minutes. This recipe works with the Simply Filling Technique.

PER SERVING: (2 slices beef with about 125 mL [½ cup] sauce and vegetables) 273 Cal, 6 g Fat, 2 g Sat Fat, 0 g Trans Fat, 101 mg Chol, 496 mg Sod, 9 g Carb, 2 g Fib, 43 g Prot, 54 mg Calc. *POINTS* value: 6.

Wild Mushroom Steak Roulades

prep 30 min • cook/slow-cook 4 hrs 10 min • serves 4 plus leftovers

20 mL (4 teaspoons) olive oil

♦ 500 g (1 pound) shiitake mushrooms, stems removed and sliced

♦ 1   (290 g [10-ounce]) package sliced cremini mushrooms

♦ 1   onion, finely chopped

2   garlic cloves, minced

3   mL (¾ teaspoon) salt

60 mL (¼ cup) Italian-seasoned dried bread crumbs

30 mL (2 tablespoons) chopped fresh thyme

♦ 1   kg 2 (500g [1-pound]) flank steaks, trimmed

♦ 125 mL (½ cup) low-sodium beef broth

125 mL (½ cup) red wine

30 mL (2 tablespoons) water

15 mL (1 tablespoon) all-purpose flour

1 To make filling, heat 10 mL (2 teaspoons) oil in large nonstick skillet over medium-high heat. Add mushrooms, onion, garlic, and 1 mL (¼ teaspoon) salt; cook, stirring occasionally, until liquid is absorbed and vegetables are very tender, 6–8 minutes. Remove skillet from heat; stir in bread crumbs and 15 mL (1 tablespoon) thyme. Transfer to medium bowl and let cool.

2 Place 1 steak on cutting board. Holding knife parallel to board and starting at one long side, cut three quarters of way through and open up steak like a book. Spoon half of filling over steak leaving 1.25 cm (½-inch) border. Starting at one narrow end, roll up jelly-roll fashion. Tie with kitchen string at 2.5 cm (1-inch) intervals. Repeat. Sprinkle with remaining 2mL (½ teaspoon) salt.

3 Heat remaining 10 mL (2 teaspoons) oil in large nonstick skillet over medium- high heat. Add roulades and cook, turning, until browned, 5 minutes. Add broth, wine, and remaining 1 tablespoon thyme; bring to boil. Transfer roulades to 5- or 6-L (5- or 6-quart) slow cooker. Pour in broth mixture. Cover and cook until roulades are fork-tender, 4–5 hours on high or 8–10 hours on low.

4 About 25 minutes before cooking time is up, whisk water and flour in small bowl until smooth; stir in about 60 mL (¼ cup) hot liquid from slow cooker until blended. Stir flour mixture into slow cooker. Cover and cook on high until mixture simmers and thickens, about 20 minutes.

5 Transfer 1 roulade and half of sauce (about 125 mL [½ cup]) to freezer container and let cool. Cover and freeze up to 2 months. Cut remaining roulade into 8 slices and serve with remaining 125 mL (½ cup) sauce.

TO REHEAT
Thaw the roulade and sauce in the refrigerator overnight. Transfer to a small baking dish; cover with foil. Bake in a 180°C (350°F) oven until heated through, 25–30 minutes.

PER SERVING (2 slices with 30 mL [2 tablespoons] sauce): 264 Cal, 7 g Fat, 2 g Sat Fat, 0 g Trans Fat, 83 mg Chol, 296 mg Sod, 11 g Carb, 2 g Fib, 36 g Prot, 33 mg Calc. *POINTS* value: *5.*

Italian Steak Rolls

prep 25 min • cook/slow-cook 4 hrs 5 min • serves 4 plus leftovers

60 mL (¼ cup) Italian-seasoned dried bread crumbs

60 mL (¼ cup) chopped fresh parsley

60 mL (¼ cup) grated Parmesan cheese

♦ 1 large hard-cooked egg, coarsely chopped

2 garlic cloves, minced

2 mL (½ teaspoon) olive oil

♦ 8 (0.5 cm [¼-inch]-thick) slices top round steak, trimmed (60 g [2 ounces] each)

2 mL (½ teaspoon) salt

4 (45 g [3-ounce]) sweet Italian turkey sausage links

1 (730 mL [25-ounce]) jar marinara sauce

125 mL (½ cup) red wine or low-sodium beef broth

1 mL (¼ teaspoon) red pepper flakes

1 To make filling, combine bread crumbs, parsley, Parmesan, egg, garlic, and oil in medium bowl.

2 Place 1 steak between 2 pieces of wax paper. Pound steak to 0.25 cm (1/8-inch) thickness. Repeat with remaining steaks. Remove and discard top sheets of wax paper. Press about 30 mL (2 tablespoons) filling onto each steak, leaving 1.25 cm (½-inch) border. From one short end, roll up each steak jelly-roll fashion. Tie each roll at 2 cm (1-inch) intervals with kitchen string. Sprinkle rolls with salt.

3 Spray large nonstick skillet with nonstick spray and set over medium-high heat. Add rolls and cook, turning occasionally, until browned, 3–4 minutes. Transfer rolls to 5- or 6-L (5- or 6-quart) slow cooker. Add sausages to skillet and cook, turning occasionally, until browned, 3–4 minutes. Transfer sausages to slow cooker. Combine marinara sauce, wine, and red pepper flakes in large bowl; pour over rolls and sausages. Cover and cook until rolls and sausages are fork-tender, 4–5 hours on high or 8–10 hours on low.

4 Transfer 4 rolls and 2 sausages with slotted spoon to freezer container. Top with half of sauce (about 425 mL [1¾ cups]) and let cool. Cover and freeze up to 2 months. Remove strings from remaining 4 rolls and cut remaining 2 sausages in half. Serve with remaining 425 mL (1¾ cups) sauce.

TO REHEAT

Thaw the steak rolls, sausages, and sauce in the refrigerator overnight. Transfer to a saucepan. Cover and cook over medium heat, stirring occasionally, until heated through, 15–20 minutes. Remove strings from rolls and cut sausages in half.

PER SERVING (1 roll with ½ sausage and scant 125 mL [½ cup] sauce): 286 Cal, 11 g Fat, 3 g Sat Fat, 0 g Trans Fat, 99 mg Chol, 969 mg Sod, 20 g Carb, 2 g Fib, 26 g Prot, 93 mg Calc. *POINTS* value: *6.*

Smoky BBQ Beef Chili

prep 20 min • cook/slow-cook 4 hrs 5 min • serves 4 plus leftovers

5　mL (1 teaspoon) canola oil

◆ 500 g (1 pound) ground extra-lean beef (5% fat or less)

◆ 1　onion, chopped

◆ 1　green bell pepper, chopped

3　garlic cloves, minced

◆ 1　small butternut squash, peeled and cubed

◆ 2　(430 g [15-ounce]) cans pinto beans, rinsed and drained

◆ 500 mL (2 cups) low-sodium chicken broth

◆ 1　(425 mL [14½-ounce]) can diced tomatoes

150 mL (²/₃ cup) chipotle barbecue sauce

2　mL (½ teaspoon) salt

30　mL (2 tablespoons) chopped fresh cilantro

125 mL (½ cup) shredded low-fat Cheddar cheese

1 Heat oil in large nonstick skillet over medium-high heat. Add beef, onion, bell pepper, and garlic. Brown beef, breaking it apart with wooden spoon, 6–8 minutes. Transfer beef mixture to 5- or 6-L (5- or 6-quart) slow cooker. Stir in squash, beans, broth, tomatoes, barbecue sauce, and salt. Cover and cook until vegetables are fork-tender, 4–5 hours on high or 8–10 hours on low.

2 Transfer half of chili (about 1.3L [5 cups]) to freezer container and let cool. Cover and freeze up to 3 months. Stir cilantro into remaining 1.3L (5 cups) chili. Serve, sprinkled with Cheddar.

TO REHEAT
Thaw the chili in the refrigerator overnight. Transfer to a saucepan. Cover and cook over medium heat, stirring occasionally, until heated through, 12–15 minutes.

PER SERVING (310 mL [1¼ cups] chili with 30 mL [2 tablespoons] cheese): 295 Cal, 9 g Fat, 4 g Sat Fat, 0 g Trans Fat, 45 mg Chol, 698 mg Sod, 32 g Carb, 8 g Fib, 24 g Prot, 157 mg Calc. *POINTS* value: *6.*

Zesty Pork Fajitas

prep 25 min • **cook/slow-cook** 4 hrs 15 min • **serves** 4 plus leftovers

- ◆ 1 (875 g [1¾-pound]) boneless pork loin roast, trimmed
- 2 mL (½ teaspoon) salt
- ◆ 500 g (1 pound) fresh tomatillos, husked, fruit rinsed, and cut into wedges
- ◆ 1 onion, sliced
- ◆ 1 (500 mL [16-ounce]) jar fat-free green salsa
- ◆ 125 mL (½ cup) low-sodium chicken broth
- ◆ 2 jalapeño peppers, seeded and chopped
- 2 garlic cloves, chopped
- ◆ 1 (450 mL [15-ounce]) can black beans, rinsed and drained
- 60 mL (¼ cup) chopped fresh cilantro
- 4 (20 cm [8-inch]) whole wheat tortillas
- ◆ 1 tomato, chopped

1 To make filling, sprinkle pork with salt. Spray large nonstick skillet with nonstick spray and set over medium-high heat. Add pork and cook, turning occasionally, until browned, 4–5 minutes. Transfer pork to 5- or 6-L (5- or 6-quart) slow cooker. Top with tomatillos, onion, salsa, broth, jalapeños, and garlic. Cover and cook until pork and vegetables are fork-tender, 4–5 hours on high or 8–10 hours on low.

2 At end of cooking time, transfer pork with slotted spoon to plate and let cool slightly, about 10 minutes. With 2 forks, shred pork into small pieces. Stir pork, beans, and cilantro into slow cooker. Cover and cook on high until filling is heated through, about 10 minutes.

3 Transfer half of filling (about 1 L [4 cups]) to freezer container and let cool. Cover and freeze up to 3 months. Spoon about 250 mL (1 cup) remaining filling onto each tortilla. Top tortillas evenly with tomato and fold in half.

TO REHEAT
Thaw the filling in the refrigerator overnight. Transfer to a saucepan. Cover and cook over medium heat, stirring occasionally, until heated through, 10–12 minutes.

PER SERVING (1 fajita): 356 Cal, 10 g Fat, 3 g Sat Fat, 0 g Trans Fat, 63 mg Chol, 709 mg Sod, 37 g Carb, 10 g Fib, 30 g Prot, 59 mg Calc.
POINTS value: *7.*

Apricot Pork Roast

prep 20 min • cook/slow-cook 4 hrs 10 min • serves 4 plus leftovers

♦ 1   (1.3 kg [2½-pound]) boneless pork loin roast, trimmed

5   mL (1 teaspoon) salt

2   mL (½ teaspoon) black pepper

5   mL (1 teaspoon) extra-virgin olive oil

♦ 1   red onion, chopped

15 mL (1 tablespoon) minced peeled fresh ginger

1   shallot, finely chopped

1   (375 mL [12-ounce]) jar apricot preserves

15 mL (1 tablespoon) whole-grain mustard

1 Sprinkle pork with salt and pepper. Heat oil in large nonstick skillet over medium-high heat. Add pork and cook, turning frequently, until browned, about 6 minutes. Transfer pork with tongs to 5- or 6-L (5- or 6-quart) slow cooker.

2 Add onion, ginger, and shallot to skillet. Reduce heat and cook, stirring frequently, until vegetables are softened, about 2 minutes. Remove skillet from heat; stir in preserves and mustard. Pour preserves mixture over pork. Cover and cook until pork is fork-tender, 4–5 hours on high or 8–10 hours on low.

3 Transfer pork to cutting board and cut crosswise into 2 pieces. Transfer half of pork to freezer container. Top with half of sauce (about 625 mL [2½ cups]) and let cool. Cover and freeze up to 2 months. Cut remaining piece of pork into 8 slices. Serve with remaining 625 mL (2½ cups) sauce.

TO REHEAT
Thaw the pork and sauce in the refrigerator overnight. Transfer to a small baking dish; cover with foil. Bake in a 160°C (325°F) oven until heated through, about 35 minutes.

PER SERVING: (2 slices pork with scant 150 mL [²/₃ cup] sauce) 323 Cal, 10 g Fat, 4 g Sat Fat, 0 g Trans Fat, 79 mg Chol, 405 mg Sod, 30 g Carb, 0 g Fib, 28 g Prot, 35 mg Calc. *POINTS* value: *7.*

Pork and Tomatillo Stew

prep 20 min • broil/cook/slow-cook 4 hrs 10 min • serves 4 plus leftovers

- 750 g (1½ pounds) fresh tomatillos, husked and fruit rinsed
- 3 poblano peppers
- 1 large onion, cut into wedges
- 2 jalapeño peppers, seeded and halved
- 625 g (1¼ pounds) boneless pork loin, trimmed and cut into 2.5 cm [1-inch] cubes
- 5 mL (1 teaspoon) ground cumin
- 3 mL (¾ teaspoon) salt
- 10 mL (2 teaspoons) olive oil
- 1 (450 mL [15-ounce]) can hominy, drained
- 1 (290 g [10-ounce]) box frozen lima beans, thawed
- 250 mL (1 cup) low-sodium chicken broth
- 5 mL (1 teaspoon) dried oregano
- 30 mL (2 tablespoons) chopped fresh cilantro

1 Preheat broiler. Spray rimmed baking sheet with nonstick spray. Arrange tomatillos, poblanos, onion, and jalapeños on baking sheet. Broil vegetables 10 cm (4 inches) from heat until lightly charred, 2–3 minutes per side. Let cool slightly. Put vegetables in food processor and puree.

2 Meanwhile, sprinkle pork with cumin and salt. Heat oil in large nonstick skillet over medium-high heat. Add pork and cook, turning frequently, until browned, 5–6 minutes. Transfer pork to 5- or 6-L (5- or 6-quart) slow cooker. Stir in tomatillo puree, hominy, beans, broth, and oregano. Cover and cook until pork is fork-tender, 4–5 hours on high or 8–10 hours on low.

3 Transfer half of stew (about 1 L [4 cups]) to freezer container and let cool. Cover and freeze up to 2 months. Stir cilantro into remaining 1 L [4 cups] stew.

TO REHEAT
Thaw the stew in the refrigerator overnight. Transfer to a saucepan. Cover and cook over medium heat, stirring occasionally, until heated through, 12–15 minutes. This recipe works with the Simply Filling technique.

PER SERVING (250 mL [1 cup]): 241 Cal, 8 g Fat, 2 g Sat Fat, 0 g Trans Fat, 45 mg Chol, 370 mg Sod, 22 g Carb, 6 g Fib, 21 g Prot, 38 mg Calc.
POINTS value: *5.*

Polish Hunter's Stew

prep 25 min • cook/slow-cook 4 hrs 10 min • serves 4 plus leftovers

- 30 g (1 ounce) dried porcini mushrooms
- **250 mL (1 cup) boiling water**
- 500 g (1 pound) pork tenderloin, trimmed and cut into 2.5 cm (1-inch) cubes
- 1 red onion, chopped
- 5 slices Canadian bacon, diced
- 1 kg (2 pounds) fresh sauerkraut, rinsed and drained
- 4 carrots, sliced
- 2 Granny Smith apples, cut into 1.25 cm (½-inch) slices
- **2 teaspoons caraway seeds**
- **1 cup dry white wine or low-sodium chicken broth**
- 45 mL (3 tablespoons) tomato paste with roasted garlic
- **500 g (1 pound) turkey kielbasa, cut into 8 pieces**
- **30 mL (2 tablespoons) chopped fresh parsley**

1 Combine mushrooms and boiling water in small bowl. Let mushrooms stand until softened, about 20 minutes.

2 Meanwhile, spray large nonstick skillet with nonstick spray and set over medium-high heat. Add pork and cook, turning occasionally, until browned, about 6 minutes. Transfer pork with slotted spoon to 5- or 6-L (5- or 6-quart) slow cooker. Add onion and bacon to skillet; cook, stirring occasionally, until browned, about 4 minutes. Transfer onion mixture to slow cooker. Stir in sauerkraut, carrots, apples, and caraway seeds.

3 Remove mushrooms with slotted spoon to sieve; rinse under cold water. Transfer mushrooms to cutting board and chop. Pour mushroom soaking liquid into skillet, discarding any grit in bottom of bowl. Stir in wine and tomato paste until smooth. Stir in chopped mushrooms. Pour wine mixture over pork and vegetables. Top with kielbasa. Cover and cook until pork, kielbasa, and vegetables are fork-tender, 4–5 hours on high or 8–10 hours on low.

4 Transfer half of stew (about 1 L [4 cups]) and 4 pieces kielbasa to freezer container and let cool. Cover and freeze up to 2 months. Stir parsley into remaining 1 L (4 cups) stew and 4 pieces kielbasa.

TO REHEAT
Thaw the stew and kielbasa in the refrigerator overnight. Transfer to a saucepan. Cover and cook over medium heat, stirring occasionally, until heated through, about 15 minutes.

PER SERVING (250 mL [1 cup] stew and 1 piece kielbasa): 278 Cal, 10 g Fat, 3 g Sat Fat, 0 g Trans Fat, 78 mg Chol, 1,139 mg Sod, 20 g Carb, 6 g Fib, 27 g Prot, 68 mg Calc. *POINTS* value: **6.**

Slow-Cooker Cassoulet

prep 30 min • cook/slow-cook 4 hrs 30 min • serves 4 plus leftovers

- ◆ 250 g (½ pound) dried cannellini (white kidney) beans, picked over, rinsed, and drained
- ◆ 3 carrots, thickly sliced
- ◆ 1 red onion, coarsely chopped
- ◆ 2 large celery stalks, sliced
- 15 mL (1 tablespoon) salt-free garlic and herb seasoning
- 1 bay leaf
- ◆ 1 (425 mL [14½-ounce]) can low-sodium chicken broth
- 125 mL (¼ cup) water
- ◆ 2 (170 g [6-ounce]) smoked bone-in centre-cut pork loin chops, trimmed
- ◆ 1 (375 g [¾-pound]) boneless pork loin, cut into 2.5 cm (1-inch)cubes
- 250 g (½ pound) fully cooked smoked chicken sausage, sliced
- ◆ 1 (425 mL [14½-ounce]) can whole tomatoes
- 2 mL (½ teaspoon) salt
- 30 mL (2 tablespoons) chopped fresh parsley parsley

1 Quick-soak beans according to package directions.

2 Combine beans, carrots, onion, celery, garlic and herb seasoning, and bay leaf in 5- or 6-L (5- or 6-quart) slow cooker. Pour broth and water over top; add pork chops. Press pork chops down into bean mixture. Cover and cook until beans are tender, 4–5 hours on high or 8–10 hours on low.

3 About 1 hour before cooking time is up, spray large nonstick skillet with nonstick spray and set over medium-high heat. Add pork cubes and sausage; cook, turning occasionally, until browned, about 6 minutes. Stir in tomatoes with juice and salt, breaking tomatoes apart with wooden spoon. Transfer pork chops to plate with slotted spoon. Stir tomato mixture into slow cooker. Cover and cook on high until pork cubes are cooked through, about 45 minutes.

4 Meanwhile, let pork chops stand until cool enough to handle, about 15 minutes. Remove and discard bones from pork chops; with 2 forks, shred pork into small pieces.

5 At end of cooking time, stir shredded pork into slow cooker. Cover and let stand until pork is heated through, about 5 minutes. Transfer half of stew (about 1 L [4 cups]) to freezer container and let cool. Cover and freeze up to 2 months. Serve remaining 1 L (4 cups) stew sprinkled with parsley.

TO REHEAT
Thaw the stew in the refrigerator overnight. Transfer to a saucepan. Cover and cook over medium heat, stirring occasionally, until heated through, about 15 minutes.

PER SERVING (about 250 mL [1 cup]): 332 Cal, 13 g Fat, 4 g Sat Fat, 0 g Trans Fat, 68 mg Chol, 1,101 mg Sod, 23 g Carb, 7 g Fib, 31 g Prot, 90 mg Calc. *POINTS* value: 7.

Cider Pork Chops with Sage

prep 25 min · cook/slow-cook 3 hrs 20 min · serves 4 plus leftovers

- ◆ 8 (150 g [5-ounce]) bone-in pork rib chops, trimmed
- 15 mL (1 tablespoon) dried sage
- 3 mL (¾ teaspoon) salt
- 3 mL (¾ teaspoon) coarsely ground black pepper
- 10 mL (2 teaspoons) canola oil
- ◆ 2 onions, thinly sliced
- ◆ 4 Granny Smith apples, cut into 1.25 cm (½-inch) wedges
- 12 dried apricots, sliced
- 175 mL (¾ cup) apple cider or unsweetened apple juice
- ◆ 175 mL (¾ cup) low-sodium chicken broth
- 3 mL (¾ teaspoon) cinnamon

1 Sprinkle pork chops with sage, salt, and pepper. Heat 5 mL (1 teaspoon) oil in large nonstick skillet over medium-high heat. Add 4 chops and cook until browned, about 2 minutes per side. Transfer to plate. Repeat with remaining 5 mL (1 teaspoon) oil and 4 chops.

2 Add onions to skillet. Reduce heat and cook, stirring occasionally, until golden, about 10 minutes.

3 Transfer half of onions to 5- or 6-L (5- or 6-quart) slow cooker. Top with half of apples, half of apricots, and pork. Repeat with remaining onions, apples, and apricots. Combine cider, broth, and cinnamon in bowl; pour into slow cooker. Cover and cook until pork and apple mixture are fork- tender, 3–4 hours on high or 6–8 hours on low.

4 Transfer 4 chops to freezer container. Top with half of apple mixture (about 625 mL [2¼ cups]) and let cool. Cover and freeze up to 2 months. Serve remaining 4 chops with remaining 625 mL (2½ cups) apple mixture.

TO REHEAT
Thaw the pork and apple mixture in the refrigerator overnight. Transfer to a saucepan. Cover and cook over medium heat, stirring occasionally, until heated through, 12–15 minutes.

PER SERVING (1 pork chop with generous 125 mL [½ cup] apple mixture): 249 Cal, 8 g Fat, 2 g Sat Fat, 0 g Trans Fat, 54 mg Chol, 264 mg Sod, 25 g Carb, 4 g Fib, 20 g Prot, 30 mg Calc. *POINTS* value: *5.*

Corn and Bacon Chowder

10 mL (2 teaspoons) olive oil

♦ 1 large onion, finely chopped

♦ 2 celery stalks, chopped

♦ 1 (930 g [32-ounce]) carton low-sodium chicken broth

♦ 500 g (1 pound) red potatoes, scrubbed and diced

2 garlic cloves, minced

60 mL (¼ cup) cold water

45 mL (3 tablespoons) all-purpose flour

♦ 125 mL (½ cup) fat-free milk

♦ 500 mL (2 cups) frozen corn kernels, thawed

♦ 3 slices Canadian bacon, diced

30 mL (2 tablespoons) chopped fresh cilantro

1 Heat oil in large nonstick saucepan over medium-high heat. Add onion and celery; cook, stirring occasionally, until softened, 6–8 minutes. Transfer vegetables to 5- or 6-L (5- or 6-quart) slow cooker. Stir in broth, potatoes, and garlic. Cover and cook until vegetables are fork-tender, 3–4 hours on high or 6–8 hours on low.

2 About 35 minutes before cooking time is up, whisk water and flour in medium bowl until smooth; whisk in milk. Stir flour mixture, corn, and bacon into slow cooker. Cover and cook on high until mixture simmers and thickens, 25–30 minutes.

3 Transfer half of chowder (about 1 L [4 cups]) to freezer container and let cool. Cover and freeze up to 2 months. Stir cilantro into remaining 1 L (4 cups) chowder.

TO REHEAT

Thaw the chowder in the refrigerator overnight. Transfer to a saucepan. Cover and cook over medium heat, stirring occasionally, until heated through, 10–12 minutes.

PER SERVING (250 mL [1 cup]): 143 Cal, 3 g Fat, 1 g Sat Fat, 0 g Trans Fat, 5 mg Chol, 175 mg Sod, 24 g Carb, 3 g Fib, 7 g Prot, 48 mg Calc.
POINTS value: *3.*

Indian Lamb Curry

prep 30 min • **cook/slow-cook** 3 hrs 10 min • **serves** 4 plus leftovers

◆ 1   small red onion, coarsely chopped

1   (5 cm [2-inch]) piece peeled fresh ginger

◆ 1   jalapeño pepper, seeded and chopped

3   garlic cloves

15   mL (1 tablespoon) curry powder

5   mL (1 teaspoon) cumin seeds

5   mL (1 teaspoon) mustard seeds

2   mL (½ teaspoon) salt

◆ 750 g (1½ pounds) boneless leg of lamb, trimmed and cut into 2cm (1-inch) cubess

10   mL (2 teaspoons) canola oil

◆ 1   (435 g [14½-ounce]) can fire-roasted diced tomatoes

◆ 125 mL (½ cup) low-sodium beef broth

◆ 500 mL (2 cups) frozen peas, thawed

45   mL (3 tablespoons) chopped fresh cilantro

1 Put onion, ginger, jalapeño, garlic, curry powder, cumin seeds, mustard seeds, and salt in mini–food processor and pulse until coarsely ground. Transfer mixture to large bowl. Add lamb and toss well to coat.

2 Heat 5 mL (1 teaspoon) oil in large nonstick skillet over medium-high heat. Add half of lamb and cook, stirring occasionally, until browned, about 5 minutes. Transfer to 5- or 6-L (5- or 6-quart) slow cooker. Repeat with remaining 1 teaspoon oil and lamb. Add tomatoes and broth to skillet; cook, scraping browned bits from bottom of pan, until mixture comes to boil. Pour tomato mixture over lamb mixture. Cover and cook until lamb is fork-tender, 3–4 hours on high or 6–8 hours on low.

3 About 20 minutes before cooking time is up, stir peas into slow cooker. Cover and cook on high until peas are just tender, about 15 minutes.

4 Transfer half of curry (about 750 mL [3 cups]) to freezer container and let cool. Cover and freeze up to 2 months. Stir cilantro into remaining 750 mL (3 cups) curry.

TO REHEAT
Thaw the curry in the refrigerator overnight. Transfer to a saucepan. Cover and cook over medium heat, stirring occasionally, until heated through, 10–12 minutes. This recipe works with the Simply Filling technique.

PER SERVING (about 175 mL [¾ cup]): 193 Cal, 8 g Fat, 2 g Sat Fat, 0 g Trans Fat, 59 mg Chol, 296 mg Sod, 10 g Carb, 2 g Fib, 21 g Prot, 41 mg Calc. *POINTS* value: *4.*

Lamb with Stout

prep 25 min • cook/slow-cook 3 hrs 10 min • serves 4 plus leftovers

- 625 g (1¼ pounds) boneless leg of lamb, trimmed and cut into 1-inch cubes
- 3 mL (¾ teaspoon) salt
- 500 g (1 pound) small red potatoes, scrubbed and halved
- 3 carrots, cut diagonally into 1.25 cm (½-inch) slices
- 8 shallots, peeled
- 2 garlic cloves, chopped
- 500 mL (2 cups) low-sodium beef broth
- 1 (375 mL [12-ounce]) bottle stout or dark beer
- 60 mL (¼ cup) all-purpose flour
- 60 mL (¼ cup) cold water
- 250 mL (1 cup) frozen peas, thawed
- 10 mL (2 teaspoons) chopped fresh rosemary or 2 mL (½ teaspoon) dried

1 Sprinkle lamb with 2 mL (½ teaspoon) salt. Spray large nonstick skillet with nonstick spray and set over medium-high heat. Add half of lamb and cook, stirring occasionally, until browned, about 5 minutes. Transfer to 5- or 6-L (5- or 6-quart) slow cooker. Repeat with remaining lamb. Top with potatoes, carrots, shallots, and garlic. Stir in broth, beer, and remaining 1 mL (¼ teaspoon) salt. Cover and cook until lamb and vegetables are fork-tender, 3–4 hours on high or 6–8 hours on low.

2 About 35 minutes before cooking time is up, whisk flour and water in small bowl until smooth; stir in about 60 mL (¼ cup) hot liquid from slow cooker until blended. Stir flour mixture into slow cooker. Cover and cook on high until mixture simmers and thickens, about 30 minutes.

3 At end of cooking time, stir peas into slow cooker. Cover and let stand until heated through, about 10 minutes.

4 Transfer half of stew (about 1 L [4 cups]) to freezer container and let cool. Cover and freeze up to 2 months. Stir rosemary into remaining 1 L (4 cups) stew.

TO REHEAT

Thaw the stew in the refrigerator overnight. Transfer to a saucepan. Cover and cook over medium heat, stirring occasionally, until heated through, 10–12 minutes.

PER SERVING (250 mL [1 cup]): 227 Cal, 5 g Fat, 2 g Sat Fat, 0 g Trans Fat, 49 mg Chol, 313 mg Sod, 24 g Carb, 3 g Fib, 19 g Prot, 44 mg Calc. *POINTS* value: 4.

Moussaka

prep 30 min • **broil/cook/slow-cook** 3 hrs 30 min • **serves** 4 plus leftovers

- 500 g (1 pound) eggplant, cut into 2.5 cm (1-inch) cubes
- **10 mL (2 teaspoons) olive oil**
- 1 onion, finely chopped
- **4 garlic cloves, minced**
- 750 g (1½ pounds) lean ground lamb
- 1 (435 mL [14½-ounce]) can diced tomatoes
- **125 mL (½ cup) red wine or low-sodium beef broth**
- **5 mL (1 teaspoon) cinnamon**
- **2 mL (½ teaspoon) ground allspice**
- **2 mL (½ teaspoon) salt**
- 425 mL (1¾ cups) fat-free milk
- **45 mL (3 tablespoons) all-purpose flour**
- 1 large egg
- **0.5 mL (⅛ teaspoon) ground nutmeg**
- **125 mL (½ cup) grated Parmesan cheese**

1 Spray broiler rack with nonstick spray; preheat broiler. Put eggplant on broiler rack and lightly spray with nonstick spray. Broil 10 cm (4 inches) from heat, turning occasionally, until lightly browned, about 8 minutes. Transfer to 5- or 6-L (5- or 6-quart) slow cooker.

2 Meanwhile, heat oil in large nonstick skillet over medium-high heat. Add onion and garlic; cook, stirring, until onion is softened, 5–6 minutes. Add lamb and brown, 5 minutes. Stir in tomatoes, wine, cinnamon, allspice, and salt; bring to boil. Simmer, stirring, until sauce thickens slightly, 10 minutes. Spoon lamb mixture over eggplant. Cover and cook until flavours are blended, 3–4 hours on high or 6–8 hours on low.

3 To make topping, about 1 hour 10 minutes before cooking time is up, whisk milk and flour in small saucepan until smooth. Cook over medium heat, whisking constantly, until mixture boils and thickens, 3 minutes. Remove saucepan from heat. Whisk egg and nutmeg in bowl; stir in about 125 mL (½ cup) hot milk mixture. Stir egg mixture into remaining hot milk mixture until blended. Stir in Parmesan. Pour topping over eggplant mixture. Cover and cook on high just until topping is set, about 1 hour.

4 Transfer stoneware to rack and let moussaka cool slightly, about 20 minutes. Transfer half of moussaka (about 750 mL [3 cups]) to freezer container and let cool. Cover and freeze up to 2 months. Divide remaining 750 mL (3 cups) moussaka among 4 plates.

TO REHEAT
Thaw the moussaka in the refrigerator overnight. Transfer to a microwavable bowl. Cover with wax paper and microwave on High until heated through, 5–6 minutes.

PER SERVING (175 mL [¾ cup]): 251 Cal, 10 g Fat, 4 g Sat Fat, 0 g Trans Fat, 91 mg Chol, 412 mg Sod, 14 g Carb, 2 g Fib, 25 g Prot, 190 mg Calc. *POINTS* value: *5.*

Stuffed Breast of Veal

prep 30 min • **cook/slow-cook** 3 hrs 10 min • **serves** 4 plus leftovers

10 mL (2 teaspoons) olive oil

♦ 1 (290 g [10-ounce]) package sliced cremini mushrooms

♦ 4 scallions, thinly sliced

2 garlic cloves, minced

3 mL (¾ teaspoon) salt

♦ 1 (170 g [6-ounce]) bag baby spinach

30 mL (2 tablespoons) whole wheat bread crumbs

♦ 1 (1.3 kg [2½-pound]) boneless veal breast, trimmed and butterflied

♦ 2 large onions, cut into wedges

125 mL (½ cup) Madeira wine

♦ 125 mL (½ cup) low-sodium beef broth

♦ 15 mL (1 tablespoon) chopped fresh thyme or 5 mL (1 teaspoon) dried

60 mL (¼ cup) water

45 mL (3 tablespoons) all-purpose flour

1 To make filling, heat 5 mL (1 teaspoon) oil in large nonstick skillet over medium-high heat. Add mushrooms, scallions, garlic, and 1 mL (¼ teaspoon) salt; cook, stirring, until mushrooms are browned, 6–8 minutes. Add spinach and cook, stirring, just until spinach wilts, 1–2 minutes. Transfer vegetable mixture to bowl. Stir in bread crumbs and let cool.

2 Place veal, cut side up, on work surface. Spread filling over veal leaving 2.5 cm (1-inch) border. Starting at one narrow end, roll up jelly-roll fashion. Tie with kitchen string at 2.5 cm (1-inch) intervals. Sprinkle with remaining 2 mL (½ teaspoon) salt.

3 Heat remaining 5 mL (1 teaspoon) oil in skillet over medium-high heat. Add veal and cook, turning, until browned, 5 minutes. Transfer to 5-or 6-L (5-or 6-quart) slow cooker. Stir in onions, wine, broth, and thyme. Cover and cook until veal is fork-tender, 3–4 hours on high or 6–8 hours on low.

4 About 35 minutes before cooking time is up, whisk water and flour in small bowl until smooth; stir in about 60 mL (¼ cup) hot liquid from slow cooker until blended. Stir flour mixture into slow cooker. Cover and cook on high until mixture simmers and thickens, about 30 minutes.

5 Transfer veal to cutting board and cut crosswise in half. Transfer half of sauce (about 375 mL [1½ cups]) and half of veal to freezer container and let cool. Cover and freeze up to 2 months. Cut remaining veal into 8 slices. Serve with remaining 375 mL (1½ cups) sauce.

TO REHEAT

Thaw the veal and sauce in the refrigerator overnight. Transfer to a saucepan. Cover and cook over medium heat, turning the veal occasionally, until heated through, 15–20 minutes.

PER SERVING (2 slices with 75 mL [⅓ cup] sauce): 252 Cal, 8 g Fat, 3 g Sat Fat, 0 g Trans Fat, 122 mg Chol, 354 mg Sod, 11 g Carb, 2 g Fib, 32 g Prot, 78 mg Calc. *POINTS* value: *5.*

White Balsamic Chicken

prep 20 min • slow-cook 4 hrs • serves 4 plus leftovers

◆ 1 (1.8 kg [3½-pound]) chicken, cut into 8 pieces and skinned

125 mL (½ cup) dry white wine

◆ 45 mL (3 tablespoons) tomato paste with Italian seasonings

6 large garlic cloves, chopped

2 mL (½ teaspoon) salt

2 mL (½ teaspoon) coarsely ground black pepper

◆ 1 (425 mL [14½-ounce]) can low-sodium chicken broth

45 mL (3 tablespoons) white balsamic vinegar

30 mL (2 tablespoons) all-purpose flourr

◆ 1 (275 g [9-ounce]) package frozen sugar-snap peas, thawed

◆ 5 plum tomatoes, sliced 1.25 cm (½ inch) thick

1 Place chicken in 5- or 6-L (5- or 6-quart) slow cooker. Whisk wine, tomato paste, garlic, salt, and pepper in small bowl until smooth; pour over chicken. Pour 375 mL (1½ cups) broth into slow cooker. Cover and cook until chicken is fork-tender, 4–5 hours on high or 8–10 hours on low. Meanwhile, cover and refrigerate remaining broth.

2 About 30 minutes before cooking time is up, whisk reserved broth, vinegar, and flour in small bowl until smooth; stir in about 60 mL (¼ cup) hot liquid from slow cooker until blended. Stir flour mixture into slow cooker without disturbing chicken. Top with even layer of snap peas then tomatoes. Cover and cook on high until mixture simmers and thickens and snap peas are just tender, about 25 minutes.

3 Transfer half of sauce and vegetables (about 500 mL [2 cups]) and 4 pieces chicken to freezer container and let cool. Cover and freeze up to 2 months. Serve remaining 4 pieces chicken with remaining 500 mL (2 cups) sauce and vegetables.

TO REHEAT
Thaw the chicken and sauce in the refrigerator overnight. Transfer to a saucepan. Cover and cook over medium heat, turning the chicken occasionally, until heated through, 15–20 minutes.

PER SERVING (1 piece chicken with 125 mL [½ cup] sauce and vegetables): 186 Cal, 6 g Fat, 2 g Sat Fat, 0 g Trans Fat, 65 mg Chol, 233 mg Sod, 10 g Carb, 2 g Fib, 24 g Prot, 44 mg Calc. *POINTS* value: *4.*

Thai Chicken and Squash Soup

prep 20 min • **cook/slow-cook** 3 hrs 10 min • **serves** 4 plus leftovers

◆ 625 g (1¼ pounds) skinless, boneless chicken breasts, cut into 2.5 cm (1-inch) cubes

2 mL (½ teaspoon) salt

10 mL (2 teaspoons) canola oil

◆ 1 onion, chopped

3 garlic cloves, minced

15 mL (1 tablespoon) minced peeled fresh ginger

5 mL (1 teaspoon) Thai red curry paste

5 mL (1 teaspoon) ground cardamom

◆ 1 L (4 cups) peeled cut-up butternut squash, cubed

◆ 1 (1 L [32-ounce]) carton low-sodium chicken broth

150 mL (²/₃ cup) light coconut milk

10 mL (2 teaspoons) packed light brown sugar

15 mL (1 tablespoon) chopped fresh chives

1 Sprinkle chicken with salt. Heat 5mL (1 teaspoon) oil in large nonstick skillet over medium-high heat. Add chicken and cook, stirring occasionally, until browned, about 5 minutes. Transfer chicken to 5- or 6-L (5- or 6-quart) slow cooker. Heat remaining 5 mL (1 teaspoon) oil in skillet over medium heat. Add onion, garlic, and ginger; cook, stirring occasionally, until onion is golden, 3–4 minutes.

2 Remove skillet from heat. Stir in curry paste and cardamom. Transfer onion mixture to slow cooker. Stir in squash and broth. Cover and cook until chicken and vegetables are fork-tender, 3–4 hours on high or 6–8 hours on low.

3 About 20 minutes before cooking time is up, stir coconut milk and brown sugar into slow cooker. Cover and cook on high until mixture simmers and flavors are blended, about 15 minutes.

4 Transfer half of soup (about 1.3 L [5 cups]) to freezer container and let cool. Cover and freeze up to 2 months. Stir chives into remaining 1.3 L (5 cups) soup.

TO REHEAT
Thaw the soup in the refrigerator overnight. Transfer to a saucepan. Cover and cook over medium heat, stirring occasionally, until heated through, 10–15 minutes.

PER SERVING (310 mL [1¼ cups]): 171 Cal, 6 g Fat, 2 g Sat Fat, 0 g Trans Fat, 44 mg Chol, 244 mg Sod, 12 g Carb, 1 g Fib, 19 g Prot, 46 mg Calc.
POINTS value: *4.*

Chicken Mole

prep 25 min • cook/slow-cook 3 hrs 15 min • serves 4 plus leftovers

3   dried pasilla chile peppers, seeded

750 mL (3 cups) boiling water

◆ 500 mL (2 cups) low-sodium chicken broth

5   mL (1 teaspoon) olive oil

◆ 1   onion, coarsely chopped

3   garlic cloves

◆ 2   tomatoes, chopped

60   mL (¼ cup) dark raisins

30   mL (2 tablespoons) sliced almonds, toasted

60   g (2 ounces) semisweet chocolate, coarsely chopped

◆ 1   (450 g [15-ounce]) can pinto beans, rinsed and drained

◆ 8   (125 g [¼-pound]) skinless chicken thighs

2   mL (½ teaspoon) salt

1 Heat large nonstick skillet over medium-high heat. Open chiles flat. Place them in skillet in single layer and press down firmly with spatula. Toast until crackly and just beginning to smoke, about 30 seconds per side. Transfer to bowl. Add boiling water and let stand until softened, about 20 minutes. Drain and discard liquid. Puree chiles and 250 mL (1 cup) broth in food processor. Transfer puree to 5- or 6-L (5- or 6-quart) slow cooker.

2 Heat oil in skillet over medium-high heat. Add onion and garlic; cook, stirring occasionally, until onion is golden, 3–4 minutes. Add tomatoes and cook, stirring occasionally, until softened, about 2 minutes. Transfer tomato mixture to food processor. Add remaining 250 mL (1 cup) broth, raisins, almonds, and chocolate and puree. Transfer mixture to slow cooker and stir in beans.

3 Wipe skillet clean. Sprinkle chicken with salt. Spray skillet with nonstick spray and set over medium-high heat. Add chicken and cook until browned, about 4 minutes per side. Transfer chicken to slow cooker. Press chicken down into chile mixture. Cover and cook until chicken is fork-tender, 3–4 hours on high or 6–8 hours on low.

4 With slotted spoon, transfer 4 thighs to freezer container. Top with half of sauce (about 625 mL [2½ cups]) and let cool. Cover and freeze up to 2 months. Divide remaining 4 thighs and 625 mL (2½ cups) sauce among 4 plates.

TO REHEAT
Thaw the chicken and sauce in the refrigerator overnight. Transfer to a saucepan. Cover and cook over medium heat, stirring occasionally, until heated through, about 15 minutes.

PER SERVING (1 chicken thigh with generous 125 mL [½ cup] sauce): 255 Cal, 10 g Fat, 3 g Sat Fat, 0 g Trans Fat, 43 mg Chol, 263 mg Sod, 23 g Carb, 5 g Fib, 20 g Prot, 54 mg Calc. *POINTS* value: 5.

Brandy Chicken with Dried Plums and Olives

prep 15 min • **cook/slow-cook** 3 hrs 20 min • **serves** 4 plus leftovers

10 mL (2 teaspoons) olive oil

♦ 4 (150 g [5-ounce]) skinless chicken thighs

♦ 4 (125 g [¼-pound]) skinless chicken drumsticks

♦ 1 large onion, thinly sliced

♦ 1 (425 mL [14½-ounce]) can stewed tomatoes

♦ 175 mL (¾ cup) low-sodium chicken broth

75 mL (⅓ cup) brandy

12 pitted dried plums

♦ 12 brine-cured green olives, pitted

3 garlic cloves, finely chopped

1 Heat 5 mL (1 teaspoon) oil in large nonstick skillet over medium-high heat. Add thighs and cook until browned, about 3 minutes per side. Transfer to 5 or 6-L (5 or 6-quart) slow cooker. Repeat with remaining 5 mL (1 teaspoon) oil and drumsticks.

2 Add onion to skillet. Reduce heat and cook, stirring occasionally, until softened, 6–8 minutes. Stir in tomatoes, broth, brandy, plums, olives, and garlic; cook, scraping browned bits from bottom of pan, until mixture comes to a boil. Pour tomato mixture over chicken. Cover and cook until chicken and onion are fork-tender, 3–4 hours on high or 6–8 hours on low.

3 Transfer 2 thighs, 2 drumsticks, and half of sauce (about 500 mL [2 cups]) to freezer container and let cool. Cover and freeze up to 2 months. Divide remaining 2 thighs, 2 drumsticks, and 500 mL (2 cups) sauce among 4 plates.

TO REHEAT
Thaw the chicken and sauce in the refrigerator overnight. Transfer to a saucepan. Cover and cook over medium heat, stirring occasionally, until heated through, about 15 minutes.

PER SERVING (1 piece chicken with 125 mL [½ cup] sauce): 190 Cal, 7 g Fat, 2 g Sat Fat, 0 g Trans Fat, 53 mg Chol, 203 mg Sod, 14 g Carb, 2 g Fib, 17 g Prot, 48 mg Calc. *POINTS* value: *4.*

Rosemary Chicken with Bell Peppers

prep 15 min • **cook/slow-cook** 3 hrs 10 min • **serves** 4 plus leftovers

10 mL (2 teaspoons) canola oil

♦ 3 assorted-colour bell peppers, sliced

♦ 1 onion, sliced

3 mL (¾ teaspoon) salt

♦ 1 (425 mL [14½-ounce]) can stewed tomatoes

♦ 250 mL (1 cup) low-sodium chicken broth

15 mL (1 tablespoon) chopped fresh rosemary or 5 mL (1 teaspoon) dried

15 mL (1 tablespoon) fennel seeds, crushed

♦ 8 skinless chicken drumsticks

♦ 250 mL (1 cup) whole wheat orzo

1 Heat 5 mL (1 teaspoon) oil in large nonstick skillet over medium-high heat. Add bell peppers, onion, and 1 mL (¼ teaspoon) salt; cook, stirring occasionally, until softened, 6–8 minutes. Transfer bell pepper mixture to 5- or 6-L (5- or 6-quart) slow cooker. Stir in tomatoes and broth.

2 Combine rosemary, fennel, and remaining 2 mL (½ teaspoon) salt in large bowl. Add chicken; toss to coat. Heat remaining 5 mL (1 teaspoon) oil in skillet over medium-high heat. Add chicken and cook, turning occasionally, until browned, 4–5 minutes. Transfer chicken to slow cooker. Press chicken down into bell pepper mixture. Cover and cook until chicken and vegetables are fork-tender, 3–4 hours on high or 6–8 hours on low.

3 About 20 minutes before cooking time is up, cook orzo according to package directions, omitting salt if desired.

4 Transfer 4 drumsticks with slotted spoon to freezer container. Top with half of sauce (about 500 mL [2 cups]) and let cool. Cover and freeze up to 2 months. Divide remaining 4 drumsticks and 500 mL (2 cups) sauce among 4 plates. Serve with orzo.

TO REHEAT
Thaw the chicken and sauce in the refrigerator overnight. Transfer to a saucepan. Cover and cook over medium heat, stirring occasionally, until heated through, 10–12 minutes. This recipe works with the Simply Filling technique.

PER SERVING (1 drumstick with125 mL [½ cup] sauce and 175mL [¾ cup] orzo): 252 Cal, 4 g Fat, 1 g Sat Fat, 0 g Trans Fat, 49 mg Chol, 549 mg Sod, 36 g Carb, 5 g Fib, 20 g Prot, 59 mg Calc. *POINTS* value: *5.*

Mexi-Style Meatball Soup

prep 25 min • **cook/slow-cook** 3 hrs 5 min • **serves** 4 plus leftovers

1   (580 g [20-ounce]) package hot or sweet Italian turkey sausage links, casings removed

♦ 60   mL (¼ cup) cornmeal

♦ 1   large egg, lightly beaten

2   mL (½ teaspoon) ground cumin

1   mL (¼ teaspoon) ground allspice

♦ 1   onion, finely chopped

♦ 1   carrot, diced

2   garlic cloves, minced

♦ 1   (1 L [32-ounce]) carton low-sodium chicken broth

♦ 1   (425 mL [14½-ounce]) can diced tomatoes with jalapeños

♦ 1   (150 g [5-ounce]) package baby spinach

♦ 30   mL (2 tablespoons) chopped scallions

1 Combine sausage, cornmeal, egg, cumin, and allspice in medium bowl. With moistened hands, form into 30 meatballs. Transfer meatballs to 5- or 6-L (5- or 6-quart) slow cooker.

2 Spray medium nonstick skillet with nonstick spray and set over medium-high heat. Add onion, carrot, and garlic; cook, stirring occasionally, until vegetables are softened, about 5 minutes. Transfer vegetables to slow cooker; stir in broth and tomatoes. Cover and cook until vegetables are fork-tender and instant-read thermometer inserted into centre of meatball registers 80 °C (180°F), 3–4 hours on high or 6–8 hours on low.

3 About 10 minutes before cooking time is up, stir spinach into slow cooker. Cover and cook on high just until spinach begins to wilt, about 5 minutes.

4 Transfer half of soup (about 1 L [4 cups]) to freezer container and let cool. Cover and freeze up to 2 months. Ladle remaining soup evenly among 4 bowls. Serve, sprinkled with scallions.

TO REHEAT

Thaw the soup in the refrigerator overnight. Transfer to a saucepan. Cover and cook over medium heat, stirring occasionally, until heated through, 10–12 minutes.

PER SERVING (250 mL [1 cup]): 209 Cal, 9 g Fat, 2 g Sat Fat, 0 g Trans Fat, 92 mg Chol, 604 mg Sod, 11 g Carb, 2 g Fib, 22 g Prot, 71 mg Calc.
POINTS value: 5.

Cod Vera Cruz

prep 25 min • **cook/slow-cook** 1 hr 10 min • **serves** 4 plus leftovers

10   mL (2 teaspoons) olive oil

♦ 1   onion, sliced

3   garlic cloves, finely chopped

♦ 2   (425 mL [14½-ounce]) can petite diced tomatoes

125 mL (½ cup) dry white wine or clam juice

♦ 60   mL (¼ cup) small pimiento-stuffed green olives (about 20)

45   mL (3 tablespoons) raisins

30   mL (2 tablespoons) capers

5   mL (1 teaspoon) dried oregano

2   mL (½ teaspoon) salt

1   mL (¼ teaspoon) red pepper flakes

♦ 8   (170 g [6-ounce]) skinless cod fillets

Grated zest of ½ lemon

1 Heat oil in large nonstick skillet over medium-high heat. Add onion and garlic; cook, stirring occasionally, until onion is softened, about 5 minutes. Stir in tomatoes, wine, olives, raisins, capers, oregano, salt, and red pepper flakes; bring to boil. Transfer tomato mixture to 5- or 6-L (5- or 6-quart) slow cooker. Add cod fillets to slow cooker. Gently press fillets down into tomato mixture. Cover and cook until onion is fork-tender and each fillet is just opaque in centre, 1–2 hours on high or 2–4 hours on low.

2 Transfer 4 fillets with slotted spoon to freezer container. Top with half of sauce (about 560 mL [2¼ cups]) and let cool. Cover and freeze up to 1 month. Divide remaining 4 fillets and 560 mL (2¼ cups) sauce among 4 plates. Serve, sprinkled with lemon zest.

TO REHEAT
Thaw the fillets and sauce in the refrigerator overnight. Transfer to a skillet. Cover and cook over medium heat until heated through, 10–15 minutes, turning the fillets once halfway through the cooking time.

PER SERVING (1 fillet with generous125 mL [½ cup] sauce): 211 Cal, 4 g Fat, 1 g Sat Fat, 0 g Trans Fat, 90 mg Chol, 571 mg Sod, 9 g Carb, 2 g Fib, 33 g Prot, 70 mg Calc. *POINTS* value: *4.*

Monkfish Ragú

- 1 (796 mL [28-ounce]) can diced tomatoes, drained (no salt added)
- 250 mL (1 cup) low-sodium chicken broth

125 mL (½ cup) clam juice

- 1 large red onion, chopped
- ½ fennel bulb, chopped
- 1 Cubanelle pepper, seeded and chopped

2 garlic cloves, minced

- 60 mL (¼ cup) tomato paste (no salt added)

30 mL (2 tablespoons) sherry vinegar

15 mL (1 tablespoon) chopped fresh thyme or 5 mL (1 teaspoon) dried

5 mL (1 teaspoon) fennel seeds

2 mL (½ teaspoon) red pepper flakes

2 mL (½ teaspoon) salt

- 1 kg (2 pounds) monkfish, cut into 2.5 cm (1-inch) chunks
- 500 g (1 pound) Swiss chard, stems removed and leaves coarsely chopped

1 Combine tomatoes, broth, clam juice, onion, fennel, Cubanelle pepper, garlic, tomato paste, vinegar, thyme, fennel seeds, red pepper flakes, and salt in 5- or 6-L (5- or 6-quart) slow cooker. Cover and cook until mixture simmers and tomatoes have softened, 2–3 hours on high.

2 At end of cooking time, gently stir in monkfish and Swiss chard. Cover and cook on high until monkfish is just opaque in centre, about 40 minutes.

3 Transfer half of ragú (about 1.3 L [5 cups]) to freezer container and let cool. Cover and freeze up to 1 month. Divide remaining 1.3 L (5 cups) ragú among 4 plates.

TO REHEAT

Thaw the ragú in the refrigerator overnight. Transfer to a saucepan. Cover and cook over medium heat until heated through, 10–15 minutes, stirring once halfway through the cooking time. This recipe works with the Simply Filling technique.

PER SERVING (310 mL [1¼ cups]): 184 Cal, 5 g Fat, 1 g Sat Fat, 0 g Trans Fat, 42 mg Chol, 511 mg Sod, 13 g Carb, 4 g Fib, 24 g Prot, 73 mg Calc.
POINTS value: *3.*

Shrimp Creole

prep 20 min • cook/slow cook 3 hrs 10 min • serves 4 plus leftovers

10 mL (2 teaspoons) olive oil

♦ **4** celery stalks, sliced

♦ **2** assorted-colour bell peppers, sliced

♦ **1** onion, sliced

♦ **4** plum tomatoes, chopped

3 garlic cloves, chopped

2 mL (½ teaspoon) Creole seasoning

♦ **375** mL (1½ cups) low-sodium chicken broth

45 mL (3 tablespoons) water

30 mL (2 tablespoons) all-purpose flourr

♦ **1** kg (2 pounds) large shrimp, shelled and deveined

♦ **1** (290 g [10-ounce]) box frozen peas, thawed

♦ **750** mL (3 cups) hot cooked brown rice

1 Heat oil in large nonstick skillet over medium-high heat. Add celery, bell peppers, and onion; cook, stirring occasionally, until vegetables are softened, 6–8 minutes. Add tomatoes, garlic, and Creole seasoning; cook, stirring occasionally, until tomatoes have softened, 5–6 minutes. Transfer mixture to 5- or 6-L (5- or 6-quart)slow cooker. Stir in broth. Cover and cook until vegetables are fork-tender, 3–4 hours on high or 6–8 hours on low.

2 About 30 minutes before cooking time is up, whisk water and flour in small bowl until smooth; stir in about 60 mL (¼ cup) hot liquid from slow cooker until blended. Stir flour mixture, shrimp, and peas into slow cooker. Cover and cook on high until mixture simmers and thickens and shrimp are just opaque in centre, about 25 minutes.

3 Transfer half of shrimp mixture (about 1 L) ([4 cups]) to freezer container and let cool. Cover and freeze up to 1 month. Serve remaining 1 L (4 cups) shrimp mixture with rice.

TO REHEAT
Thaw the shrimp mixture in the refrigerator overnight. Transfer to a saucepan. Cover and cook over medium heat, stirring occasionally, until heated through, 12–15 minutes.

PER SERVING (310 mL [1¼ cups] shrimp mixture with 175 mL [¾ cup] rice): 293 Cal, 4 g Fat, 1 g Sat Fat, 0 g Trans Fat, 107 mg Chol, 219 mg Sod, 46 g Carb, 8 g Fib, 19 g Prot, 66 mg Calc. *POINTS* value: *5.*

Root Vegetable Tagine

prep 25 min • cook/slow-cook 3 hr 5 min • serves 4 plus leftovers

10 mL (2 teaspoons) canola oil

◆ 1 onion, sliced

2 garlic cloves, chopped

5 mL (1 teaspoon) cinnamon

2 mL (½ teaspoon) ground cumin

2 mL (½ teaspoon ground ginger

◆ 2 sweet potatoes, peeled and cut into 2.5 cm (1-inch) chunks

◆ 2 carrots, sliced 1.25 cm (½ inch) thick

◆ 2 small tomatoes, chopped

◆ 1 parsnip, peeled and cut into 2.5 cm (1-inch) chunks

125 mL (½ cup) pitted dried plums

◆ 750 mL (3 cups) vegetable broth

15 mL (1 tablespoon) honey

◆ 175 mL (¾ cup) whole wheat couscous

60 mL (¼ cup) sliced almonds, toasted

1 Heat oil in medium nonstick skillet over medium-high heat. Add onion and garlic; cook, stirring occasionally, until onion is softened, 5–6 minutes. Remove skillet from heat; stir in cinnamon, cumin, and ginger. Transfer onion mixture to 5- or 6-L (5- or 6-quart) slow cooker. Add potatoes, carrots, tomatoes, parsnip, and dried plums. Combine broth and honey in large bowl; stir into vegetable mixture. Cover and cook until vegetables are fork-tender, 3–4 hours on high or 6–8 hours on low.

2 About 15 minutes before cooking time is up, cook couscous according to package directions, omitting salt if desired.

3 Transfer half of tagine 1.1 L (about 4½ cups) to freezer container and let cool. Cover and freeze up to 2 months. Divide remain]ing 1.1 L (4½ cups) tagine among 4 plates. Sprinkle with almonds and serve with couscous.

TO REHEAT
Thaw the tagine in the refrigerator overnight. Transfer to a saucepan. Cover and cook over medium heat, stirring occasionally, until heated through, 12–15 minutes.

PER SERVING (generous 250 mL [1 cup] tagine with 15 mL [1 tablespoon] almonds and 125 mL [½ cup] couscous): 231 Cal, 4 g Fat, 0 g Sat Fat, 0 g Trans Fat, 0 mg Chol, 378 mg Sod, 47 g Carb, 8 g Fib, 6 g Prot, 68 mg Calc. *POINTS* value: *4.*

CATALAN SEAFOOD STEW
PAGE 150

Chapter 5

Beans and Grains

Hearty main dishes, soups,
sides, (even breads!) the whole
family will love.

Barley, Beef, and Root Vegetable Stew

prep 25 min • **cook/slow-cook** 3 hrs 10 min • **serves** 4

- 250 g (½ pound) bottom round steak, trimmed and cut into 1.25 cm (½-inch) cubes
- 1 onion, chopped
- **250 mL (1 cup) water**
- 4 carrots, quartered lengthwise and cut into 1.25 cm (½-inch) chunks
- 1 celeriac, peeled and cut into 2 cm (¾-inch) chunks
- 2 parsnips, peeled and cut into 2 cm (¾-inch) chunks
- 1 turnip, peeled and cut into 2 cm (¾-inch) chunks
- 1 (425 mL [14½-ounce]) can low-sodium beef broth
- 125 mL (½ cup) pearl barley
- 3 garlic cloves, minced
- 15 mL (1 tablespoon) chopped fresh thyme or 5 mL (1 teaspoon) dried
- 2 mL (½ teaspoon) salt
- 1 mL (¼ teaspoon) black pepper

1 Spray large nonstick skillet with nonstick spray and set over medium-high heat. Add beef and cook, stirring frequently, until browned, about 4 minutes. Transfer beef to 5- or 6-L (5- or 6-quart) slow cooker.

2 Add onion to skillet and cook, stirring frequently, until lightly browned, about 4 minutes. Add water and cook, scraping up browned bits from bottom of pan. Pour onion mixture into slow cooker. Stir in carrots, celeriac, parsnips, turnip, broth, barley, garlic, thyme, salt, and pepper. Cover and cook until beef and vegetables are fork-tender, 3–4 hours on high or 6–8 hours on low.

◆ **FILLING EXTRA**

For even heartier flavour, add a 290 g (10-ounce) package sliced cremini or white mushrooms with the vegetables in step 2. This recipe works with the Simply Filling technique.

PER SERVING (375 mL [1½ cups]): 306 Cal, 4 g Fat, 1 g Sat Fat, 0 g Trans Fat, 42 mg Chol, 477 mg Sod, 46 g Carb, 10 g Fib, 24 g Prot, 100 mg Calc.
POINTS value: *6.*

Pinto, Pork, and Hominy Stew

prep 20 min • **cook/slow-cook** 3 hrs 5 min • **serves** 4

- 250 g (½ pound) boneless pork loin, trimmed and cut into 1.25 cm (½-inch) cubes
- 1 onion, chopped

  125 mL (½ cup) water
- 1 (475 mL [15½-ounce]) can pinto beans, rinsed and drained
- 1 (425 mL [14½-ounce]) can low-sodium chicken broth
- 1 large red bell pepper, thinly sliced
- 250 mL (1 cup) fresh or thawed frozen corn kernels
- 2 **garlic cloves, minced**
- 1 **(35 g [1¼-ounce]) envelope low- sodium chili seasoning mix**
- 5 **mL (1 teaspoon) ground cumin**
- 1 (450 mL [15-ounce]) can hominy, rinsed and drained
- 4 radishes, chopped
- 30 **mL (2 tablespoons) chopped fresh cilantro**

1 Spray large nonstick skillet with nonstick spray and set over medium-high heat. Add pork and onion; cook, stirring frequently, until browned, about 5 minutes. Transfer pork mixture to 5- or 6-L (5- or 6-quart) slow cooker.

2 Add water to skillet and cook, scraping up browned bits from bottom of pan. Pour liquid into slow cooker; stir in beans, broth, bell pepper, corn, garlic, seasoning mix, and cumin. Top with hominy. Cover and cook until pork and vegetables are fork-tender, 3–4 hours on high or 6–8 hours on low. Serve, sprinkled with radishes and cilantro.

IN THE KITCHEN
Hominy are dried corn kernels with a pleasantly chewy texture and mild flavour. Look for the canned variety near the canned beans at the supermarket.

PER SERVING (310 mL [1¼ cups]): 362 Cal, 7 g Fat, 2 g Sat Fat, 0 g Trans Fat, 36 mg Chol, 520 mg Sod, 51 g Carb, 13 g Fib, 25 g Prot, 95 mg Calc.
POINTS value: *7.*

Pasta e Fagioli Soup

prep 20 min • **cook/slow-cook** 4 hrs 5 min • **serves** 6

10 mL (2 teaspoons) extra-virgin olive oil

◆ 1 large red onion, finely chopped

3 garlic cloves, finely chopped

15 mL (1 tablespoon) chopped fresh rosemary or 5 mL (1 teaspoon) dried

◆ 1 (540 mL [19-ounce]) can cannellini (white kidney) beans, rinsed and drained

◆ 3 carrots, finely chopped

◆ 1 fennel bulb, finely chopped

1 (90 g [3-ounce]) piece smoked ham hock

12 fresh flat-leaf parsley sprigs

2 mL (½ teaspoon) salt

1 mL (¼ teaspoon) black pepper

◆ 1 (1 L [32-ounce]) carton low-sodium chicken broth

250 mL (1 cup) ditalini

60 mL (¼ cup) grated pecorino cheese

1 Heat oil in large nonstick skillet over medium heat. Add onion, garlic, and rosemary; cook, stirring occasionally, until onion is softened, about 5 minutes. Transfer onion mixture to 5- or 6-L (5- or 6-quart) slow cooker. Stir in beans, carrots, fennel, ham hock, parsley, salt, and pepper. Pour broth over beans and vegetables. Cover and cook until vegetables are fork-tender, 4–5 hours on high or 8–10 hours on low. Discard ham hock and parsley. Skim any fat from soup.

2 About 20 minutes before cooking time is up, cook ditalini according to package directions, omitting salt if desired.

3 At end of cooking time, stir ditalini into slow cooker. Serve, sprinkled with pecorino.

◆ **FILLING EXTRA**
If you like, before sprinkling the soup with the pecorino in step 3, top it evenly with 3 seeded and finely diced plum tomatoes.

PER SERVING (500 mL [2 cups]): 247 Cal, 7 g Fat, 2 g Sat Fat, 0 g Trans Fat, 18 mg Chol, 1,027 mg Sod, 30 g Carb, 6 g Fib, 17 g Prot, 101 mg Calc. *POINTS* value: *5.*

Escarole, Bean, and Chicken Soup

prep 20 min • **slow-cook** 3 hrs 25 min • **serves** 6

- ◆ 2 (290 g [10-ounce]) bone-in chicken breasts, skinned
- ◆ 4 carrots, sliced
- ◆ 2 celery stalks, sliced
- ◆ 1.3 L (5cups) low-sodium chicken broth
- 2 garlic cloves, minced
- ◆ 5 cups low-sodium chicken broth
- 2 mL (½ teaspoon) Italian seasoning
- 2 mL (½ teaspoon) salt
- 1 mL (¼ teaspoon) black pepper
- ◆ 1 small head escarole, trimmed and cut into 2.5 cm (1-inch) pieces
- ◆ 1 (450 g [15-ounce]) can white beans, rinsed and drained
- 90 g (3 ounces) multigrain spaghetti, broken into 3.5 cm (1½-inch) lengths
- 60 mL (¼ cup) grated Parmesan cheese

1 Place chicken in 5- or 6- (5- or 6-quart) slow cooker. Top with carrots, celery, onion, and garlic. Add broth, Italian seasoning, salt, and pepper. Cover and cook until chicken and vegetables are fork-tender, 3–4 hours on high or 6–8 hours on low.

2 At end of cooking time, transfer chicken with slotted spoon to plate and let stand until cool enough to handle, about 20 minutes.

3 Meanwhile, stir escarole, beans, and spaghetti into slow cooker. Cover and cook on high until escarole and spaghetti are tender, about 20 minutes, stirring once halfway through cooking time.

4 Remove chicken from bones and coarsely shred. Stir chicken into slow cooker. Cover and cook on high until heated through, about 5 minutes. Serve, sprinkled with Parmesan.

IN THE KITCHEN
If the soup seems thick after cooking the escarole and spaghetti, add an additional 1 cup low-sodium chicken broth with the shredded chicken in step 4.

PER SERVING (about 400 mL [1⅔ cups] soup with 10 mL [2 teaspoons] cheese): 326 Cal, 6 g Fat, 2 g Sat Fat, 0 g Trans Fat, 62 mg Chol, 579 mg Sod, 34 g Carb, 6 g Fib, 35 g Prot, 161 mg Calc. *POINTS* value: **6.**

Brown and Wild Rice Casserole with Chicken

prep 15 min • **cook/slow-cook** 2 hrs 35 min • **serves** 6

- 1 small onion, chopped
- 625 mL (2½ cups) low-sodium chicken broth
- 6 small carrots, cut diagonally into 1.25 cm (½-inch) slices
- 1 (250g [8-ounce]) package sliced mushrooms
- 250 mL (1 cup) brown and wild rice blend or 125 mL (½ cup) each brown rice and wild rice
- 2 celery stalks, cut diagonally into 1.25 cm (½-inch) slices
- 2 garlic cloves, minced
- 2 mL (½ teaspoon) poultry seasoning
- 1 mL (¼ teaspoon) salt
- 625 g (1¼ pounds) chicken tenders
- 1 (275 mL [10¾-ounce]) can low-fat condensed cream of mushroom soup

1 Spray large nonstick skillet with nonstick spray and set over medium heat. Add onion and cook, stirring occasionally, until softened, about 5 minutes. Transfer onion to 5- or 6- (5- or 6-quart) slow cooker. Stir in broth, carrots, mushrooms, rice blend, celery, garlic, poultry seasoning, and salt; mix well. Top with chicken, placing it towards centre of slow cooker. Cover and cook until chicken and vegetables are fork-tender and rice is tender but still slightly chewy, 2½–3 hours on high or 5–6 hours on low.

2 About 25 minutes before cooking time is up, stir soup into slow cooker. Cover and cook on high until mixture simmers, about 20 minutes.

◆ **FILLING EXTRA**
Prepare the recipe as directed, but add 750 mL (3 cups) thawed frozen peas to the slow cooker with the soup in step 2 and up the per-serving *POINTS* value by *1.*

PER SERVING (325 mL [1⅓ cups]): 309 Cal, 6 g Fat, 2 g Sat Fat, 0 g Trans Fat, 60 mg Chol, 625 mg Sod, 35 g Carb, 5 g Fib, 29 g Prot, 63 mg Calc.
POINTS value: *6.*

Cornmeal Dumplings with Beans, Greens, and Chicken

prep 25 min • **slow-cook** 3 hrs 25 min • **serves** 6

- 1 onion, finely chopped
- **2 garlic cloves, minced**
- **1 mL (¼ teaspoon) salt**
- 375 g (¾ pound) skinless, boneless chicken thighs, halved
- 1 (450 mL [15-ounce]) can white beans, rinsed and drained
- 500 g (1 pound) collard greens, stems discarded, leaves cut into 2.5 cm (1-inch) pieces
- 250 g (8 oz) kale, stems discarded, leaves cut into 2.5 cm (1-inch) pieces
- 2 (400 mL [14-ounce]) cans low-sodium chicken broth
- **175 mL (¾ cup) low-fat buttermilk baking mix**
- 60 mL (¼ cup) cornmeal
- 75 mL (⅓ cup) fat-free milk
- **White vinegar and hot pepper sauce (optional)**

1 Combine onion, garlic, and salt in 5- or 6-L (5- or 6-quart) slow cooker. In single layers, top with chicken, beans, collard greens, and kale. Press greens down into slow cooker to fit. Pour broth over greens. Cover and cook until chicken and greens are fork-tender, 3–4 hours on high or 6–8 hours on low.

2 At end of cooking time, transfer greens with slotted spoon to bowl; cover and keep warm.

3 Combine baking mix and cornmeal in medium bowl. Stir in milk just until soft dough forms. Drop dough by heaping tablespoonfuls about 2.5 cm (1 inch) apart onto simmering stew, making 6 dumplings. Cover and cook on high until toothpick inserted in centre of each dumpling comes out clean, 25–30 minutes.

4 Divide greens among 6 shallow bowls. Top evenly with chicken and beans mixture and dumplings. Serve with vinegar and pepper sauce (if using).

PER SERVING (150 mL [⅔ cup] greens with about 150 mL [⅔ cup] chicken and bean mixture and 1 dumpling): 298 Cal, 7 g Fat, 2 g Sat Fat, 0 g Trans Fat, 35 mg Chol, 507 mg Sod, 37 g Carb, 7 g Fib, 24 g Prot, 253 mg Calc. *POINTS* value: **6.**

Golden Split Pea Soup

prep 20 min • **slow-cook/cook** 4 hrs 5 min • **serves** 6

◆ 1 (1.5 L [48-ounce]) can low-sodium chicken broth

500 mL (2 cups) water

◆ 250 mL (1 cup) dried yellow split peas, picked over, rinsed, and drained

◆ 250 mL (1 cup) dried red lentils, picked over, rinsed, and drained

◆ 2 carrots, diced

◆ 2 celery stalks, diced

◆ 1 onion, chopped

◆ 1 sweet potato, peeled and diced

2 **garlic cloves, minced**

15 **mL (1 tablespoon) curry powder**

2 **mL (½ teaspoon) salt**

◆ 1 (290 g [10-ounce]) smoked turkey drumstick

1 Combine broth, water, split peas, lentils, carrots, celery, onion, potato, garlic, curry powder, and salt in 5- or 6-L (5- or 6-quart) slow cooker. Add turkey, pressing it down into broth mixture. Cover and cook until peas, lentils, and vegetables are fork-tender, 4–5 hours on high or 8–10 hours on low.

2 At end of cooking time, transfer turkey with slotted spoon to plate and let stand until cool enough to handle, about 15 minutes.

3 Remove and discard skin and bones from turkey; cut turkey into bite-size chunks. Stir turkey into slow cooker. Cover and cook on high until hot, about 5 minutes.

◆ **FILLING EXTRA**

Top each serving of this chunky soup with 15 mL (1 tablespoon) plain fat-free yogourt. This recipe works with the Simply Filling technique.

PER SERVING (375 mL [1½ cups]): 312 Cal, 3 g Fat, 1 g Sat Fat, 0 g Trans Fat, 25 mg Chol, 655 mg Sod, 47 g Carb, 16 g Fib, 27 g Prot, 75 mg Calc. *POINTS* value: *6.*

Turkey-and-Bean Burrito Bake

prep 30 min • cook/slow-cook 2 hrs 35 min • serves 6

- 375 g (¾ pound) ground skinless turkey breast
- 1 onion, finely chopped
- 15 mL (1 tablespoon) chili powder
- 1 (425 mL [14½-ounce] can diced tomatoes
- 1 (300 mL [10-ounce]) can enchilada sauce
- 250 mL (1 cup) fat-free salsa
- 6 fat-free corn tortillas
- 125 mL (½ cup) quick-cooking brown rice
- 1 zucchini, chopped
- 1 (450 mL [15-ounce]) can pink or red beans, rinsed and drained
- 325 mL (1⅓ cups) shredded low-fat Mexican cheese blend
- 750 mL (3 cups) shredded lettuce
- 75 mL (⅓ cup) fat-free sour cream

1 Spray large nonstick skillet with nonstick spray and set over medium-high heat. Add turkey and onion; cook, breaking turkey apart with wooden spoon, until turkey is no longer pink, about 5 minutes. Stir in chili powder and remove skillet from heat.

2 Spray 5- or 6-L (5- or 6-quart) slow cooker stoneware with nonstick spray. Combine tomatoes, enchilada sauce, and 75 mL (⅓ cup) salsa in medium bowl. Spread 125 mL (½ cup) tomato mixture over bottom of slow cooker. Top with 2 tortillas, tearing one of the tortillas in half so tortillas cover tomato mixture. Top evenly with half of turkey mixture, half of rice, and half of zucchini. Spoon 250 mL (1 cup) tomato mixture evenly over zucchini. Top with half of beans and 125 mL (½ cup) cheese blend. Repeat with 2 tortillas, remaining turkey mixture, rice, and zucchini, 250mL (1 cup) tomato mixture, remaining beans, and 125 mL (½ cup) cheese blend. Top with remaining 2 tortillas and spread with remaining tomato mixture. Cover and cook until hot and bubbling at edges, 2½–3 hours on high or 5–6 hours on low.

3 Sprinkle burrito bake with remaining 75 mL (⅓ cup) cheese blend. Cover and let stand until cheese melts, about 5 minutes. Serve with remaining 150 mL (⅔ cup) salsa, the lettuce and sour cream.

PER SERVING (375 mL [1½ cups] burrito bake with 22 mL [1½ tablespoons] salsa, 125 mL (½ cup) lettuce, and 15 mL [1 tablespoon] sour cream): 341 Cal, 7 g Fat, 3 g Sat Fat, 0 g Trans Fat, 53 mg Chol, 956 mg Sod, 45 g Carb, 10 g Fib, 28 g Prot, 380 mg Calc. *POINTS* value: 7.

Polenta Lasagna

prep 30 min • **cook/slow-cook** 2 hrs 45 min • **serves** 6

375 g (¾ pound) hot Italian turkey sausage links, casings removed

◆ 1 (250 g [8-ounce]) package sliced mushrooms

1 (680 mL [24-ounce]) jar fat-free marinara sauce

◆ 1 (560 g [18-ounce]) tube refrigerated fat-free plain polenta, cut into 18 rounds

◆ 1 (290 g [10-ounce]) package frozen chopped spinach, thawed and squeezed dry

◆ 250 mL (1 cup) fat-free ricotta cheese

◆ 1 zucchini, very thinly sliced

◆ 175 mL (¾ cup) shredded fat-free mozzarella cheese

60 mL (¼ cup grated Parmesan cheese

1 Place large nonstick skillet over medium heat. Add sausage and cook, breaking it apart with wooden spoon, until no longer pink, about 8 minutes. Transfer sausage with slotted spoon to plate. Add mushrooms to skillet and cook, stirring occasionally, until liquid is absorbed and mushrooms are tender, about 5 minutes.

2 Spray 5- or 6-L (5- or 6-quart) slow cooker stoneware with nonstick spray. Spread 75 mL (⅓ cup) marinara sauce in bottom of slow cooker. Top with 6 slices polenta (if they don't cover bottom completely that's okay), half of spinach, and half of mushrooms. Spread 125 mL (½ cup) ricotta over mushrooms and spinach. Top with half of sausage, 250 mL (1 cup) marinara sauce, and half of zucchini. Repeat with 6 slices polenta, remaining spinach, mushrooms, ricotta, and sausage, 250 mL (1 cup) marinara sauce, and remaining zucchini. Top with remaining 6 polenta slices and marinara sauce. Cover and cook until lasagna is hot and bubbling, 2½–3 hours on high or 5–6 hours on low.

3 Turn off slow cooker. Sprinkle lasagna with mozzarella and Parmesan. Cover and let stand 20 minutes before serving. Cut into 6 wedges.

PER SERVING (1 wedge): 297 Cal, 8 g Fat, 2 g Sat Fat, 0 g Trans Fat, 62 mg Chol, 1,147 mg Sod, 27 g Carb, 4 g Fib, 30 g Prot, 350 mg Calc. *POINTS* value: *6.*

Salmon Risotto

prep 15 min • **cook/slow-cook** 2 hrs 15 min • **serves** 6

- 1 onion, chopped
- 375 mL (1½ cups) red and brown rice blend or brown rice
- 2 garlic cloves, crushed through a press
- 125 mL (½ cup) dry white wine or clam juice
- 1 (1 L [32-ounce]) carton low-sodium chicken broth
- 1½ cups shredded carrots
- 3 mL (¾ teaspoon) salt
- 1 L (¼ teaspoon) black pepper
- 500 g (1 pound) skinless salmon fillet, cut into 2.5 cm (1-inch) chunks
- 250 mL (1 cup) frozen peas, thawed

1 Spray large nonstick skillet with nonstick spray and set over medium heat. Add onion and cook, stirring frequently, until softened, about 5 minutes. Add rice blend and garlic; cook, stirring frequently, until rice is translucent, about 2 minutes. Add wine and cook, stirring frequently, until wine is absorbed, about 1 minute.

2 Transfer rice mixture to 5- or 6-L (5- or 6-quart) slow cooker. Stir in broth, carrots, salt, and pepper. Cover and cook until rice is tender, but still slightly chewy, 2–2½ hours on high or 4–5 hours on low.

3 About 15 minutes before cooking time is up, stir salmon and peas into slow cooker. Cover and cook on high until salmon is just opaque in centre and peas are just tender, 15–20 minutes, stirring once halfway through cooking time.

◆ FILLING EXTRA

For an extra-fancy seafood risotto, prepare the recipe as directed but add 375 g (¾ pound) shelled and deveined cooked shrimp along with the salmon in step 3 (and up the per-serving *POINTS* value by *1*).

PER SERVING (325 mL [1⅓ cups]): 345 Cal, 7 g Fat, 2 g Sat Fat, 0 g Trans Fat, 50 mg Chol, 429 mg Sod, 46 g Carb, 7 g Fib, 25 g Prot, 53 mg Calc. *POINTS* value: *7*.

Catalan Seafood Stew

....

prep 25 min • **cook/slow-cook** 3 hrs 15 min • **serves** 6

....

◆ 1   onion, sliced

  2   garlic cloves, crushed through a press

  7   mL (1½ teaspoons) ground cumin

  7   mL (1½ teaspoons) smoked paprika

  1   mL (¼ teaspoon) salt

  0.5 mL (⅛ to ¼ teaspoon) red pepper flakes

◆ 1   (450 mL [15-ounce] can kidney beans, rinsed and drained

◆ 1   (450 mL [15-ounce]) can chickpeas, rinsed and drained

◆ 1   (425 mL [14½-ounce]) can fire-roasted diced tomatoes

◆ 250 mL (1 cup) low-sodium chicken broth

◆ 1   bell pepper (any colour), cut into 2.5 cm (1-inch) chunks

◆ 150 mL (⅔ cup) farro or brown rice

◆ 250 g (½ pound) skinless halibut or cod fillet, cut into 2.5 cm (1-inch) chunks

◆ 250 g (½ pound) large shrimp, peeled and deveined

  125 mL (½ cup) fresh cilantro leaves

1 Spray large nonstick skillet with nonstick spray and set over medium heat. Add onion and cook until softened, about 5 minutes. Stir in garlic, cumin, paprika, salt, and red pepper flakes. Transfer onion mixture to 5- or 6-L (5- or 6-quart) slow cooker. Stir in beans, chickpeas, tomatoes, bell pepper, and broth. Cover and cook until vegetables are fork-tender, 3–4 hours on high or 6–8 hours on low.

2 About 40 minutes before cooking time is up, cook farro according to package directions.

3 At end of cooking time, stir halibut and shrimp into slow cooker. Cover and cook on high until halibut and shrimp are just opaque in centre, 8–10 minutes.

4 Divide farro evenly among 4 plates; top evenly with stew. Serve, sprinkled with cilantro.

IN THE KITCHEN

Farro are whole wheat kernels from Italy prized for their sweet and nutty flavour. Look for semi-pearled farro, which requires no presoaking. This recipe works with the Simply Filling technique.

....

PER SERVING (generous 250 mL [1 cup] stew with about 75 mL [1/3 cup] farro): 297 Cal, 3 g Fat, 1 g Sat Fat, 0 g Trans Fat, 56 mg Chol, 470 mg Sod, 46 g Carb, 10 g Fib, 24 g Prot, 101 mg Calc. *POINTS* value: *5.*

Shrimp and Lentil Curry

prep 20 min • **slow-cook** 2 hrs 15 min • **serves** 4

♦ 625 mL (2½ cups) low-sodium vegetable broth

♦ 250 mL (1 cup) dried red lentils, picked over, rinsed, and drained

♦ 1 large red onion, chopped

♦ 2 celery stalks, thinly sliced

30 mL (2 tablespoons) minced peeled fresh ginger

1 garlic clove, minced

20 mL (4 teaspoons) curry powder

2 mL (½ teaspoon) cinnamon

2 mL (½ teaspoon) salt

0.5 mL (⅛ teaspoon) cayenne

♦ 1 kg (2 pounds) medium shrimp, peeled and deveined

1 Combine broth, lentils, onion, celery, ginger, garlic, curry powder, cinnamon, salt, and cayenne in 5- or 6-L (5- or 6-quart) slow cooker. Cover and cook until lentils are tender, 2–3 hours on high or 4–6 hours on low.

2 At end of cooking time, stir in shrimp. Cover and cook on high until shrimp are just opaque in centre, about 15 minutes.

♦ **FILLING EXTRA**
If you like, add 4 stalks of sliced celery instead of 2 in step 1.
This recipe works with the Simply Filling technique.

PER SERVING (about 425 mL [1¾ cups]): 363 Cal, 3 g Fat, 0 g Sat Fat, 0 g Trans Fat, 336 mg Chol, 1,052 g Sod, 36 g Carb, 9 g Fib, 48 g Prot, 155 mg Calc. *POINTS value: 7.*

Quinoa-and-Corn Stuffed Peppers

prep 20 min • **slow-cook** 2 hrs 20 min • **serves** 4

- 125 mL (½ cup) quinoa
- 1 (450 mL [15-ounce]) can black beans, rinsed and drained
- 500 mL (2 cups) packed baby spinach, coarsely chopped
- 250 mL (1 cup) fresh or thawed frozen corn kernels
- 125 mL (½ cup) crumbled fat-free feta cheese
- 2 scallions, chopped
- 7 mL (1½ teaspoons) ground cumin
- 1 (425 mL [14½-ounce]) can diced tomatoes
- 125 mL (½ cup) + 60 mL (4 tablespoons) fat-free green salsa
- 45 mL (3 tablespoons) chopped fresh cilantro
- 4 large assorted-colour bell peppers, tops cut off

1 To make filling, cook quinoa according to package directions. Drain. Transfer to large bowl and let cool slightly, about 10 minutes.

2 Stir in beans, spinach, corn, feta, scallions, cumin, 60 mL (¼ cup) tomatoes, 30 mL (2 tablespoons) salsa, and 30 mL (2 tablespoons) cilantro.

3 Spoon filling evenly into bell peppers. Transfer bell peppers, top side up, to 5- or 6-L (5- or 6-quart) slow cooker. Combine remaining tomatoes and 125 mL (½ cup) + 30 mL (2 tablespoons) salsa in small bowl. Spoon tomato mixture over and around bell peppers. Cover and cook until bell peppers are fork-tender, 2–3 hours on high or 4–6 hours on low. Serve, sprinkled with remaining 15mL (1 tablespoon) cilantro.

IN THE KITCHEN
To add extra-flavour to the quinoa filling, toast it first. Place the quinoa in a small skillet and set over medium-high heat. Toast, stirring frequently, until fragrant, about 3 minutes. This recipe works with the Simply Filling technique.

PER SERVING (1 stuffed pepper with 60 mL [¼ cup] sauce): 318 Cal, 3 g Fat, 0 g Sat Fat, 0 g Trans Fat, 1 mg Chol, 823 mg Sod, 59 g Carb, 16 g Fib, 17 g Prot, 189 mg Calc. *POINTS* value: *6.*

Bean and Sweet Potato Soup

10 mL (2 teaspoons) olive oil

♦ 2 red onions, finely chopped

3 garlic cloves, finely chopped

15 mL (1 tablespoon) curry powder

♦ 1 (826 mL [29-ounce]) can black beans, rinsed and drained

♦ 1 (826 mL [29-ounce]) can red kidney beans, rinsed and drained

♦ 1 large sweet potato, peeled and diced

2 mL (½ teaspoon) salt

1 mL (¼ teaspoon) black pepper

♦ 1.5 mL (6 cups) low-sodium vegetable broth

♦ 60 mL (¼ cup) plain fat-free yogourt

30 mL (2 tablespoons) chopped fresh cilantro

Grated zest of ½ lime

1 Heat oil in large nonstick skillet over medium heat. Add onions and garlic; cook, stirring occasionally, until onion is softened, about 5 minutes. Add curry powder and cook, stirring constantly, until fragrant, about 30 seconds. Transfer onion mixture to 5- or 6-L (5- or 6-quart) slow cooker. Stir in beans, potato, salt, and pepper. Pour broth over beans and vegetables. Cover and cook until vegetables are fork-tender, 4–5 hours on high or 8–10 hours on low.

2 Meanwhile, combine yogourt, cilantro, and lime zest in small bowl.

3 At end of cooking time, let mixture cool 10 minutes. Puree in batches in food processor or blender. Serve, topped with yogourt mixture.

This recipe works with the Simply Filling technique.

PER SERVING (500 mL [2 cups] and 15 mL (1 scant tablespoon) yogourt mixture): 322 Cal, 3 g Fat, 0 g Sat Fat, 0 g Trans Fat, 0 mg Chol, 1,083 mg Sod, 59 g Carb, 18 g Fib, 17 g Prot, 148 mg Calc. *POINTS* value: 6.

Bulgur and Bean Chili

prep 20 min • **cook/slow-cook** 3 hrs 5 min • **serves** 6

15 mL (1 tablespoon) ground cumin

♦ 1 onion, chopped

♦ 2 assorted-colour bell peppers, cut into 2.5 cm (1-inch) chunks

♦ 1 (580 g [20-ounce]) bag peeled cut-up butternut squash, cut into 2.5 cm (1-inch) chunks

♦ 1 (450 mL [15-ounce) can kidney beans, rinsed and drained

♦ 1 (450 mL [15-ounce]) can black beans, rinsed and drained

♦ 1 (425 mL [14½-ounce]) can vegetable broth

♦ 1 (300 mL [10-ounce]) can diced tomatoes with green chiles

♦ 1 (250 g [8-ounce]) can tomato sauce

3 garlic cloves, crushed through a press

15 mL (1 tablespoon) chili powder

1 mL (¼ teaspoon) salt

♦ 125 mL (½ cup) bulgur

♦ 1 (275 g [9-ounce]) box frozen cut green beans, thawed

♦ 175 mL (¾ cup) shredded fat-free Monterey Jack cheese

♦ 75 mL (⅓ cup) fat-free sour cream

1 Set large nonstick skillet over medium heat. Add cumin and cook, stirring constantly, until toasted and fragrant, about 1 minute; transfer to 5- or 6-L (5- or 6-quart) slow cooker.

2 Spray skillet with nonstick spray and set over medium heat. Add onion and cook, stirring occasionally, until softened, about 4 minutes. Transfer onion to slow cooker. Stir in bell peppers, squash, kidney beans, black beans, broth, diced tomatoes, tomato sauce, garlic, chili powder, and salt. Top vegetable mixture with bulgur, leaving 1.25 cm (½-inch) from side of slow cooker. Cover and cook until bulgur and vegetables are fork-tender, 3–4 hours on high or 6–8 hours on low.

3 About 30 minutes before cooking time is up, stir in green beans. Cover and cook on high until green beans are just tender, about 25 minutes. Serve, topped with Monterey Jack and sour cream.

IN THE KITCHEN

If peeled cut-up butternut squash is not available at your supermarket, buy a 1 kg (2-pound) butternut squash and prep it yourself. The recipe works with the Simply Filling technique.

PER SERVING (about 425 mL [1¾ cups] chili with 30 mL [2 tablespoons] cheese and 15 mL [1 scant Tablespoon] sour cream): 298 Cal, 2 g Fat, 0 g Sat Fat, 0 g Trans Fat, 4 mg Chol, 1,147 mg Sod, 58 g Carb, 15 g Fib, 17 g Prot, 291 mg Calc. *POINTS* value: *5.*

Three-Bean Chili

prep 15 min • **cook/slow-cook** 4 hrs • **serves** 4

- ◆ 1 large red onion, chopped
- ◆ 2 yellow bell peppers, diced
- ◆ 1 small rutabaga, peeled and diced
- ◆ 250 mL (1 cup) frozen baby lima beans, thawed
- ◆ 1 (450 mL [15-ounce]) can pinto beans, rinsed and drained
- ◆ 1 (450 mL [15-ounce]) can black beans, rinsed and drained
- ◆ 1 (450 mL [15-ounce]) can diced tomatoes in sauce
- ◆ 1 (250 mL [8-ounce]) can tomato sauce (no salt added)
- 75 mL (⅓ cup) cayenne pepper sauce
- 30 mL (2 tablespoons) honey
- 45 mL (3 tablespoons) ancho chile powder
- 4 garlic cloves, coarsely chopped
- 15 mL (1 tablespoon) ground cumin
- 45 mL (3 tablespoons) shredded pepperjack cheese
- ◆ 2 scallions, sliced

Combine onion, bell peppers, rutabaga, lima beans, pinto beans, black beans, diced tomatoes, tomato sauce, pepper sauce, honey, chile powder, garlic, and cumin in 5- or 6-L (5- or 6-quart) slow cooker. Cover and cook until vegetables are fork-tender, 4–5 hours on high or 8–10 hours on low. Serve, sprinkled with pepperjack and scallions.

IN THE KITCHEN
Don't let the amount of pepper sauce throw you in this recipe! Cayenne pepper sauce has a milder flavour than hot pepper sauce, which is made from fiery Tabasco peppers.

PER SERVING (425 mL [1¾ cups] chili with about 10 mL [2 teaspoons] cheese and 7 mL [½ tablespoon] scallions): 324 Cal, 4 g Fat, 1 g Sat Fat, 0 g Trans Fat, 5 mg Chol, 1,000 mg Sod, 60 g Carb, 18 g Fib, 15 g Prot, 171 mg Calc.
POINTS value: *6.*

Green Lentil Stew with Hot Spinach Salad

prep 15 min • slow-cook/cook 3 hrs 10 min • serves 6

- 875 mL (3½ cups) low-sodium chicken or vegetable broth
- 375 mL (1½ cups) dried green (French) lentils, picked over, rinsed, and drained
- 3 carrots, thinly sliced
- 3 celery stalks, sliced
- 3 garlic cloves, minced
- 30 mL (2 tablespoons) tomato paste
- 2 mL (½ teaspoon) dried thyme
- 2 mL (½ teaspoon) salt
- 10 mL (2 teaspoons) olive oil
- 1 large red onion, chopped
- 30 mL (2 tablespoons) red-wine vinegar
- 5 mL (1 teaspoon) Dijon mustard
- 0.5 mL (⅛ teaspoon) black pepper
- 1 (170 g [6-ounce]) bag baby spinach

1 Combine broth, lentils, carrots, celery, garlic, tomato paste, thyme, and 1 mL (¼ teaspoon) salt in 5- or 6-L (5- or 6-quart) slow cooker. Cover and cook until lentils are fork-tender, 3–4 hours on high or 6–8 hours on low.

2 At end of cooking time, heat oil in large nonstick skillet over medium heat. Add onion and cook, stirring frequently, until softened and lightly browned, about 8 minutes. Remove skillet from heat. Stir in vinegar, mustard, pepper, and remaining 1 mL (¼ teaspoon) salt. Return skillet to heat and cook just until vinegar comes to a simmer.

3 Put spinach in large bowl; add onion mixture and toss to combine. Serve with lentils.

IN THE KITCHEN
Green lentils are smaller than brown lentils, have a slightly peppery flavour, and hold their shape well. They can be found in some supermarkets, specialty food stores, or health food stores. This recipe works with the Simply Filling technique.

PER SERVING (generous 250 mL [1 cup] lentils with generous 375 mL [1½ cups] spinach mixture): 345 Cal, 5 g Fat, 1 g Sat Fat, 0 g Trans Fat, 0 mg Chol, 549 mg Sod, 55 g Carb, 15 g Fib, 25 g Prot, 135 mg Calc. *POINTS* value: 7.

Lentil-Winter Squash Stew

prep 20 min • slow-cook 4 hrs 20 min • serves 6

- ◆ 375 mL (1½ cups) dried lentils, picked over, rinsed, and drained
- ◆ 1 (450 mL [15½ounce]) can chickpeas, rinsed and drained
- 30 mL (2 tablespoons) minced peeled fresh ginger
- 4 large garlic cloves, minced
- 1 mL (¼ teaspoon) red pepper flakes
- ◆ 425 g (1¾ pounds) buttercup or butternut squash, peeled, seeded and cut into 2.5 cm (1-inch) chunks
- ◆ 625 mL (2½ cups) vegetable broth
- ◆ 1 (425 mL [14½-ounce]) can Italian-style stewed tomatoes
- ◆ 1 (170 g [6-ounce]) bag baby spinach
- ◆ 2 (290 g [10-ounce]) bags frozen broccoli, cauliflower, carrot, and zucchini blend, thawed

1 Combine lentils, chickpeas, ginger, garlic, and red pepper flakes in 5- or 6-L (5- or 6-quart) slow cooker. Top with squash. Pour broth into slow cooker. Cover and cook until lentils and squash are fork-tender, 4–5 hours on high or 8–10 hours on low.

2 About 20 minutes before cooking time is up, stir tomatoes and half of spinach into slow cooker. When spinach begins to wilt, after about 5 minutes, stir in remaining spinach. Cover and cook on high until spinach wilts completely, about 10 minutes.

3 At end of cooking time, stir vegetable blend into slow cooker. Cover and cook on high until vegetables are crisp-tender, about 20 minutes.

This recipe works with the Simply Filling technique.

PER SERVING (375 mL [1½ cups]): 306 Cal, 2 g Fat, 0 g Sat Fat, 0 g Trans Fat, 0 mg Chol, 741 mg Sod, 59 g Carb, 19 g Fib, 19 g Prot, 137 mg Calc. *POINTS* value: 5.

Mixed-Grain Quick Bread

prep 20 min • **slow-cook** 2 hrs 30 min • **serves** 12

250 mL (1 cup) whole wheat flour

250 mL (1 cup) all-purpose flourr

♦ 75 mL (⅓ cup) old-fashioned oats

♦ 60 mL (¼ cup) cornmeal

30 mL (2 tablespoons) sunflower seeds

15 mL (1 tablespoon) millet (optional)

5 mL (1 teaspoon) baking powder

3 mL (¾ teaspoon) salt

1 mL (¼ teaspoon) baking soda

♦ 310 mL (1¼ cups) fat-free buttermilk

♦ 1 large egg

30 mL (2 tablespoons) honey

15 mL (1 tablespoon) olive or canola oil

1 Spray 1.5L (1½-quart) soufflé dish with nonstick spray. Place small rack in bottom of 5- or 6-L (5- or 6-quart) slow cooker.

2 Combine whole wheat flour, all-purpose flour, 60 mL (¼ cup) oats, cornmeal, sunflower seeds, millet (if using), baking powder, salt, and baking soda in large bowl. Whisk buttermilk, egg, honey, and oil in medium bowl. Add buttermilk mixture to flour mixture and stir just until flour mixture is moistened. Transfer dough to prepared dish and spread evenly. Sprinkle with remaining oats.

3 Spray 30 cm (12-inch) square of foil with nonstick spray. Cover dish tightly with foil, sprayed side down. Transfer dish to slow cooker. Pour 250 mL (1 cup) hot water around dish. Cover and cook until toothpick inserted into centre of bread comes out clean, 2½–3 hours on high.

4 Transfer dish to another rack and let cool 10 minutes. Run thin knife around bread to loosen it from dish. Remove bread from dish and let cool completely on rack. Cut into 12 wedges.

♦ **FILLING EXTRA**

For a satisfying snack, toast a wedge of the bread and spread it with 30 mL (2 tablespoons) mashed avocado. The per-serving *POINTS* value will increase by *1*.

PER SERVING (1 wedge): 139 Cal, 3 g Fat, 1 g Sat Fat, 0 g Trans Fat, 19 mg Chol, 100 mg Sod, 24 g Carb, 2 g Fib, 5 g Prot, 62 mg Calc. *POINTS* value: *3*.

Spiced Apple-Nut Bread

prep 20 min • **slow-cook** 2 hrs 30 min • **serves** 12

- 125 mL (½ cup) unsweetened applesauce
- 1 large egg
- 1 large egg white
- 30 mL (2 tablespoons) canola oil
- 375 mL (1½ cups) white whole wheat flour
- 125 mL (½ cup) packed brown sugar
- 5 mL (1 teaspoon) apple pie spice
- 5 mL (1 teaspoon) baking powder
- 2 mL (½ teaspoon) salt
- 1 mL (¼ teaspoon) baking soda
- 1 Granny Smith apple, peeled and chopped
- 120 mL (8 tablespoons) walnuts, chopped

1 Spray 1.5 L (1½-quart) soufflé dish with nonstick spray. Place small rack in bottom of 5- or 6-L (5- or 6-quart) slow cooker.

2 Whisk applesauce, egg, egg white, and oil in medium bowl. Combine flour, brown sugar, pie spice, baking powder, salt, and baking soda in large bowl, breaking up any lumps of sugar. Stir in applesauce mixture, apple, and 90 mL (6 tablespoons) walnuts just until flour mixture is moistened (dough will be stiff). Transfer dough to prepared dish and spread evenly. Sprinkle with remaining 30 mL (2 tablespoons) walnuts.

3 Spray 30 cm (12-inch) square of foil with nonstick spray. Cover dish tightly with foil, sprayed side down. Transfer dish to slow cooker. Pour 250 mL (1 cup) hot water around dish. Cover and cook until toothpick inserted into centre of bread comes out clean, 2½–3 hours on high.

4 Transfer dish to another rack and let cool 15 minutes. Run thin knife around bread to loosen it from dish. Remove bread from dish and let cool completely on rack. Cut into 12 wedges.

IN THE KITCHEN
Look for white whole wheat flour at the supermarket or health food store. It has all the fiber and nutrition of traditional whole wheat flour, but with a milder flavour and lighter colour. Or substitute 250 mL (1 cup) whole wheat flour and 125 mL (½ cup) all-purpose flour in this recipe.

PER SERVING (1 wedge): 154 Cal, 6 g Fat, 1 g Sat Fat, 0 g Trans Fat, 18 mg Chol, 179 mg Sod, 24 g Carb, 3 g Fib, 4 g Prot, 44 mg Calc.
POINTS value: *3.*

VEGGIE-STUFFED ONIONS,
PAGE 162

Chapter 6

Vegetarian Main Dishes and Sides

Looking for new veggie ideas? Only 20 minutes prep (or less) is required—and the slow cooker does the rest!

Veggie-Stuffed Onions

prep 25 min • slow-cook 3 hrs • serves 4

♦ 4 (375 g [¾-pound each) Vidalia onions

♦ 1 (375 g [12-ounce]) package frozen soy crumbles, thawed

♦ 250 mL (1 cup) cooked brown rice

♦ 1 (290 g [10-ounce) bag frozen peas and carrots, thawed

Grated zest and juice of ½ lemon

5 mL (1 teaspoon) dried sage

2 mL (½ teaspoon) salt

2 mL (½ teaspoon) black pepper

1 mL (¼ teaspoon) ground allspice

♦ 500 mL (2 cups tomato puree (no salt added)

♦ 125 mL (½ cup) low-sodium chicken broth

45 mL (3 tablespoons) chopped fresh dill

15 mL (1 tablespoon) Worcestershire sauce

1 Trim bottom of each onion to stand onions upright, making sure bottoms are left intact to hold filling. Trim little more than 0.5 cm (¼ inch) from top of each onion. With melon baller, or small sharp knife, cut out onion centres, leaving all but outer layer. Discard onion centres (or chop and freeze for another use).

2 To make filling, combine soy crumbles, rice, 250 mL (1 cup) peas and carrots, lemon zest, sage, salt, pepper, and allspice in medium bowl. Fill onion cavities evenly with filling, packing firmly. Transfer onions to 5- or 6-L (5- or 6-quart) slow cooker. Sprinkle remaining peas and carrots around onions.

3 Mix tomato puree, broth, lemon juice, 30 mL (2 tablespoons) dill, and Worcestershire sauce in medium bowl; pour around onions (not over tops). Cover and cook until onions are fork-tender, 3–4 hours on high or 6–8 hours on low. Serve, sprinkled with remaining 15 mL (1 tablespoon) dill.

IN THE KITCHEN
If the outer layer of an onion is too thin when cutting out the centre in step 1, leave 2 layers so it doesn't collapse while cooking.

PER SERVING (1 stuffed onion with 125 mL [½ cup] sauce): 313 Cal, 2 g Fat, 0 g Sat Fat, 0 g Trans Fat, 0 mg Chol, 447 mg Sod, 42 g Carb, 9 g Fib, 35 g Prot, 127 mg Calc. *POINTS* value: 6.

Thai Tempeh with Vegetables

prep 15 min • **slow-cook/cook** 3 hrs 5 min • **serves** 4

- 375 g (¾ pound) small red potatoes, scrubbed and quartered
- 1 (250 g [8-ounce]) package tempeh
- 500 mL (2 cups) baby carrots
- 500 mL (2 cups) fresh cauliflower florets
- 1 small tomato, diced
- 1 small onion, thinly sliced
- 125 mL (½ cup) light coconut milk
- 3 garlic cloves, minced
- 30 mL (2 tablespoons) unsweetened shredded coconut
- 60 mL (¼ cup) chutney

1 Combine potatoes, tempeh, carrots, cauliflower, tomato, onion, coconut milk, and garlic in 5- or 6-L (5- or 6-quart) slow cooker. Cover and cook until vegetables are fork-tender, 3–4 hours on high or 6–8 hours on low.

2 Meanwhile spread coconut in small nonstick skillet and set over medium-high heat. Cook, stirring frequently, until lightly browned, about 5 minutes. Let cool.

3 At end of cooking time, stir chutney into stew until blended. Serve, sprinkled with coconut.

◆ FILLING EXTRA

Add peas to this mild Thai stew. Prepare the recipe as directed but 20 minutes before the end of the cooking time, stir in 500 mL (2 cups) thawed frozen peas. Cover and cook on high until the peas are heated through, about 15 minutes. Increase the per-serving *POINTS* value by *1.*

PER SERVING (310 mL [1¼ cups): 281 Cal, 10 g Fat, 4 g Sat Fat, 0 g Trans Fat, 0 mg Chol, 116 mg Sod, 39 g Carb, 8 g Fib, 15 g Prot, 128 mg Calc.
POINTS value: 6.

Tofu Vegetable Stew

prep 15 min • **slow-cook** 3 hrs • **serves** 4

- 500 g (1 pound) extra-firm tofu, cut into 2.5 cm (1-inch) cubes
- 500 mL (2 cups) low-sodium vegetable broth or water
- 4 large carrots, thinly sliced
- 1 large red onion, chopped
- 170 g (6 ounces) shiitake mushrooms, stems discarded and quartered
- 30 mL (2 tablespoons) low-sodium soy sauce
- 5 mL (1 teaspoon) Asian (dark) sesame oil
- 500 mL (2 cups) thinly sliced Napa cabbage
- 125 mL (½ cup) water
- 45 mL (3 tablespoons) miso
- 2 scallions, thinly sliced

1 Combine tofu, broth, carrots, onion, mushrooms, soy sauce, and sesame oil in 5- or 6-L (5- or 6-quart) slow cooker. Cover and cook until vegetables are fork-tender, 3–4 hours on high or 6–8 hours on low.

2 About 35 minutes before cooking time is up, stir cabbage into slow cooker. Cover and cook on high until cabbage is crisp-tender, about 30 minutes.

3 At end of cooking time, whisk water and miso in small bowl until smooth. Stir miso mixture into stew. Serve, sprinkled with scallions.

◈ FILLING EXTRA

Keep an 265 g (8.8-ounce) bag of shelf-stable cooked brown rice on hand for saucy stews like this one. It reheats in the microwave in just 90 seconds. A 125 mL (½ cup) of cooked brown rice per serving will increase the *POINTS* value by *2.*

PER SERVING (375 mL [1½ cups]): 216 Cal, 9 g Fat, 1 g Sat Fat, 0 g Trans Fat, 0 mg Chol, 976 mg Sod, 22 g Carb, 6 g Fib, 16 g Prot, 285 mg Calc. *POINTS* value: *4.*

Barbecue Tofu Chili

prep 20 min • **slow-cook** 4 hrs • **serves** 4

- 625 mL (2½ cups) peeled and diced acorn squash
- 1 (290 g [10-ounce]) package sliced cremini mushrooms
- 2 celery stalks, chopped
- 1 large red onion, chopped
- 1 poblano pepper, diced
- 1 (425 mL [14½-ounce]) can diced tomatoes with roasted garlic
- 1 (450 mL [15-ounce]) can black beans, rinsed and drained
- 45 mL (3 tablespoons) cayenne pepper saucee
- 45 mL (3 tablespoons) tomato paste
- 45 mL (3 tablespoons) ancho chlle powder
- 30 mL (2 tablespoons) honey
- 15 mL (1 tablespoon) ground cumin
- 10 mL (2 teaspoons) dried oregano
- 2 (175 g [6¼-ounce]) packages barbecue-flavored tofu, cut into 2 cm (¾-inch) cubes
- 30 mL (2 tablespoons) cornmeal
- 45 mL (3 tablespoons) shredded low-fat Monterey Jack cheese

1 Combine squash, mushrooms, celery, onion, poblano, tomatoes, beans, pepper sauce, tomato paste, chile powder, honey, cumin, and oregano in 5- or 6-L (5- or 6-quart) slow cooker. Press vegetables down into tomato mixture to form even layer. Top with tofu, leaving 2.5 cm (1-inch) border from side of slow cooker. Cover and cook until vegetables are fork-tender, 4–5 hours on high or 8–10 hours on low.

2 About 20 minutes before cooking time is up, gradually stir cornmeal into slow cooker until blended. Cover and cook on high until mixture simmers and thickens, about 15 minutes. Serve, sprinkled with Monterey Jack.

♦ FILLING EXTRA
Serve each portion of this hearty chili topped with 30mL (2 tablespoons) of your favorite fat-free salsa.

PER SERVING (500 mL [2 cups] chili with about 10 mL [2 teaspoons] cheese): 329 Cal, 7 g Fat, 1 g Sat Fat, 0 g Trans Fat, 3 mg Chol, 1,129 mg Sod, 56 g Carb, 12 g Fib, 18 g Prot, 323 mg Calc. *POINTS* value: 6.

"Sausage"-Stuffed Eggplant

prep 15 min • **cook/slow-cook** 3 hrs 5 min • **serves** 4

- 1   (625 g [1¼-pound]) eggplant, halved lengthwise

  10   mL (2 teaspoons) extra-virgin olive oil

- 1   large onion, chopped

  125 g (¼ pound) frozen vegetarian sausage patties, chopped

  2   garlic cloves, minced

- 250 mL (1 cup) cooked brown rice

  30   mL (2 tablespoons) chopped fresh dill

  30   mL (2 tablespoons) chopped fresh mint

  2   mL (½ teaspoon) salt

  2   mL (½ teaspoon) coarsely ground black pepper

- 1   (250 mL [8-ounce]) can tomato sauce

  60   mL (¼ cup) crumbled low-fat feta cheese

1 With grapefruit spoon, scoop out flesh from each eggplant half leaving 1.25 cm (½-inch) shell. Coarsely chop scooped flesh and set aside.

2 To make stuffing, heat oil in large nonstick skillet over medium-high heat. Add onion, sausage, chopped eggplant, and garlic; cook, stirring frequently, until onion is softened, about 3 minutes. Remove skillet from heat. Stir in rice, dill, mint, salt, and pepper.

3 Fill each eggplant shell with half of stuffing. Transfer stuffed halves to 5- or 6-L (5- or 6-quart) slow cooker. Top with tomato sauce. Cover and cook until eggplant and filling are fork-tender, 3–4 hours on high or 6–8 hours on low. Serve, sprinkled with feta.

IN THE KITCHEN

To make the eggplant flesh easier to scoop out, score the cut side of each eggplant half with a small sharp knife, taking care not to pierce the skin.

PER SERVING (¼ stuffed eggplant with about 30 mL [2 tablespoons] sauce and 15 mL [1 tablespoon] cheese): 224 Cal, 7 g Fat, 1 g Sat Fat, 0 g Trans Fat, 3 mg Chol, 849 mg Sod, 33 g Carb, 7 g Fib, 11 g Prot, 86 mg Calc. *POINTS* value: *4.*

Cheese and Spinach–Stuffed Savoy Cabbage

prep 20 min • **microwave/slow-cook** 3 hrs 5 min • **serves** 4

- 8 large Savoy cabbage leaves
- 1 (450 mL [15-ounce]) container low-fat ricotta cheese
- 375 mL (1½ cups) baby spinach, chopped
- 125 g (¼ pound) shallots, minced
- 60 mL (¼ cup) chopped fresh parsley
- 1 large egg
- 60 mL (4 tablespoons) grated pecorino cheese
- 2 mL (½ teaspoon) salt
- 1 mL (¼ teaspoon) black pepper
- 1 (250 mL [8-ounce]) can tomato sauce
- 30 mL (2 tablespoons) chopped fresh basil

1 Spread cabbage leaves on large microwavable plate and cover with paper towel. Microwave on High until softened, 3–4 minutes. Transfer leaves to cutting board. When cool enough to handle, trim thick ribs from leaves.

2 Meanwhile, to make filling, mix ricotta, spinach, shallots, parsley, egg, 30 mL (2 tablespoons) pecorino, salt, and pepper.

3 Place 75 mL (⅓ cup) filling on centre of each cabbage leaf. Fold in sides and roll up. Transfer rolls, seam side down, to 5- or 6-L (5- or 6-quart) slow cooker. Top with tomato sauce. Cover and cook until cabbage is fork-tender, 3–4 hours on high or 6–8 hours on low. Serve, sprinkled with basil and remaining 30 mL (2 tablespoons) pecorino.

IN THE KITCHEN

To remove the cabbage leaves from the head of cabbage, cut around the core of the cabbage with a small sharp knife (it's not necessary to remove the core). Carefully peel off each leaf, one at a time, taking not to tear them.

PER SERVING (2 rolls with 30 mL [2 tablespoons] sauce and 7 mL [½ tablespoon] each basil and cheese): 225 Cal, 11 g Fat, 6 g Sat Fat, 0 g Trans Fat, 88 mg Chol, 795 mg Sod, 17 g Carb, 3 g Fib, 17 g Prot, 373 mg Calc. *POINTS* value: *5.*

Broccoflower and Cheese Soup

prep 20 min • **roast/slow-cook** 4 hrs 30 min • **serves** 4

◆ 1 head broccoflower, cored and cut into 2.5 cm (1-inch) pieces

◆ 2 medium red onions, chopped

◆ 3 carrots, chopped

10 mL (2 teaspoons) olive oil

5 mL (1 teaspoon) dried thyme

1 mL (¼ teaspoon) salt

1 mL (¼ teaspoon) black pepper

◆ 1 (1 L [4 cups]) carton vegetable broth

125 mL (½ cup) coarsely shredded low-fat Cheddar cheese

1 Preheat oven to 230°C (450°F). Combine broccoflower, onions, carrots, oil, and thyme in large bowl. Transfer vegetables to large rimmed baking sheet and spread in single layer. Roast until lightly browned, about 30 minutes, stirring vegetables every 10 minutes. Transfer vegetables to 5- or 6-L (5- or 6-quart) slow cooker. Add salt and pepper. Pour broth over vegetable mixture. Cover and cook until vegetables are fork-tender, 4–5 hours on high or 8–10 hours on low.

2 At end of cooking time, let mixture cool 5 minutes. Puree in batches in food processor or blender. Serve, topped with Cheddar.

◆ **FILLING EXTRA**

For a creamier soup, add 250 mL (1 cup) fat-free ricotta cheese to the soup mixture before pureeing it in step 2. The per-serving *POINTS* value will increase by *1.*

PER SERVING (500 mL [2 cups] soup with 30 mL [2 tablespoons] cheese): 206 Cal, 9 g Fat, 4 g Sat Fat, 0 g Trans Fat, 18 mg Chol, 516 mg Sod, 22 g Carb, 6 g Fib, 14 g Prot, 214 mg Calc. *POINTS* value: *4.*

Cauliflower and Lentils with Feta

prep 15 min • **slow-cook** 1 hr 30 min • **serves** 4

♦ 1 (750 g [1½-pound]) cauliflower, cut into 5 cm (2-inch) florets

♦ 1 large yellow onion, chopped

♦ 125 mL (½ cup) vegetable or chicken broth

3 garlic cloves, chopped

5 mL (1 teaspoon) ground cumin

5 mL (1 teaspoon) salt

0.5 mL (⅛ teaspoon) cayenne

♦ 1 (250 g [8-ounce]) package cooked black Beluga lentils or 375 mL [1½ cups] cooked green (French) lentils

250 mL (1 cup) crumbled low-fat feta cheese

1 lime, cut into 4 wedges

1 Combine cauliflower, onion, broth, garlic, cumin, salt, and cayenne in 5- or 6-L (5- or 6-quart) s slow cooker. Cover and cook until cauliflower is just tender, 1½–2 hours on high or 3–4 hours on low.

2 About 15 minutes before cooking time is up, stir lentils into slow cooker. Cover and cook on high until heated through, about 10 minutes.

3 At end of cooking time, sprinkle cauliflower and lentil mixture with feta. Serve with lime wedges.

IN THE KITCHEN
Black beluga lentils (which look like caviar after cooking, hence the name) are one of the smallest varieties of the lentil family. Like green lentils, they hold their shape well after cooking and are terrific hot and in salads.

PER SERVING (250 mL [1 cup] cauliflower and lentils with 60 mL [¼ cup] cheese and 1 lime wedge): 187 Cal, 4 g Fat, 2 g Sat Fat, 0 g Trans Fat, 12 mg Chol, 1,170 mg Sod, 28 g Carb, 7 g Fib, 13 g Prot, 193 mg Calc. *POINTS* value: *3.*

Greens and Black-Eyed Peas

prep 10 min • slow-cook 3 hrs • serves 4

- 500 mL (2 cups) frozen black-eyed peas, thawed
- 250 mL (1 cup) vegetable broth or water
- 1 large onion, chopped
- 1 celery stalk, diced
- 3 **garlic cloves, minced**
- 2 **mL (½ teaspoon) salt**
- 2 **mL (½ teaspoon) dried thyme**
- 2 **mL (½ teaspoon) ground allspice**
- 1 **mL (¼ teaspoon) red pepper flakes**
- 375 g (¾ pound) collard greens, stems discarded and leaves sliced 1.25 cm (½ inch) thick
- 500 mL (2 cups) hot cooked brown rice

1 Combine black-eyed peas, broth, onion, celery, garlic, salt, thyme, allspice, and red pepper flakes in 5- or 6-L (5- or 6-quart) slow cooker. Cover and cook until vegetables are fork-tender, 3–4 hours on high or 6–8 hours on low.

2 About 35 minutes before cooking time is up, stir greens into slow cooker. Cover and cook on high until greens are crisp-tender, about 30 minutes. Serve with rice.

◆ **FILLING EXTRA**
Add 2 chopped carrots with the vegetables in step 1. This recipe works with the Simply Filling technique.

PER SERVING (250 mL [1 cup] black-eyed peas and greens with 125 mL [½ cup] rice): 263 Cal, 2 g Fat, 0 g Sat Fat, 0 g Trans Fat, 0 mg Chol, 562 mg Sod, 52 g Carb, 12 g Fib, 12 g Prot, 143 mg Calc. *POINTS* value: *5.*

Veggie and Bean Chipotle Chili

prep 15 min • **slow-cook** 4 hrs • **serves** 4

- 1   (450 g [15-ounce]) can pinto beans, rinsed and drained
- 1   (425 mL [14½-ounce]) can diced tomatoes in sauce
- 1   (250 mL [8-ounce]) can Italian-style tomato sauce
- 1   (250 g [8-ounce]) package cremini mushrooms, halved
- 2   large yellow bell peppers, diced
- 1   large red onion, chopped
- 37 **mL (2½ tablespoons) chipotle chile powder**
- 15 **mL (1 tablespoon) packed brown sugar**
- 2   **mL (½ teaspoon) salt**
- 500 g (1 pound) zucchini, cut into 2.5 cm (1-inch) chunks
- 30 mL (2 tablespoons) cornmeal
- 60 **mL (¼ cup) low-fat Greek yogourt**

1 Combine beans, diced tomatoes, tomato sauce, mushrooms, bell peppers, onion, chile powder, brown sugar, and salt in 5- or 6-L (5- or 6-quart) slow cooker. Press vegetables down into tomato mixture to form even layer. Top with zucchini. Cover and cook until vegetables are fork-tender, 4–5 hours on high or 8–10 hours on low.

2 About 20 minutes before cooking time is up, gradually stir cornmeal into slow cooker until blended. Cover and cook on high until mixture simmers and thickens, about 15 minutes. Serve with yogourt.

◆ FILLING EXTRA

Microwave 2 (175 g [6-ounce]) baking potatoes until fork-tender. Split the potatoes, then spoon each serving of chili over a potato half (and up the *POINTS* value by *1*).

PER SERVING (about 425 mL [1¾ cups] with 15 mL [1 tablespoon] yogourt): 290 Cal, 2 g Fat, 1 g Sat Fat, 0 g Trans Fat, 1 mg Chol, 926 mg Sod, 59 g Carb, 13 g Fib, 14 g Prot, 168 mg Calc. *POINTS* value: *5.*

Squash and Cranberry Soup with Yogourt Drizzle

prep 20 min • **slow-cook** 4 hrs 5 min • **serves** 4

- 750 g (1½ pounds) butternut or kabocha squash, peeled, seeded, and cut into 2.5 cm (1-inch) chunks
- 2 Granny Smith apples, peeled and chopped
- 1 large onion, chopped
- 250 mL (1 cup) fresh or thawed frozen cranberries
- 250 mL (1 cup) unsweetened apple juice
- 250 mL (1 cup) water
- 15 mL (1 tablespoon) minced peeled fresh ginger
- 10 mL (2 teaspoons) extra-virgin olive oil
- 2 mL (½ teaspoon) salt
- 125 mL (½ cup) plain fat-free yogourt
- 15 mL (1 tablespoon) maple syrup
- Pinch black pepper

1 Combine squash, apples, onion, cranberries, apple juice, water, ginger, oil, and salt in 5- or 6-L (5- or 6-quart) slow cooker. Cover and cook until vegetables are fork-tender, 4–5 hours on high or 8–10 hours on low.

2 At end of cooking time, uncover and let mixture cool 5 minutes. Puree in batches in blender. Return puree to slow cooker. Cover and cook on high until soup is heated through, about 5 minutes.

3 Meanwhile, mix yogourt, maple syrup, and pepper in small bowl. Divide soup among 4 bowls. Serve, drizzled with yogourt mixture.

IN THE KITCHEN
Love ginger? Add another tablespoon of minced peeled fresh ginger to the soup before you puree it in step 2.

PER SERVING (250 mL [1 cup] soup with 22 mL [1½ tablespoons] yogourt mixture): 198 Cal, 3 g Fat, 0 g Sat Fat, 0 g Trans Fat, 1 mg Chol, 331 mg Sod, 44 g Carb, 5 g Fib, 4 g Prot, 137 mg Calc. *POINTS* value: *3.*

Leeks with Dill Sauce

prep 10 min • slow-cook/cook 3 hrs 5 min • serves 4

- ◆ 8 (25-30 cm [10- to 12-inch]) trimmed and cleaned whole leeks
- ◆ 60 mL (¼ cup) vegetable broth
- 15 mL (1 tablespoon) unsalted butter
- 3 mL (¾ teaspoon) salt
- ◆ 1 large egg
- Juice of 1 small lemon
- 15 mL (1 tablespoon) chopped fresh dill
- 1 mL (¼ teaspoon) black pepper

1 Combine leeks, broth, butter, and 2 mL (½ teaspoon) salt in 5- or 6-L (5- or 6-quart)slow cooker. Cover and cook until leeks are fork-tender, 3–4 hours on high or 6–8 hours on low.

2 At end of cooking time, transfer leeks with slotted spoon to platter; cover and keep warm.

3 Whisk egg, lemon juice, dill, pepper, and remaining 1 mL (¼ teaspoon) salt in small bowl. Pour hot liquid from slow cooker into small saucepan. Cook over medium heat until liquid comes to a simmer, about 2 minutes. Remove saucepan from heat. Slowly pour in egg mixture, whisking constantly. Return saucepan to heat and cook, whisking constantly, until sauce is thickened, about 1 minute. Pour sauce over leeks.

IN THE KITCHEN

Cook 4 frozen vegetarian patties according to the package directions to serve alongside this elegant vegetable dish (and up the per-serving *POINTS* value by *2*).

PER SERVING (2 leeks with 30 mL [2 tablespoons] sauce): 156 Cal, 5 g Fat, 3 g Sat Fat, 0 g Trans Fat, 61 mg Chol, 552 mg Sod, 26 g Carb, 3 g Fib, 4 g Prot, 114 mg Calc. *POINTS* value: *3.*

Vegetable Sancocho

prep 15 min • **slow-cook** 2 hrs • **serves** 4

6   garlic cloves, chopped

♦ 1   (250 g [½-pound]) yucca, peeled and cut into 5 cm (2-inch) chunks

♦ 250 g (½ pound) red potatoes, scrubbed and halved

♦ 250 g (½ pound) acorn squash or fresh pumpkin, peeled, seeded, and cut into 5 cm (2-inch) chunks

♦ 1   large red onion, thinly sliced

♦ 1   red bell pepper, cut into 2.5 cm (1-inch) chunks

♦ 250 mL (1 cup) canned diced tomatoes

250 mL (1 cup) water

5   mL (1 teaspoon) kosher salt

2   mL (½ teaspoon) dried oregano

♦ 2   ears corn on the cob, husked and cut crosswise into 2 cm (¾-inch) pieces

60 mL (¼ cup) chopped fresh cilantro

15 mL (1 tablespoon) red-wine vinegar

Hot pepper sauce (optional)

1 Set aside 10 mL (2 teaspoons) garlic. Combine yucca, potatoes, squash, onion, bell pepper, tomatoes, water, salt, oregano, and remaining garlic in 5- or 6-L (5- or 6-quart) slow cooker. Cover and cook until vegetables are fork-tender, 2–3 hours on high or 4–6 hours on low.

2 About 35 minutes before cooking time is up, stir corn into slow cooker. Cover and cook on high until corn is fork-tender, about 30 minutes.

3 Just before serving, stir reserved 10 mL (2 teaspoons) garlic, cilantro, and vinegar into slow cooker. Serve with pepper sauce (if using).

IN THE KITCHEN

Sancocho, a traditional Latin American stew, usually includes large pieces of meat as well as vegetables. But our vegetarian version is equally satisfying. Serve this dish with 650 mL (2⅔ cups) cooked whole wheat couscous (150 mL [⅔ cup] cooked couscous per serving will up the *POINTS* value by *2*). This recipe works with the Simply Filling technique.

PER SERVING (375 mL [1½ cups]): 231 Cal, 1 g Fat, 0 g Sat Fat, 0 g Trans Fat, 0 mg Chol, 495 mg Sod, 53 g Carb, 8 g Fib, 6 g Prot, 122 mg Calc.
POINTS value: *4.*

Fennel and Onions with Saffron

prep 10 min • cook/slow-cook 3 hrs 15 min • serves 4

10 mL (2 teaspoons) extra-virgin olive oil

♦ 2 fennel bulbs, quartered

♦ 4 small onions, each halved through the root end

♦ 125 mL (½ cup) low-sodium chicken broth or water

5 mL (1 teaspoon) kosher salt

2 mL (½ teaspoon) ground coriander

1 mL (¼ teaspoon) black pepper

♦ 1 plum tomato, seeded and chopped

1 Heat 5 mL (1 teaspoon) oil in large nonstick skillet over medium-high heat. Add enough of fennel (about two thirds) so that it fits in single layer and cook until browned, 3–4 minutes per side. Transfer fennel to 5- or 6-L (5- or 6-quart) slow cooker. Heat remaining 5 mL (1 teaspoon) oil in skillet. Add single layer of remaining fennel and onions; cook until browned, 3–4 minutes per side. Transfer fennel and onions to slow cooker.

2 Add broth to skillet and bring to boil, scraping up browned bits from bottom of pan. Stir broth mixture, salt, coriander, pepper, and saffron into slow cooker. Cover and cook until vegetables are fork-tender, 3–4 hours on high or 6–8 hours on low. Serve warm or at room temperature sprinkled with tomato.

IN THE KITCHEN
In addition to the tomato, top this dish with a combination of 30 mL (2 tablespoons) coarsely chopped fennel fronds or fresh basil and the grated zest of ½ small lemon. This recipe works with the Simply Filling technique.

PER SERVING (375 mL [1½ cups]): 93 Cal, 3 g Fat, 0 g Sat Fat, 0 g Trans Fat, 0 mg Chol, 469 mg Sod, 16 g Carb, 5 g Fib, 3 g Prot, 79 mg Calc. *POINTS* value: *1.*

Chayote with Five-Spice Sauce

prep 10 min • slow-cook/cook 2 hrs 5 min • serves 4

♦ 2   chayote, each quartered through root end

60   mL (¼ cup) water

15   mL (1 tablespoon) sherry or vegetable broth

15   mL (1 tablespoon) soy sauce

15   mL (1 tablespoon) packed brown sugar

2   garlic cloves, minced

10   mL (2 teaspoons) minced peeled fresh ginger

1   mL (¼ teaspoon) five-spice powder

1   mL (¼ teaspoon) black pepper

2   mL (½ teaspoon) cornstarch

1 Combine chayote, water, sherry, soy sauce, brown sugar, garlic, ginger, five-spice powder, and pepper in 5- or 6-L (5- or 6-quart) slow cooker. Cover and cook until chayote is fork-tender, 2–3 hours on high or 4–6 hours on low.

2 Transfer chayote with slotted spoon to plate; cover and keep warm. Pour hot liquid from slow cooker into small saucepan; whisk in cornstarch until smooth. Cook over medium-high heat, stirring occasionally, until mixture comes to boil. Cook, stirring occasionally, just until thickened, about 1 minute. Pour sauce over chayote.

IN THE KITCHEN

Pale green, pear-shaped chayote is a popular vegetable in Asian and Latin American cuisines. Its taste and texture are between that of a cucumber and an apple.

PER SERVING (2 pieces chayote with 15 mL [1 tablespoon] sauce): 50 Cal, 1 g Fat, 0 g Sat Fat, 0 g Trans Fat, 0 mg Chol, 79 mg Sod, 11 g Carb, 3 g Fib, 1 g Prot, 24 mg Calc. *POINTS* value: *0.*

Lemon-Glazed Carrots and Parsnips

prep 15 min • **slow-cook/cook** 2 hrs 5 min • **serves** 4

- 500 g (1 pound) parsnips, peeled and cut matchstick strips
- 500 g (1 pound) baby carrots

Grated zest and juice of 1 lemon

30 mL (2 tablespoons) mirin or other rice wine, such as sake

30 mL (2 tablespoons) water

2 mL (½ teaspoon) salt

1 Combine parsnips, carrots, lemon juice, mirin, water, and salt in 5- or 6-L (5- or 6-quart) slow cooker. Cover and cook until vegetables are fork-tender, 2–3 hours on high or 4–6 hours on low.

2 Transfer vegetables with slotted spoon to plate; cover and keep warm. Pour hot liquid from slow cooker into small saucepan and bring to boil. Reduce heat and simmer until liquid becomes syrupy glaze, 3–4 minutes. Pour glaze over vegetables. Sprinkle with lemon zest and toss to blend.

◈ **FILLING EXTRA**

Add 1 turnip, peeled and cut into matchstick strips, along with the carrots and parsnips in step 1.

PER SERVING (generous 250 mL [1 cup]): 126 Cal, 1 g Fat, 0 g Sat Fat, 0 g Trans Fat, 0 mg Chol, 386 mg Sod, 30 g Carb, 8 g Fib, 2 g Prot, 77 mg Calc. *POINTS* value: **2.**

Beets with Dried Cherries

prep 10 min • **slow-cook** 1 hr • **serves** 4

◆ 500 g (1 pound) beets, trimmed, peeled, and cut into 2.5 cm (1-inch) chunks

125 g (¼ pound) shallots, thinly sliced

75 mL (⅓ cup) orange juice

1 bay leaf

2 mL (½ teaspoon) dried thyme or herbes de Provence

2 mL (½ teaspoon) salt

30 mL (2 tablespoons) dried cherries

5 mL (1 teaspoon) red-wine vinegar

15 mL (1 tablespoon) chopped fresh parsley

1 mL (¼ teaspoon) black pepper

1 Combine beets, shallots, orange juice, bay leaf, thyme, and salt in 5- or 6-L (5- or 6-quart) slow cooker. Cover and cook until beets are fork-tender, 1–2 hours on high or 2–4 hours on low.

2 About 10 minutes before cooking time is up, stir cherries into slow cooker. Cover and cook on high until cherries are softened, about 5 minutes. Discard bay leaf. Stir in vinegar, parsley, and pepper. Serve warm or at room temperature.

IN THE KITCHEN

To peel raw beets most easily, use a swivel-blade peeler. Also wear plastic gloves and an apron, so your hands and clothing won't turn beet red.

PER SERVING (175 mL [¾ cup]): 80 Cal, 0 g Fat, 0 g Sat Fat, 0 g Trans Fat, 0 mg Chol, 359 mg Sod, 18 g Carb, 3 g Fib, 2 g Prot, 33 mg Calc. *POINTS* value: *1.*

Green Beans Olivada

- 500 g (1 pound) fresh green beans, trimmed
- 250 mL (1 cup) cherry tomatoes, halved
- 1 small onion, thinly sliced
- 3 garlic cloves, thinly sliced
- 10 brine-cured Kalamata olives, pitted and chopped
- 60 mL (¼ cup) water
- 2 mL (½ teaspoon) salt
- 1 mL (¼ teaspoon) black pepper
- 1 mL (¼ teaspoon) dried thyme
- 15 mL (1 tablespoon) chopped fresh basil

Combine green beans, tomatoes, onion, garlic, olives, water, salt, pepper, and thyme in 5- or 6-L (5- or 6-quart) slow cooker. Cover and cook until green beans are fork-tender, 2–3 hours on high or 4–6 hours on low. Serve, sprinkled with basil.

◆ FILLING EXTRA

If you like, toss these Mediterranean-inspired green beans with 1 L (4 cups) cooked whole wheat penne and up the per-serving POINTS value by 3. This recipe works with the Simply Filling technique.

PER SERVING (250 mL [1 cup]): 62 Cal, 1 g Fat, 0 g Sat Fat, 0 g Trans Fat, 0 mg Chol, 392 mg Sod, 12 g Carb, 5 g Fib, 3 g Prot, 62 mg Calc. POINTS value: 1.

APRICOT-ALMOND CRISP,
PAGE 189

Chapter 7

Easy Sweets

Thanks to the slow cooker, these foolproof cakes, cobblers, and puddings practically cook themselves.

Carrot Cake

prep 15 min • **slow-cook** 1 hr 30 min • **serves** 12

250 mL (1 cup) all-purpose flour

125 mL (½ cup) whole wheat flour

5 mL (1 teaspoon) baking powder

2 mL (½ teaspoon) baking soda

5 mL (1 teaspoon) cinnamon

2 mL (½ teaspoon) ground nutmeg

175 mL (¾ cup) granulated sugar

75 mL (⅓ cup) canola oil

60 mL (¼ cup) water

♦ 175 mL (¾ cup) fat-free egg substitute

5 mL (1 teaspoon) vanilla extract

♦ 750 mL (3 cups) coarsely shredded carrots

250 mL (1 cup) raisins

15 mL (1 tablespoon) confectioners' sugar

1 Preheat heating base of 3½- or 4-L (3½- or 4-quart) slow cooker to high. Spray stoneware with nonstick spray. Line bottom with wax paper and lightly spray paper with nonstick spray.

2 Whisk all purpose flour, whole wheat flour, baking powder, baking soda, cinnamon, and nutmeg in medium bowl. With electric mixer on medium-high speed, beat granulated sugar, oil, water, egg substitute, and vanilla about 2 minutes. Reduce speed to low, add flour mixture, and beat just until blended. Stir in carrots and raisins. Pour batter into stoneware and place it in heating base. Cover slow cooker with 2 double layers paper towels; then place lid on top. Cook until toothpick inserted into centre of cake comes out clean, $1\frac{1}{2}$–2 hours.

3 Transfer stoneware to rack and let cool 15 minutes. Run thin knife around cake to loosen it from stoneware. Invert onto rack; remove wax paper. Let cool completely. Serve dusted with confectioners' sugar.

IN THE KITCHEN

Placing several layers of paper towels between the top of the slow cooker and the lid absorbs excess steam while the cake cooks. The result? A pleasantly moist-textured cake.

PER SERVING ($\frac{1}{12}$ of cake): 219 Cal, 6 g Fat, 1 g Sat Fat, 0 g Trans Fat, 0 mg Chol, 152 mg Sod, 38 g Carb, 2 g Fib, 5 g Prot, 69 mg Calc.
POINTS value: *4.*

Lemon Sponge Pudding with Blueberries

125 mL (½ cup) granulated sugar

45 mL (3 tablespoons) all-purpose flour

250 mL (1 cup) low-fat (1%) milk

Grated zest and juice of 2 large lemons

◆ 3 large eggs, separated

15 mL (1 tablespoon) unsalted butter, melted

1 mL (¼ teaspoon) salt

15 mL (1 tablespoon) confectioners'sugar

◆ 1 (175 g [6¼-oz]) container fresh blueberries

1 Preheat heating base of 5- or 6- (5- or 6-quart) slow cooker to high.

2 Combine granulated sugar and flour in medium bowl. Whisk in milk, lemon zest and juice, egg yolks, and melted butter. With electric mixer on high speed, beat egg whites and salt until stiff peaks form. With rubber spatula, gently fold beaten whites into lemon mixture just until no streaks of white remain.

3 Pour mixture into 2-L (2-quart) glass bowl. Cover bowl tightly with foil, securing foil with rubber band. Place bowl in stoneware and place it in heating base; pour enough boiling water into stoneware to come halfway up outside of bowl. Cover and cook until top is set, about 2 hours.

4 Carefully transfer bowl to rack and let cool. Dust top of cake with confectioners' sugar and serve warm or at room temperature with blueberries.

IN THE KITCHEN
When cooking in bowls or baking dishes in the slow cooker, make sure there's at least 2.5 cm (1 inch) between the side of the bowl and the stoneware. If it's too tight, there will be insufficient room for the heat to circulate, resulting in a flat or undercooked dessert.

PER SERVING (250 mL [1 cup] pudding with 30 mL [2 tablespoons] blueberries): 177 Cal, 5 g Fat, 2 g Sat Fat, 0 g Trans Fat, 113 mg Chol, 152 mg Sod, 29 g Carb, 1 g Fib, 5 g Prot, 68 mg Calc. *POINTS* value: *4.*

Apple-Rum Raisin Bread Pudding

prep 20 min • **slow-cook** 2 hrs • **serves** 8

1   L (4 cups) cubed day-old crusty bread (2.5cm [1-inch] pieces)

♦ 2   large apples, peeled and coarsely chopped (about 750 mL [3 cups])

125 mL (½ cup) golden raisins

500 mL (2 cups) low-fat (1%) milk

250 mL (1 cup) fat-free half-and-half

125 mL (½ cup) packed brown sugar

♦ 2   large eggs

♦ 1   large egg white

15   mL (1 tablespoon) dark rum or 2 mL (½ teaspoon) rum extract

10   mL (2 teaspoons) vanilla extract

2   mL (½ teaspoon) cinnamon

2   mL (½ teaspoon) ground nutmeg

15   mL (1 tablespoon) confectioners' sugar

1 Spray 5- or 6- (5- or 6-quart) slow cooker stoneware with nonstick spray. Add bread cubes, apples, and raisins; toss to combine. Whisk milk, half-and-half, brown sugar, eggs, egg white, rum, vanilla, cinnamon, and nutmeg in large bowl; pour into slow cooker. Cover slow cooker tightly with foil, then place lid on top. Cook until toothpick inserted into centre of pudding comes out clean, about 2 hours on high or 4 hours on low.

2 Transfer stoneware to rack and let pudding cool 15 minutes. Run thin knife around pudding to loosen it from stoneware. Invert onto large serving plate. Serve warm or at room temperature, dusted with confectioners' sugar.

IN THE KITCHEN

For the same *POINTS* value, this comfort classic is equally delicious prepared with an equal amount of pears and brandy in lieu of the apples and rum.

PER SERVING (175 mL [¾ cup]): 203 Cal, 3 g Fat, 1 g Sat Fat, 0 g Trans Fat, 55 mg Chol, 190 mg Sod, 41 g Carb, 2 g Fib, 5 g Prot, 83 mg Calc. *POINTS* value: *4.*

Rice Pudding with Indian Spices

500 mL (2 cups) low-fat (1%) milk

250 mL (1 cup) basmati or other long- grain rice

125 mL (½ cup) golden raisins

60 mL (¼ cup) sugar

30 mL (2 tablespoons) light stick butter, melted

2 mL (½ teaspoon) vanilla extract

2 mL (½ teaspoon) ground cardamom

1 (10 cm [4-inch]) cinnamon stick

1 Spray 3½- or 4-L (3½- or 4-quart) slow cooker stoneware with nonstick spray. Add milk, rice, raisins, sugar, melted butter, vanilla, and cardamom; mix well. Stir in cinnamon stick. Cover and cook until rice is very soft and mixture is thick and creamy, 2–2½ hours on high or 4–5 hours on low.

2 Remove cinnamon stick. Serve warm or at room temperature.

◈ FILLING EXTRA
Serve each portion of this luscious pudding with ½ sliced large banana and up the *POINTS* value by *1.*

PER SERVING (175 mL [¾ cup]): 229 Cal, 3 g Fat, 2 g Sat Fat, 0 g Trans Fat, 9 mg Chol, 61 mg Sod, 47 g Carb, 1 g Fib, 5 g Prot, 111 mg Calc.
POINTS value: *5.*

Peach-Blackberry Cobbler

prep 15 min • microwave/slow-cook 2 hrs 35 min • serves 6

- 2 (500 g [16-ounce]) bags frozen sliced peaches, thawed
- 2 (175 g [6-ounce]) containers fresh blackberries
- 45 mL (3 tablespoons) sugar + 15 mL (3 teaspoons)
- Juice of ½ lemon
- 15 mL (1 tablespoon) cornstarch
- 175 mL (¾ cup) all-purpose flour
- 2 mL (½ teaspoon) salt
- 2 mL (½ teaspoon) baking powder
- 1 mL (¼ teaspoon) baking soda
- 75 mL (⅓ cup) low-fat buttermilk
- 30 mL (2 tablespoons) light stick butter, melted
- 5 mL (1 teaspoon) vanilla extract

1 Place small rack in bottom of 6-L (6-quart) slow cooker.

2 To make filling, combine peaches, blackberries, 45 mL (3 tablespoons) sugar, lemon juice, and cornstarch in 1½- to 2-L (1½- to 2-quart) round microwavable casserole. Cover with wax paper. Microwave on High until mixture is bubbling and starts to thicken, about 7 minutes, stirring once halfway through cooking time.

3 Meanwhile, to make topping, whisk flour, 12 mL (2½ teaspoons) sugar, salt, baking powder, and baking soda in medium bowl. Stir in buttermilk, melted butter, and vanilla just until blended. Drop dough by tablespoonfuls onto hot filling, making 6 mounds. Sprinkle with remaining 2 mL (½ teaspoon) sugar.

4 Transfer casserole to rack in slow cooker. Cover and cook until toothpick inserted into centre of each biscuit comes out clean, about 2½ hours on high.

PER SERVING (75 mL [⅓ cup] filling with 1 biscuit): 180 Cal, 2 g Fat, 1 g Sat Fat, 0 g Trans Fat, 5 mg Chol, 312 mg Sod, 37 g Carb, 5 g Fib, 4 g Prot, 61 mg Calc. *POINTS* value: *3.*

Apricot-Almond Crisp

prep 15 min • **slow-cook** 4 hrs • **serves** 6

- 125 mL (½ cup) quick-cooking oats

75 mL (⅓ cup) packed brown sugar

60 mL (¼ cup) all-purpose flour

60 mL (¼ cup) toasted wheat germ

60 mL (¼ cup) whole blanched almonds, finely chopped

15 mL (1 tablespoon) cold butter

- 15 to 39 mL (1 to 2 tablespoons) fat-free milk

15 mL (1 tablespoon) granulated sugar

3 mL (¾ teaspoon) ground ginger

2 (420 g [14-ounce]) cans apricot halves in juice, drained and cut in half

3 mL (¾ teaspoon) almond extract

1 Spray 5- or 6-L (5- or 6-quart) slow cooker stoneware with nonstick spray.

2 To make topping, combine oats, brown sugar, flour, wheat germ, and almonds in medium bowl. With fork, cut in butter until mixture resembles coarse crumbs. Gradually add milk, tossing lightly with fork, just until mixture resembles fine crumbs.

3 Mix granulated sugar and ginger in medium bowl. Add apricots and almond extract; toss to coat. Transfer apricot mixture to slow cooker. Sprinkle with topping; lightly spray with nonstick spray. Cover and cook until topping is crisp and begins to brown, about 4 hours on low.

IN THE KITCHEN

Top each serving with 60 mL (¼ cup) fat-free vanilla frozen yogourt and 5 mL (1 teaspoon) chopped crystallized ginger and up the *POINTS* value by *1*.

PER SERVING (125 mL [½ cup]): 219 Cal, 6 g Fat, 2 g Sat Fat, 0 g Trans Fat, 5 mg Chol, 25 mg Sod, 39 g Carb, 4 g Fib, 5 g Prot, 46 mg Calc. *POINTS* value: *4*.

"Baked" Apples with Gingersnaps

prep 15 min • **slow-cook** 3 hrs • **serves** 8

◆ 4 large Granny Smith or Rome Beauty apples

8 (5 cm [2-inch]) gingersnap cookies, coarsely crushed (about 125 mL [½ cup])

60 mL (¼ cup packed brown sugar

1 mL (¼ teaspoon) cinnamon

Juice of 1 lemon

250 mL (1 cup) apple cider

15 mL (1 tablespoon) cold butter, cut into small pieces

30 mL (2 tablespoons) honey

1 Peel top half of each apple. With melon baller, cut out apple cores without cutting all the way through apples. Trim bottoms, if necessary, to stand apples upright.

2 Combine cookie crumbs, brown sugar, cinnamon, and half of lemon juice in small bowl. Fill apple cavities evenly with crumb mixture.

3 Transfer apples to 5- or 6-L (5- or 6-quart) slow cooker. Pour cider and remaining lemon juice over apples. Dot apples evenly with butter and drizzle with honey. Cover slow cooker tightly with foil, then place lid on top. Cook until apples are fork-tender but still hold their shape, 3–3½ hours on low. Serve with cooking liquid.

IN THE KITCHEN
To crush the gingersnaps, place the cookies in a small zip-close plastic bag and gently pound them with a rolling pin or the bottom of a small skillet.

PER SERVING (½ stuffed apple with 7 mL [½ tablespoon] cooking liquid): 155 Cal, 2 g Fat, 1 g Sat Fat, 0 g Trans Fat, 4 mg Chol, 58 mg Sod, 35 g Carb, 3 g Fib, 1 g Prot, 23 mg Calc. *POINTS* value: *3.*

Spiced Applesauce

- ◆ 6 Newton Pippin or other green apples, peeled and sliced
- 75 mL (1/3 cup) tiny red cinnamon candies
- 60 mL (1/4 cup) packed brown sugar
- Juice of 1/2 lemon
- 1 mL (1/4 teaspoon) cinnamon
- Pinch ground cloves
- Pinch salt
- 18 tiny red cinnamon candies, for garnish

1 75 mL (1/3 cup) candies, brown sugar, lemon juice, cinnamon, cloves, and salt in 4-L (4-quart) slow cooker. Press apples down so they form even layer. Cover and cook until mixture simmers and apples break apart, 4 hours on high or 8 hours on low.

2 At end of cooking time, let mixture cool 5 minutes. Coarsely mash apples with potato masher or puree in batches in blender or food processor. Garnish each serving with 3 candies. Serve warm or chilled.

◆ FILLING EXTRA

In addition to the candy garnish, top each serving of applesauce with 15 mL (1 tablespoon) fat-free sour cream then sprinkle with a pinch of freshly grated nutmeg.

PER SERVING 125 mL [1/2 cup]): 122 Cal, 0 g Fat, 0 g Sat Fat, 0 g Trans Fat, 0 mg Chol, 27 mg Sod, 32 g Carb, 3 g Fib, 0 g Prot, 14 mg Calc. *POINTS* value: *2.*

Raspberry-Rhubarb Compote

prep 15 min • **slow-cook** 2 hrs 30 min • **serves** 4

- 750 mL (3 cups) sliced fresh or thawed frozen rhubarb
- 175 mL (¾ cup) water
- 75 mL (⅓ cup) sugar
- 60 mL (¼ cup) honey
- 15 mL (1 tablespoon) quick-cooking tapioca
- 2 (175g [6-ounce]) containers fresh raspberries
- Grated zest of 1 lemon
- 15 mL (1 tablespoon) finely chopped crystallized ginger
- 2 mL (½ teaspoon) cinnamon
- 2 mL (½ teaspoon) vanilla extract

1 Combine rhubarb, water, sugar, honey, and tapioca in 4-L (4-quart) slow cooker. Press mixture down so it forms even layer. Cover and cook until rhubarb is fork-tender, 2½ hours on high or 5 hours on low.

2 About 35 minutes before cooking time is up, stir in raspberries, lemon zest, ginger, and cinnamon. Cover and cook on high until mixture begins to simmer and raspberries are tender, about 30 minutes.

3 At end of cooking time, stir in vanilla until blended. Serve warm or at room temperature.

IN THE KITCHEN
Stuck with rock-hard crystallized ginger? Place it in a sieve set over a small saucepan of simmering water. Cover and steam until softened, about 5 minutes.

PER SERVING (about 175 mL [¾ cup]): 191 Cal, 0 g Fat, 0 g Sat Fat, 0 g Trans Fat, 0 mg Chol, 8 mg Sod, 49 g Carb, 6 g Fib, 2 g Prot, 206 mg Calc.
POINTS value: *3.*

Vanilla Custards with Lavender-Rosemary Drizzle

prep 15 min • **microwave/cook/slow-cook** 1 hr 5 min • **serves** 4

1   (7.5 cm [3-inch]) sprig fresh rosemary or 15 mL (1 tablespoon) dried

1   (7.5 cm [3-inch]) sprig fresh lavender or 15 mL (1 tablespoon) dried

60 mL (4 tablespoons) honey

1   vanilla bean

1   (375 mL [12-ounce]) can low-fat evaporated milk

125 mL (½ cup) low-fat (1%) milk

♦ 2   large eggs

♦ 2   large egg whites

60 mL (¼ cup) sugar

0.5 mL (⅛ teaspoon) salt

1 Preheat heating base of 6-L (6-quart) slow cooker to high.

2 Remove leaves from fresh rosemary and buds from fresh lavender. Combine rosemary leaves, lavender buds, and honey in small microwavable bowl. Microwave on High 30 seconds. Let stand until flavours are blended, about 5 minutes. Strain honey mixture through sieve into another small bowl and discard herbs.

3 With small, sharp knife, split vanilla bean lengthwise and scrape out seeds (reserve bean for another use such as making vanilla sugar). Combine evaporated milk, low-fat milk, 30 mL (2 tablespoons) honey mixture, and vanilla-bean seeds in small saucepan. Cook over medium heat until small bubbles appear around edge of pan, about 3 minutes. Let cool slightly, about 5 minutes.

4 Whisk eggs, egg whites, sugar, and salt in medium bowl. Slowly add hot milk mixture, whisking constantly, in thin steady stream. Pour mixture evenly into 4 (175 g [6-ounce]) custard cups or ramekins. Place cups in stoneware and place it in heating base; add enough boiling water to stoneware to come halfway up outsides of cups. Cover and cook until each custard is set in centre and jiggles slightly, 1–1½ hours.

5 Carefully transfer custards to racks and let cool completely. Serve, drizzled with remaining 30 mL (2 tablespoons) honey mixture.

IN THE KITCHEN
These luscious custards can be made ahead. Cover and refrigerate up to 3 days.

PER SERVING (1 custard with 7 mL [½ tablespoon] honey): 266 Cal, 6 g Fat, 3 g Sat Fat, 0 g Trans Fat, 122 mg Chol, 239 mg Sod, 41 g Carb, 0 g Fib, 12 g Prot, 293 mg Calc. *POINTS* value: *6.*

Spicy Chocolate-Orange Flan

prep 20 min • cook/slow-cook 1 hr 50 min • serves 8

250 mL (1 cup) sugar

Juice of ½ small lemon or 15 mL (1 tablespoon) water

1 (375 g [12-ounce]) can low-fat evaporated milk

125 mL (½ cup) low-fat (1%) milk

125 mL (½ cup) semisweet chocolate chips, melted

1 (10 cm [4-inch]) cinnamon stick

0.5 mL (⅛ teaspoon) cayenne

♦ 2 large eggs

♦ 2 large egg whites

2 mL (½ teaspoon) vanilla extract

2 mL (½ teaspoon) orange extract

0.5 mL (⅛ teaspoon) salt

1 Preheat heating base of 5- or 6-L (5- or 6-quart) slow cooker to high.

2 Combine ½ cup sugar and lemon juice in small heavy saucepan. Cook over medium heat, stirring constantly, until sugar is dissolved. Bring to boil. Cook, stirring occasionally, until it turns a deep golden caramel, about 10 minutes. Pour hot caramel into bottom of 2-L (2-quart) soufflé dish. Quickly tilt dish so that bottom and halfway up side are coated with caramel.

3 Combine evaporated milk, low-fat milk, remaining 125 mL (½ cup) sugar, melted chocolate, cinnamon stick, and cayenne in medium saucepan. Cook over medium heat until small bubbles appear around edge of pan, about 5 minutes. Let cool slightly, about 5 minutes. Remove cinnamon stick.

4 Whisk eggs, egg whites, vanilla and orange extracts, and salt in medium bowl. Slowly add hot milk mixture, whisking constantly, in thin steady stream. Pour mixture into prepared dish and tightly cover with foil. Place dish in stoneware and place it in heating base; add enough boiling water to stoneware to come halfway up outside of dish. Cover and cook until centre of flan is set and jiggles slightly, about 1½ hours.

5 Carefully transfer dish to rack and let cool completely. Cover and refrigerate until completely chilled, at least 4 hours or overnight. Run thin knife around flan to loosen it from dish. Invert onto large serving plate, scraping out any extra caramel sauce from bottom of dish. Cut flan into 8 wedges and serve with caramel sauce.

PER SERVING (1 wedge with about 15 mL [1 tablespoon] sauce): 224 Cal, 6 g Fat, 3 g Sat Fat, 0 g Trans Fat, 61 mg Chol, 120 mg Sod, 37 g Carb, 1 g Fib, 7 g Prot, 147 mg Calc. *POINTS* value: *5.*

Summer Berry Parfaits

- ♦ 1 (500 g [1 pound]) container fresh strawberries, hulled and quartered
- ♦ 1 (170 g [6-ounce]) container fresh blueberries
- ♦ 1 (170 g [6-ounce]) container fresh blackberries
- ♦ 1 (170 g [6-ounce]) container fresh raspberries
- 75 mL (⅓ cup) sugar
- 60 mL (¼ cup) water
- Juice of 1 small lemon
- 15 mL (1 tablespoon) cassis or other fruit brandy
- 1 (250 g [8-ounce]) package fat-free cream cheese, at room temperature
- 250 mL (1 cup) plain low-fat (2%) Greek yogourt
- 5 mL (1 teaspoon) vanilla extract
- 1 (375 g [12-ounce]) plain angel food cake, cut into 1.25 cm (½-inch) cubes
- 8 fresh mint leaves, thinly sliced

1 Combine berries, sugar, water, lemon juice, and cassis in 6-L (5- or 6-quart) slow cooker. Cover and cook until berries are softened and mixture is juicy, 1–1½ hours on low. Transfer berry mixture to large bowl and let cool.

2 Whisk cream cheese, yogourt, and vanilla in medium bowl until smooth. Alternately layer one eighth of cake cubes and berry mixture in each of 8 parfait glasses. Top evenly with yogourt mixture and mint.

IN THE KITCHEN

Greek yogourt is sought after for its rich, velvety texture, similar to that of sour cream or crème fraîche. It is thick and creamy because it has been strained of its whey during processing. The sheep's milk variety has a distinctive sour tang while the cow's milk version is milder. Both make equally delicious toppers on these refreshing fruit parfaits.

PER SERVING (1 parfait with scant 30 mL [2 tablespoons] yogourt mixture): 256 Cal, 1 g Fat, 1 g Sat Fat, 0 g Trans Fat, 4 mg Chol, 497 mg Sod, 52 g Carb, 4 g Fib, 10 g Prot, 134 mg Calc. *POINTS* value: *4.*

SOUTHWEST STEAK
TACOS, PAGE 39

Recipe Index

Recipes by *POINTS* value

0 POINTS value
Chayote with Five-Spice Sauce, 178

1 POINTS value
Beets with Dried Cherries, 180
Caponata, 25
Fennel and Onions with Saffron, 177
Green Beans Olivada, 181
Mini Falafels, 24

2 POINTS value
Baja Shrimp Boil, 22
Black Bean Salsa Dip, 26
Broccoli Frittata Bites, 23
Chicken, Apple, and Cheese Meatballs, 20
Hot Chocolate Latte, 31
Italian Snack Mix, 30
Lemon-Glazed Carrots and Parsnips, 179
Moo Shu Rolls, 18
Southern Artichoke Dip, 29
Spiced Applesauce, 191
Warm Cheese and Cannellini Dip, 28

3 POINTS value
African Peanut Chicken, 88
"Baked" Apples with Gingersnaps, 190
Cauliflower and Lentils with Feta, 169
Corn and Bacon Chowder, 123
Leeks with Dill Sauce, 175
Mixed-Grain Quick Bread, 158
Mumbai Chai, 32
Monkfish Ragù, 135

Peach-Blackberry Cobbler, 188
Pork-Pineapple Skewers, 19
Raspberry-Rhubarb Compote, 192
Spiced Apple-Nut Bread, 159
Squash and Cranberry Soup with Yogourt Drizzle, 174
Tomatillo-Pinto Bean Dip, 27
White Vegetable Soup, 173
Zesty Sausage and Tomato, 21

4 POINTS value
Apple-Rum Raisin Bread Pudding, 186
Apricot-Almond Crisp, 189
Brandy Chicken with Dried Plums and Olives, 131
Broccoflower and Cheese Soup, 168
Carrot Cake, 184
Classic Chicken Noodle Soup, 81
Cod Vera Cruz, 134
Corned Beef with Beet Relish, 112
Glogg, 33
Hearty Beef and Vegetable Soup, 46
Indian Lamb Curry, 124
Lamb with Stout, 125
Lemon Sponge Pudding with Blueberries, 185
Minestrone, 172
Osso Buco–Style Drumsticks, 95
Root Vegetable Tagine, 137
Rotisserie-Style Chicken, 76
"Sausage"-Stuffed Eggplant, 166
Summer Berry Parfaits, 195
Thai Chicken and Squash Soup, 129
Thai-Style Chicken Thighs, 89

Tofu Vegetable Stew, 164
Vegetable Sancocho, 176
White Balsamic Chicken, 128

5 POINTS value
Beef Burgoo, 48
Belgian Beef Stew, 44
Catalan Seafood Stew, 150
Bulgur and Bean Chili, 154
Cheese and Spinach–Stuffed Savoy Cabbage, 167
Chicken Mole, 130
Chicken, Sausage, and White Bean Stew, 92
Cider Pork Chops with Sage, 122
Country Captain Chicken, 77
Cranberry-Orange Turkey, 103
Creamy Turkey Meatballs, 104
Double Mushroom–Smothered Pork Chops, 59
Greens and Black-Eyed Peas, 170
Ham and Vegetable Chowder, 66
Harvest Pot Roast Dinner, 36
Hot-and-Spicy Turkey Curry, 100
Kentucky Pork Chili, 65
Kung Pao Chicken, 86
Lamb and Spinach Stew, 70
Latin-Style Meatball Soup, 51
Lentil-Winter Squash Stew, 157
Mexicali Turkey Breast, 98
Mexi-Style Meatball Soup, 133
Moussaka, 126
Mushroom and Cheese–Stuffed Chicken Breasts, 85

Dry and Liquid Measurement Equivalents

If you are converting the recipes in this book to metric measurements, use the following chart as a guide.

TEASPOONS	TABLESPOONS	CUPS	FLUID OUNCES
3 teaspoons	1 tablespoon		½ fluid ounce
6 teaspoons	2 tablespoons	⅛ cup	1 fluid ounce
8 teaspoons	tablespoons plus teaspoons	⅙ cup	
12 teaspoons	tablespoons	¼ cup	2 fluid ounces
15 teaspoons	5 tablespoons	⅓ cup minus 1 teaspoon	
16 teaspoons	5 tablespoons plus 1 teaspoon	⅓ cup	
18 teaspoons	6 tablespoons	¼ cup plus 2 tablespoons	3 fluid ounces
24 teaspoons	8 tablespoons	½ cup	4 fluid ounces
30 teaspoons	10 tablespoons	½ cup plus 2 tablespoons	5 fluid ounces
32 teaspoons	10 tablespoons plus 2 teaspoons	⅔ cup	
36 teaspoons	12 tablespoons	¾ cup	6 fluid ounces
42 teaspoons	14 tablespoons	1 cup minus 2 tablespoons	7 fluid ounces
45 teaspoons	15 tablespoons	1 cup minus 1 tablespoon	
48 teaspoons	16 tablespoons	1 cup	8 fluid ounces

TEASPOONS	
¼ teaspoon	1 milliliter
½ teaspoon	2 milliliters
1 teaspoon	5 milliliters
1 tablespoon	15 milliliters
2 tablespoons	30 milliliters
3 tablespoons	45 milliliters
¼ cup	60 milliliters
⅓ cup	80 milliliters
½ cup	125 milliliters
⅔ cup	160 milliliters
¾ cup	175 milliliters
1 cup	250 milliliters
1 quart	1 L

OVEN TEMPERATURE			
250°F	120°C	400°F	200°C
275°F	140°C	425°F	220°C
300°F	150°C	450°F	230°C
325°F	160°C	475°F	250°C
350°F	180°C	500°F	260°C
375°F	190°C	525°F	270°C

LENGTH	
1 inch	25 millimeters
1 inch	2.5 centimeters

WEIGHT	
1 ounce	30 grams
¼ pound	125 grams
½ pound	250 grams
1 pound	500 grams

Note: Measurement of less than 0.5ml (⅛ teaspoon) is considered a dash or a pinch. Metric volume measurements are approximate.